DERIVED SENTENCE LOG

Argument by Cases

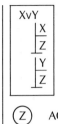

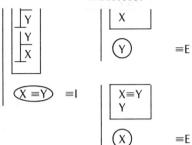

Disjunction Elimination

Reductio Ad Absurdum

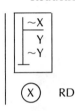

Weakening

Denying the Consequent

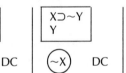

Negation Introduction

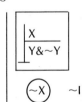

Contradiction

De Morgan's Rules

~(XvY) and ~X&~Y are mutually derivable (DM)
~(X&Y) and ~Xv~Y are mutually derivable (DM)

Contraposition

X⊃Y and ~Y⊃~X are mutually derivable (CP)
~X⊃Y and ~Y⊃X are mutually derivable (CP)
X⊃~Y and Y⊃~X are mutually derivable (CP)

Conditional Rules

X⊃Y and ~XvY are mutually derivable (C)
~(X⊃Y) and X&~Y are mutually derivable (C)

A Modern Formal Logic Primer

Volume
II

A Modern Formal Logic Primer

Volume
II

Predicate Logic and Metatheory

Paul Teller

*University of Illinois
at Chicago*

PRENTICE HALL, Englewood Cliffs, New Jersey 07632

Library of Congress Cataloging-in-Publication Data

TELLER, PAUL, (date)
  A modern formal logic primer / Paul Teller.

  Includes index.
  Contents: —v. 2. Predicate and metatheory.
  ISBN 0-13-903196-0 (v. 2)
  1. Logic. I Title.
BC71. T42 1989
160—dc19   88-28912
                                           CIP

Editorial/production supervision and
  interior design: Marianne Peters
Cover design: George Cornell
Manufacturing buyer: Peter Havens

 © 1989 by Prentice-Hall, Inc.
A Division of Simon & Schuster
Englewood Cliffs, New Jersey 07632

Printed in the United States of America
10 9 8 7 6 5 4 3 2 1

ISBN 0-13-903196-0

Prentice-Hall International (UK) Limited, *London*
Prentice-Hall of Australia Pty. Limited, *Sydney*
Prentice-Hall Canada Inc., *Toronto*
Prentice-Hall Hispanoamericana, S.A., *Mexico*
Prentice-Hall of India Private Limited, *New Delhi*
Prentice-Hall of Japan, Inc., *Tokyo*
Simon & Schuster Asia Pte. Ltd., *Singapore*
Editora Prentice-Hall do Brasil, Ltda., *Rio de Janeiro*

Contents

Preface to Volumes I and II

A Guide to the Primer

This text is a primer in the best sense of the word: A book which presents the basic elements of a subject. In other respects, I have sought to write a different kind of text, breaking with what I regard as an unfortunate tradition in teaching formal logic. From truth tables through completeness, I seek to explain, as opposed to merely presenting my subject matter. Most logic texts (indeed, most texts) put their readers to sleep with a formal, dry style. I have aimed for a livelier lecture style, which treats students as human beings and not as knowledge receptacles. In a text, as in the classroom, students need to be encouraged and to hear their difficulties acknowledged. They need variation in pace. They need shifts in focus among "I," "we," and "you," just as most of us speak in the classroom. From time to time students simply need to rest their brains.

One fault of logic textbooks especially bothers me: Some authors feel so concerned to teach rigor that they end up beating their students over the head with it. I have not sacrificed rigor. But I have sought to cultivate it rather than rubbing it in.

Now to the contents of the **Primer.** Volume I presents sentence logic. Volume II, Part I lays out predicate logic, including identity, functions, and definite descriptions; Part II introduces metatheory, including mathematical induction, soundness, and completeness. The text includes completely independent presentations of Fitch-style natural deduction and the tree method as developed by Richard Jeffrey. I have presented the material with a great deal of modularity.

I have presented the text in two volumes to maximize flexibility of use in a variety of courses. Many introductory courses cover a mix of informal and formal logic. Too often I have heard instructors express dissatisfaction with what they find available for the formal portion of such a course. Volume I provides a new option. Using it in tandem with any of the many available inexpensive informal texts, instructors can combine the best of both subjects. Volume I will present a serious-minded introduction to formal logic, which at the same time should prove accessible and encouraging to those students who will never again take another logic course. The relatively small numbers who continue to a second course, devoted exclusively to formal logic, need only purchase Volume II to build on the foundation already laid.

The **Primer** incorporates a number of unusual features. Chapters 1, 3, and 4 emphasize the concept of a truth function. Though the idea is simple once you get it, many students need several passes. The optional section 3–4, on disjunctive normal form and the Scheffer stroke, serves the didactic function of providing yet more drill on truth functionality.

Following Richard Jeffrey, I have thoroughly presented '&', 'v', and '~' before treating '⊃' and '≡'. '&', 'v', and '~' are much less controversial correlates of their English counterparts than is '⊃'. Using '&', 'v' and '~' as a vehicle for introducing the idea of a truth function, I can deal honestly with the difficulties of giving a truth functional formulation of conditionals. In turn, this honest examination provides further drill with the concept of a truth function.

Sentences in English and logic often do not correspond very accurately. Consequently, I speak of transcription, not translation between logic and English. I treat sentence logic transcription quite briefly in chapter 1 of Volume I and further in the short, optional chapter 2. Predicate logic transcription gets a minimal introduction in chapter 1 of Volume II and then comes in for a thorough workout in chapter 4, also optional. There I deal with the subject matter of domains and the traditional square of opposition by using the much more general method of restricted quantifier subscripts and their elimination. This technique provides an all-purpose tool for untangling complicated transcription problems. Chapter 4 of Volume II also examines quantificational ambiguity in English, which most logic texts strangely ignore.

Training in metatheory begins in Volume I, chapter 1. But the training is largely implicit: I use elementary ideas, such as metavariables, and then call attention to them as use makes their point apparent. After thorough preparation throughout the text, chapter 10 of Volume II brings together the fundamental ideas of metatheory.

Standard treatments of sentence logic present sentence logic semantics, in the form of truth tables, before sentence logic derivation rules. Only in this way do students find the rules clearly intelligible, as opposed to poorly understood cookbook recipes. Often texts do not follow this heuristic for predicate logic, or they do so only half-heartedly. Presumedly, authors fear that the concept of an interpretation is too difficult. However, one can transparently define interpretations if one makes the simplifying assumption of including a name for each object in an interpretation's domain, in effect adopting a substitutional interpretation of the quantifiers. I further smooth the way by stressing the analogy of form and function between interpretations and truth value assignments in sentence logic.

This approach is ample for fixing basic ideas of semantics and for making predicate logic rules intelligible. After introducing predicate logic syntax in Volume II, chapter 1, and semantics in chapters 2 and 3, tree rules are almost trivial to teach; and derivation rules, because they can be better motivated, come more easily. I have clearly noted the limitation in my definition of an interpretation, and I have set students thinking, in an exercise, why one may well not want to settle for a substitutional interpretation. Finally, with the ground prepared by the limited but intuitive definitions of chapters 2 and 3 of Volume II students have a relatively easy time with the full characterization of an interpretation in chapter 15.

No one has an easy time learning—or teaching—natural deduction quantifier rules. I have worked hard to motivate them in the context of informal argument. I have made some minor modifications in detail of formulation, modifications which I believe make the rules a little easier to grasp and understand. For existential elimination, I employ the superficially restrictive requirement that the instantiating name be restricted to the sub-derivation. I explain how this restriction works to impose the more complex and traditional restrictions, and I set this up in the presentation so that instructors can use the more traditional restrictions if they prefer.

For the proof of completeness of the natural deduction system I have fashioned my own semantic tableau proof. I believe that on its own it is at least as accessible as the Henkin and other more familiar proofs. In addition, if you do tree completeness first, you can explain the natural deduction completeness proof literally in a few minutes.

I have been especially careful not to dive into unexplained proofs of soundness and completeness. Instructors will find, in separate sections, informal and intuitive explanations of the sentence logic proofs, unencumbered with formal details, giving an understanding of how the proofs work. These sections require only the first short section of the induction chapter. Instructors teaching metatheory at a more elementary level may want to conclude with some of these sections. Those ready for the tonic of rigor will find much to satisfy them in the succeeding sections.

In some chapters I have worked as hard on the exercises as on the text. I have graded the skill problems, beginning with easy comprehension checkers, through skill builders, to some problems which will test real skill mastery. I think few will not find enough problems.

Exercises should exercise understanding as well as skills. Any decent mathematics text puts problems to this task, as well as uses them to present auxiliary material. Too few logic texts fall in this tradition. I hope that students and instructors will enjoy my efforts in some of the exercises to introduce auxiliary material, to lay foundations for succeeding material, to engage creative understanding, and to join in the activity of conceptual exploration.

For teaching plans the key word is "modularity." Those using just Volume I in an informal/formal course may teach chapters 1, 2 (optional), 3, and 4 to introduce sentence logic. Then, as taste and time permit, you may do natural deduction (chapters 5, 6, and 7) or trees (chapters 8 and 9), or both, in either order.

Volumes I and II together provide great flexibility in a first symbolic logic course. Given your introduction of sentence logic with chapters 1, 3, and 4 of Volume I and grounding of predicate logic with chapters 1, 2, and 3 of Volume II you can do almost anything you want. I have made treatment of derivations and trees completely independent. You can run through the one from sentence to predicate logic, and then go back and do the other. Or you can treat both natural deduction and trees for sentence logic before continuing to predicate logic. You can spend up to two weeks on transcription in chapter 2 of Volume I and chapter 4 of Volume II, or you can rely on the minimal discussion of transcription in the first chapters of Volumes I and II and omit chapter 2 of Volume I and chapter 4 of Volume II altogether.

If you do both trees and natural deduction, the order is up to you. Trees further familiarize students with semantics, which helps in explaining natural deduction rules. On the other hand, I have found that after teaching natural deduction I can introduce trees almost trivially and still get their benefit for doing semantics and metatheory.

Your only limitation is time. Teaching at an urban commuter university, in one quarter I cover natural deduction (Volume I, chapters 1, 2, 3, 4, 5, 6, 7; Volume II, chapters 1, 2, 3, 5, and perhaps 6), or trees and sentence logic natural deduction (Volume I, chapters 1, 2, 3, 4, 8, 9; Volume II, chapters 1, 2, 3, 7, 8; Volume I, chapters 5, 6, and 7). A semester should suffice for all of Volume I and Volume II through chapter 8, and perhaps 9. Again, you may want to follow the chapter sequencing, or you may want to do natural deduction first, all the way through predicate logic, or trees first.

If you do just natural deduction or just trees you have more time for identity, functions, definite descriptions, and metatheory. Chapter 10 of Volume II, basic metatheoretical concepts, can provide a very satisfying conclusion to a first course. A two quarter sequence may suffice for all of the metatheory chapters, especially if you do not do both natural deduction and trees thoroughly. To this end the metatheory chapters cover soundness and completeness for both natural deduction and trees independently. Or, you may choose to end with the sections presenting the informal explanations of induction and the soundness and completeness proofs. The text will provide a leisurely full year course or a faster paced full year course if you supplement it a bit at the end of the year.

I want to mention several features of my usage. I use single quotes to form names of expressions. I depart from logically correct use of quotation makes in one respect. In stating generalizations about arguments I need a formulation which makes explicit use of metavariables for premise and conclusion. But before chapter 10 of Volume II, where I make the metalanguage/object language distinction explicit, I do not want to introduce a special argument forming operator because I want to be sure that students do not mistake such an operator for a new symbol in the object language. Consequently I use the English word 'therefore'. I found, however, that the resulting expressions were not well enough set off from their context. For clarity I have used double quotes when, for example, I discuss what one means by saying that an argument, "**X**. Therefore **Y**." is valid.

Throughout I have worked to avoid sexist usage. This proves difficult with anaphoric reference to quantified variables, where English grammar calls for constructions such as 'If someone is from Chicago he likes big cities.' and 'Anyone who loves Eve loves himself.' My solution is to embrace grammatical reform and use a plural pronoun: 'If someone is from Chicago they like big cities.' and 'Anyone who loves Eve loves themself.' I know. It grates. But the offense to grammar is less than the offense to social attitudes. As this reform takes hold it will sound right to all of us.

I thank the many friends and family who have actively supported this project, and who have born with me patiently when the toil has made me hard to live with. I do not regard the project as finished. Far from it. I hope that you—instructors and students—will write me. Let me know where I am still unclear. Give me your suggestions for further clarification, for alternative ways to explain, and for a richer slate of problems. Hearing your advice on how to make this a better text will be the best sign that I have part way succeeded.

Paul Teller
Chicago

A Modern
Formal Logic
Primer

Volume

II

Predicate Logic   1
Syntax

In Volume I you gained a firm foundation in sentence logic. But there must be more to logic, as you can see from the next examples. Consider the following two English arguments and their transcriptions into sentence logic:

(1) Everyone loves Adam.   A
     Eve loves Adam.   B

(2) Eve loves Adam.   B
     Someone loves Adam.   C

In sentence logic, we can only transcribe the sentences in these arguments as atomic sentence letters. But represented with sentence letters, both natural deduction and truth trees tell us that these arguments are invalid. No derivation will allow us to derive 'B' from 'A' or 'C' from 'B'. A&~B is a counterexample to the first argument, and B&~C is a counterexample to the second. An argument is valid only if it has no counterexamples.

Something has gone terribly wrong. Clearly, if everyone loves Adam, then so does Eve. If the premise is true, without fail the conclusion will be true also. In the same way, if Eve loves Adam, then someone loves Adam. Once again, there is no way in which the premise could be true and the conclusion false. But to say that if the premises are true, then without fail the conclusion will be true also is just what we intend when we say that an argument is valid. Since sentence logic describes these arguments as invalid, it looks like something has to be wrong with sentence logic.

Sentence logic is fine as far as it goes. The trouble is that it does not go far enough. These two arguments owe their validity to the internal logical structure of the sentences appearing in the arguments, and sentence logic does not describe this internal logical structure. To deal with this shortcoming, we must extend sentence logic in a way which will display the needed logical structure and show how to use this structure in testing arguments for validity. We will keep the sentence logic we have learned in Volume I. But we will extend it to what logicians call *Predicate Logic* (also sometimes called *Quantificational Logic*).

Predicate logic deals with sentences which say something about someone or something. Consider the sentence 'Adam is blond.' This sentence attributes the property of being blond to the person named 'Adam'. The sentence does this by applying the predicate (the word) 'blond' to the name 'Adam'. A sentence of predicate logic does the same thing but in a simplified way.

We will put capital letters to a new use. Let us use the capital letter 'B', not now as a sentence letter, but to transcribe the English word 'blond'. And let us use 'a' to transcribe the name 'Adam'. For 'Adam is blond.', predicate logic simply writes 'Ba', which you should understand as the predicate 'B' being applied to the name 'a'. This, in turn, you should understand as stating that the person named by 'a' (namely, Adam) has the property indicated by 'B' (namely, the property of being blond).

Of course, on a different occasion, we could use 'B' to transcribe a different English predicate, such as 'bachelor', 'short', or 'funny'. And we could use 'a' as a name for different people or things. It is only important to stick to the same transcription use throughout one problem or example.

Predicate logic can also express relations which hold between things or people. Let's consider the simple statement that Eve loves Adam. This tells us that there is something holding true of Eve and Adam together, namely, that the first loves the second. To express this in predicate logic we will again use our name for Adam, 'a'. We will use a name for Eve, say, the letter 'e'. And we will need a capital letter to stand for the relation of loving, say, the letter 'L'. Predicate logic writes the sentence 'Eve loves Adam.' as 'Lea'. This is to be read as saying that the relation indicated by 'L' holds between the two things named by the lowercase letters 'e' and 'a'. Once again, in a different example or problem, 'L', 'a', and 'e' could be used for different relations, people, or things.

You might be a little surprised by the order in which the letters occur in 'Lea'. But don't let that bother you. It's just the convention most often used in logic: To write a sentence which says that a relation holds between two things, first write the letter which indicates the relation and then write the names of the things between which the relation is supposed to hold. Some logicians write 'Lea' as 'L(e,a)', but we will not use this notation.

Note, also, the order in which the names 'e' and 'a' appear in 'Lea'. 'Lea' is a different sentence from 'Lae'. 'Lea' says that Eve loves Adam. 'Lae' says that Adam loves Eve. One of these sentences might be true while the other one is false! Think of 'L' as expressing the relation, which holds just in case the **first** thing named loves the **second** thing named.

Here is a nasty piece of terminology which I have to give you because it is traditional and you will run into it if you continue your study of logic. Logicians use the word *Argument* for a letter which occurs after a predicate or a relation symbol. The letter 'a' in 'Ba' is the argument of the predicate 'B'. The letters 'e' and 'a' in 'Lea' are the arguments of the relation symbol 'L'. This use of the word 'argument' has nothing to do with the use in which we talk about an argument from premises to a conclusion.

At this point you might be perplexed by the following question. I have now used capital letters for three different things. I have used them to indicate atomic sentences. I have used them as predicates. And I have used them as relation symbols. Suppose you encounter a capital letter in a sentence of predicate logic. How are you supposed to know whether it is an atomic sentence letter, a predicate, or a relation symbol?

Easy. If the capital letter is followed by two lowercase letters, as in 'Lea', you know the capital letter is a relation symbol. If the capital letter is followed by one lowercase letter, as in 'Ba', you know the capital letter is a predicate. And if the capital letter is followed by no lowercase letters at all, as in 'A', you know it is an atomic sentence letter.

There is an advantage to listing the arguments of a relation symbol after the relation symbol, as in 'Lea'. We can see that there is something important in common between relation symbols and predicates. To attribute a relation as holding between two things is to say that something is true about the two things taken together and in the order specified. To attribute a property as holding of one thing is to say that something is true about that one thing. In the one case we attribute something to one thing, and in the other we attribute something to two things.

We can call attention to this similarity between predicates and relations in a way which also makes our terminology a bit smoother. We can indicate the connection by calling a relation symbol a *Two Place Predicate*, that is, a symbol which is very like an ordinary predicate except that it has two argument places instead of one. In fact, we may sometimes want to talk about **three** place predicates (equally well called 'three place relation symbols'). For example, to transcribe 'Eve is between Adam and Cid', I introduce 'c' as a name for Cid and the three place predicate 'K' to indicate the three place relation of being between. My transcription is 'Keac', which you can think of as saying that the three place relation of being between holds among Eve, Adam, and Cid, with the first being between the second and the third.

This is why our new logic is called 'predicate logic': It involves predicates of one place, two places, three places, or indeed, any number of places. As I mentioned, logicians also refer to these symbols as one place, two place, or many place relation symbols. But logicians never call the resulting system of logic 'relation logic'. I have no idea why not.

Our familiar sentence logic built up all sentences from atomic sentence letters. Predicate logic likewise builds up compound sentences from atomic sentences. But we have expanded our list of what counts as an atomic sentence. In addition to atomic sentence letters, we will include sentences such as 'Ba' and 'Lea'. Indeed, any one place predicate followed by one name, any two place predicate followed by two names, and so on, will now also count as an atomic sentence. We can use our expanded stock of atomic sentences to build up compound sentences with the help of the connectives, just as before.

How would you say, for example, 'Either Eve loves Adam or Adam is not blond.'? 'Lea ∨ ~Ba'. Try 'Adam loves himself and if he is blond then he loves Eve too.': 'Laa & (Ba ⊃ Lae)'.

In summarizing this section, we say

> In predicate logic, a capital letter without a following lowercase letter is (as in sentence logic) an atomic sentence. Predicate logic also includes predicates applied to names among its atomic sentences. A capital letter followed by one name is a *One Place Predicate* applied to one name. A capital letter followed by two names is a *Two Place Predicate* applied to two names, where the order of the names is important. Predicates with three or more places are used similarly.

EXERCISES

In the following exercises, use this transcription guide:

a:	Adam
e:	Eve
c:	Cid
Bx:	x is blond
Cx:	x is a cat
Lxy:	x loves y
Txy:	x is taller than y

1–1. Transcribe the following predicate logic sentences into English:

a) Tce
b) Lce
c) ~Tcc
d) Bc
e) Tce ⊃ Lce
f) Lce ∨ Lcc
g) ~(Lce & Lca)
h) Bc ≡ (Lce ∨ Lcc)

1–2. Transcribe the following English sentences into sentences of predicate logic;

a) Cid is a cat.
b) Cid is taller than Adam.
c) Either Cid is a cat or he is taller than Adam.
d) If Cid is taller than Eve then he loves her.
e) Cid loves Eve if he is taller than she is.
f) Eve loves both Adam and Cid.
g) Eve loves either Adam or Cid.
h) Either Adam loves Eve or Eve loves Adam, but both love Cid.
i) Only if Cid is a cat does Eve love him.
j) Eve is taller than but does not love Cid.

1–2. QUANTIFIERS AND VARIABLES

We still have not done enough to deal with arguments (1) and (2). The sentences in these arguments not only attribute properties and relations to things, but they involve a certain kind of generality. We need to be able to express this generality, and we must be careful to do it in a way which will make the relevant logical form quite clear. This involves a way of writing general sentences which seems very awkward from the point of view of English. But you will see how smoothly everything works when we begin proving the validity of arguments.

English has two ways of expressing general statements. We can say 'Everyone loves Adam.' (Throughout, 'everybody' would do as well as 'everyone'.) This formulation puts the general word 'everyone' where ordinarily we might put a name, such as 'Eve'. Predicate logic does not work this way. The second way of expressing general statements in English uses expressions such as 'Everyone is such that they love Adam.' or 'Everything is such that it loves Adam.' Predicate logic uses a formulation of this kind.

Read the symbol '(∀x)' as 'Every x is such that'. Then we transcribe 'Everyone loves Adam.' as '(∀x)Lxa'. In words, we read this as "Every x is such that x loves Adam." '(∀x)' is called a *Universal Quantifier*. In other logic books you may see it written as (x).

We are going to need not only a way of saying that **everyone** loves Adam but also a way of saying that **someone** loves Adam. Again, English does this most smoothly by putting the general word 'someone' where we might have placed a name like 'Eve'. And again logic does not imitate this style. Instead, it imitates English expressions such as 'Someone is such that he or she loves Adam.', or 'Some person is such that he or she loves Adam.', or 'Something is such that it loves Adam.' Read the symbol '(∃x)' as 'Some x is such that'. Then we transcribe 'Someone loves Adam.' as '(∃x)Lxa'. '(∃x)' is called an *Existential Quantifier*.

In one respect, '(∃x)' corresponds imperfectly to English expressions which use words such as 'some', 'there is a', and 'there are'. For example, we say 'Some cat has caught a mouse' and 'There is a cat which has caught a mouse' when we think that there is exactly one such cat. We say 'Some cats have caught a mouse' or 'There are cats which have caught a mouse' when we think that there are more than one. Predicate logic has only the one expression, '(∃x)', which does not distinguish between 'exactly one' and 'more than one'. '(∃x)' means that there is **one or more** x such that. (In chapter 9 we will learn about an extension of our logic which will enable us to make this distinction not made by '(∃x)'.)

In English, we also make a distinction by using words such as 'Every**one**' and 'every**body**' as opposed to words like 'every**thing**'. That is, English uses one word to talk about all people and another word to talk about all things which are not people. The universal quantifier, '(∀x)', does not mark this distinction. If we make no qualification, '(∀x), means all people **and** things. The same comments apply to the existential quantifier. English contrasts 'some**one**' and 'some**body**' with 'some**thing**'. But in logic, if we make no qualification, '(∃x)' means something, which can be a person or a thing. All this is very inconvenient when we want to transcribe sentences such as 'Someone loves Adam.' and 'Everybody loves Eve.' into predicate logic.

Many logicians try to deal with this difficulty by putting restrictions on the things to which the 'x' in '(∀x)' and '(∃x)' can refer. For example, in dealing with a problem which deals only with people, they say at the outset: For this problem 'x' will refer only to people. This practice is called establishing a *Universe of Discourse* or *Restricting the Domain of Discourse*. I am not going to fill in the details of this common logical practice because it really does not solve our present problem. If we resolved to talk only about people, how would we say something such as 'Every**body** likes some**thing**.'? In chapter 4 I will show you how to get the effect of restricting the domain of discourse in a more general way which will also allow us to talk at the same time about people, things, places, or whatever we like.

But until chapter 4 we will make do with the intuitive idea of restricting 'x' to refer only to people when we are transcribing sentences using expressions such as 'anybody', 'no one', and 'someone'. In other words, we will, for the time being indulge in the not quite correct practice of transcribing '(∀x)' as 'everyone', 'anybody', etc., and '(∃x)' as 'someone', 'somebody', or the like, when this is the intuitively right way to proceed, instead of the strictly correct 'everything', 'something', and similar expressions.

The letter 'x' in '(∀x)' and '(∃x)' is called a *Variable*. Variables will do an amazing amount of work for us, work very similar to that done by English pronouns, such as 'he', 'she', and 'it'. For example, watch the work 'it' does for me when I say the following: "I felt something in the closed bag. It felt cold. I pulled it out." This little discourse involves existential quantification. The discourse begins by talking about **something** without saying just which thing this something is. But then the discourse goes on to make several comments about this thing. The important point is that all the comments are about the **same** thing. This is the work that 'it' does for us. It enables us to cross-reference, making clear that we are always referring to the same thing, even though we have not been told exactly what that thing is.

A variable in logic functions in exactly the same way. For example, once we introduce the variable 'x' with the existential quantifier, '(∃x)' we can use 'x' repeatedly to refer to the same (unknown) thing. So I can say, 'Someone is blond and he or she loves Eve' with the sentence '(∃x)(Bx &Lxe)'. Note the use of parentheses here. They make clear that the quantifier '(∃x)' applies to all of the sentence 'Bx & Lxe'. Like negation, a quantifier applies to the shortest full sentence which follows it, where the shortest full following sentence may be marked with parentheses. And the 'x' in the quantifier applies to, or is linked to, all the occurrences of 'x' in this shortest full following sentence. We say that

> A quantifier *Governs* the shortest full sentence which follows it and *Binds* the variables in the sentence it governs. The latter means that the variable in the quantifier applies to all occurrences of the same variable in the shortest full following sentence.

Unlike English pronouns, variables in logic do not make cross-references between sentences.

These notions actually involve some complications in sentences which use two quantifiers, complications which we will study in chapter 3. But this rough characterization will suffice until then.

Let us look at an example with the universal quantifier, '(∀x)'. Consider the English sentences 'Anyone blond loves Eve.', 'All blonds love Eve.',

'Any blond loves Eve.', and 'All who are blond love Eve.' All these sentences say the same thing, at least so far as logic is concerned. We can express what they say more painstakingly by saying, 'Any people are such that if they are blond then they love Eve.' This formulation guides us in transcribing into logic. Let us first transcribe a part of this sentence, the conditional, which talks about some unnamed people referred to with the pronoun 'they': 'If they are blond then they love Eve.' Using the variable 'x' for the English pronoun 'they', this comes out as 'Bx ⊃ Lxe'. Now all we have to do is to say that this is true whoever "they" may be. This gives us '(∀x)(Bx ⊃ Lxe)'. Note that I have enclosed 'Bx ⊃ Lxe' in parentheses before prefixing the quantifier. This is to make clear that the quantifier applies to the whole sentence.

I have been using 'x' as a variable which appears in quantifiers and in sentences governed by quantifiers. Obviously, I would just as well have used some other letter, such as 'y' or 'z'. In fact, later on, we will need to use more than one variable at the same time with more than one quantifier. So we will take '(∀x)', '(∀y)', and '(∀z)' all to be universal quantifiers, as well as any other variable prefixed with '∀' and surrounded by parentheses if we should need still more universal quantifiers. In the same way, '(∃x)', '(∃y)', and '(∃z)' will all function as existential quantifiers, as will any similar symbol obtained by substituting some other variable for 'x', 'y', or 'z'.

To make all this work smoothly, we should clearly distinguish the letters which will serve as variables from other letters. Henceforth, I will reserve lowercase 'w', 'x', 'y', and 'z' to use as variables. I will use lowercase 'a' through 'r' as names. If one ever wanted more variables or names, one could add to these lists indefinitely by using subscripts. Thus 'a_1' and 'd_{17}' are both names, and 'x_1' and 'z_{34}' are both variables. But in practice we will never need that many variables or names.

What happened to 's', 't', 'u', and 'v'? I am going to reserve these letters to talk generally **about** names and variables. The point is this: As I have mentioned, when I want to talk generally in English about sentences in sentence logic, I use boldface capital '**X**', '**Y**', and '**Z**'. For example, when I stated the & rule I wrote, "For any sentences **X** and **Y**. . . ." The idea is that what I wrote is true no matter what sentence you might write in for '**X**' and '**Y**'. I will need to do the same thing when I state the new rules for quantifiers. I will need to say something which will be true no matter what names you might use and no matter what variables you might use. I will do this by using boldface '**s**' and '**t**' when I talk about names and boldface '**u**' and '**v**' when I talk about variables.

To summarize our conventions for notation:

> We will use lowercase letter 'a' through 'r' as names, and 'w', 'x', 'y' and 'z' as variables. We will use boldface '**s**' and '**t**' to talk generally about names and boldface '**u**' and '**v**' to talk generally about variables.

1–3. THE SENTENCES OF PREDICATE LOGIC

We now have all the pieces for saying exactly which expressions are going to count as sentences of predicate logic. First, all the sentences of sentence logic count as sentences of predicate logic. Second, we expand our stock of atomic sentences. I have already said that we will include among the atomic sentences predicates followed by the right number of names (one name for one place predicates, two names for two place predicates, and so on). We will do the same thing with variables and with variables mixed with names. So 'Bx' will count as an atomic sentence, as will 'Lxx', 'Lxy', and 'Lxa'. In general, any predicate followed by the right number of names and/or variables will count as an atomic sentence.

We get all the rest of the sentences of predicate logic by using connectives to build longer sentences from shorter sentences, starting from atomic sentences. We use all the connectives of sentence logic. And we add to these '(∀x)', '(∀y)', '(∃x)', '(∃y)', and other quantifiers, all of which count as new connectives. We use a quantifier to build a longer sentence from a shorter one in exactly the same way that we use the negation sign to build up sentences. Just put the quantifier in front of any expression which is already itself a sentence. We always understand the quantifier to apply to the shortest full sentence which follows the quantifier, as indicated by parentheses. Thus, if we start with 'Lxa', '(∀x)Lxa' counts as a sentence. We could have correctly written '(∀x)(Lxa)', though the parentheses around 'Lxa' are not needed in this case. To give another example, we can start with the atomic sentences 'Bx' and 'Lxe'. We build a compound by joining these with the conditional, '⊃', giving 'Bx ⊃ Lxe'. Finally, we apply '(∀x)' to this compound sentence. We want to be clear that '(∀x)' applies to the whole of 'Bx ⊃ Lxe', so we have to put parentheses around it before prefixing '(∀x)'. This gives '(∀x)(Bx ⊃ Lxe)'.

Here is a formal definition of sentences of predicate logic:

> All sentence letters and predicates followed by the appropriate number of names and/or variables are sentences of predicate logic. (These are the atomic sentences.) If **X** is any sentence of predicate logic and **u** is any variable, then (∀u)**X** (a universally quantified sentence) and (∃u)**X** (an existentially quantified sentence) are both sentences of predicate logic. If **X** and **Y** are both sentences of predicate logic, then any expression formed from **X** and **Y** using the connectives of sentence logic are sentences of predicate logic. Finally, only these expressions are sentences of predicate logic.

Logicians often use the words *Well Formed Formula* (Abbreviated *wff*) for any expression which this definition classifies as a predicate logic sentence.

You may have noticed something a little strange about the definition. It tells us that an expression such as '(∀x)Ba' is a predicate logic sentence. If 'A' is a sentence letter, even '(∀x)A' is going to count as a sentence! But how should we understand '(∀x)Ba' and '(∀x)A'? Since the variable 'x' of the quantifier does not occur in the rest of the sentence, it is not clear what these sentences are supposed to mean.

To have a satisfying definition of predicate logic sentence, one might want to rule out expressions such as '(∀x)Ba' and '(∀x)A'. But it will turn out that keeping these as official predicate logic sentences will do no harm, and ruling them out in the definition makes the definition messier. It is just not worth the effort to rule them out. In the next chapter we will give a more exact characterization of how to understand the quantifiers, and this characterization will tell us that "vacuous quantifiers," as in '(∀x)Ba' and '(∀x)A', have no effect at all. These sentences can be understood as the sentences 'Ba' and 'A', exactly as if the quantifiers were not there.

The definition also counts sentences such as 'By', 'Lze', and 'Bx & Lxe' as sentences, where 'x' and 'z' are variables not governed by a quantifier. Such sentences are called *Open Sentences*. Open sentences can be a problem in logic in the same way that English sentences are a problem when they contain "open" pronouns. You fail to communicate if you say, 'He has a funny nose,' without saying or otherwise indicating who "he" is.

Many logicians prefer not to count open sentences as real sentences at all. Where I use the expression 'open sentence', often logicians talk about 'open formulas' or 'propositional functions'. If you go on in your study of logic, you will quickly get used to these alternative expressions, but in an introductory course I prefer to keep the terminology as simple as possible.

Have you been wondering what the word 'syntax' means in the title of this chapter? The *Syntax* of a language is the set of rules which tell you what counts as a sentence of the language. You now know what constitutes a sentence of predicate logic, and you have a rough and ready idea of how to understand such a sentence. Our next job will be to make the interpretation of these sentences precise. We call this giving the *Semantics* for predicate logic, which will be the subject of the next chapter. But, first, you should practice what you have learned about the syntax of predicate logic to make sure that your understanding is secure.

EXERCISES

1–3. Which of the following expressions are sentences of predicate logic?

    a) Ca
    b) Tab
    c) aTb
    d) Ca ⊃ Tab
    e) (∃x)~Cx

f) $(\forall x)(Cx \supset Tax)$
g) $(\forall x)Cx \ \& \ Tax(\forall x)$
h) $\sim(\forall x)(Txa \lor Tax)$
i) $[(\exists x)Cx \lor(\exists x)\sim Cx] \equiv (\forall x)(Txa \ \& \ Tax)$

In the following exercises, use this transcription guide:

a: Adam
e: Eve
c: Cid
Bx: x is blond
Cx: x is a cat
Lxy: x loves y
Txy: x is taller than y

Before you begin, I should point out something about transcribing between logic and pronouns in English. I used the analogy to English pronouns to help explain the idea of a variable. But that does not mean that you should always transcribe variables as pronouns or that you should always transcribe pronouns as variables. For example, you should transcribe 'If Eve is a cat, then she loves herself.' with the predicate logic sentence 'Ce ⊃ Lee'. Notice that 'she' and 'herself' are both transcribed as 'e'. That is because in this case we have been told who she and herself are. We know that they are Eve, and so we use the name for Eve, namely, 'e' to transcribe these pronouns. How should we describe 'Ca ⊃ ~Ba'? We could transcribe this as 'If Adam is a cat then Adam is not blond.' But a nicer transcription is simply 'If Adam is a cat then he is not blond.'

Now do your best with the following transcriptions.

1–4. Transcribe the following predicate logic sentences into English:

a) $\sim Laa$
b) $Laa \supset \sim Taa$
c) $\sim(Bc \lor Lce)$
d) $Ca \equiv (Ba \lor Lae)$
e) $(\exists x)Txc$
f) $(\forall x)Lax \ \& \ (\forall x)Lcx$
g) $(\forall x)(Lax \ \& \ Lcx)$
h) $(\exists x)Txa \lor (\exists x)Txc$
i) $(\exists x)(Txa \lor Txc)$
j) $(\forall x)(Cx \supset Lxe)$
k) $(\exists x)(Cx \ \& \ \sim Lex)$
l) $\sim(\forall x)(Cx \supset Lex)$
m) $(\forall x)[Cx \supset (Lcx \lor Lex)]$
n) $(\exists x)[Cx \ \& \ (Bx \ \& \ Txc)]$

1–5. Transcribe the following English sentences into sentences of predicate logic:

a)   Everyone loves Eve.
b)   Everyone is loved by either Cid or Adam.
c)   Either everyone is loved by Adam or everyone is loved by Cid.
d)   Someone is taller than both Adam and Cid.
e)   Someone is taller than Adam and someone is taller than Cid.
f)   Eve loves all cats.
g)   All cats love Eve.
h)   Eve loves some cats.
i)   Eve loves no cats.
j)   Anyone who loves Eve is not a cat.
k)   No one who loves Eve is a cat.
l)   Somebody who loves Adam loves Cid.
m)   No one loves both Adam and Cid.

CHAPTER SUMMARY EXERCISES

Provide short explanations for each of the following. Check against the text to make sure that your explanations are correct, and keep your explanations in your notebook for reference and review.

a)   Predicate Logic
b)   Name
c)   Predicate
d)   One Place Predicate
e)   Two Place Predicate
f)   Relation
g)   Variable
h)   Universal Quantifier
i)   Existential Quantifier
j)   Universe, or Domain of Discourse
k)   Govern
l)   Bind
m)   Open Sentence
n)   Sentence of Predicate Logic
o)   Well Formed Formula (wff)
p)   Syntax
q)   Semantics

Predicate Logic $\overline{2}$

Semantics and Validity

2–1. INTERPRETATIONS

Recall that we used truth tables to give very precise definitions of the meaning of '&', 'v' '~', '⊃', and '≡'. We would like to do the same for the meaning of quantifiers. But, as you will see very soon, truth tables won't do the job. We need something more complicated.

When we were doing sentence logic, our atomic sentences were just sentence letters. By specifying truth values for all the sentence letters with which we started, we already fixed the truth values of **any** sentence which we could build up from these smallest pieces. Now that we are doing predicate logic, things are not so easy. Suppose we are thinking about all the sentences which we could build up using the one place predicate 'B', the two place predicate 'L', the name 'a', and the name 'e'. We can form six atomic sentences from these ingredients: 'Ba', 'Be', 'Laa', 'Lae', 'Lea', and 'Lee'. The truth table formed with these six atomic sentences would have 64 lines. Neither you nor I are going to write out a 64-line truth table, so let's consider just one quite typical line from the truth table:

Ba, Be, Laa, Lae, Lea, Lee	
t f f t f t	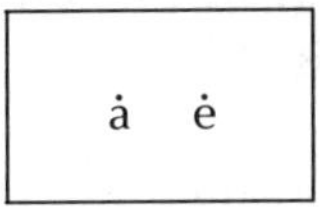 ȧ ė

Figure 2–1

Even such an elementary case in predicate logic begins to get quite complicated, so I have introduced a pictorial device to help in thinking about such cases (see figure 2–1). I have drawn a box with two dots inside, one labeled 'a' and the other labeled 'e'. This box is very different from a Venn diagram. This box is supposed to picture just one way the whole world might be. In this very simple picture of the world, there are just two things, Adam and Eve. The line of the truth table on the left gives you a completed description of what is true and what is false about Adam and Eve in this very simple world: Adam is blond, Eve is not blond, Adam does not love himself, Adam does love Eve, Eve does not love Adam, and Eve does love herself.

You can also think of the box and the description on the left as a very short novel. The box gives you the list of characters, and the truth table line on the left tells you what happens in this novel. Of course, the novel is not true. But if the novel were true, if it described the whole world, we would have a simple world with just Adam and Eve having the properties and relations described on the left.

Now, in writing this novel, I only specified the truth value for atomic sentences formed from the one and two place predicates and from the two names. What about the truth value of more complicated sentences? We can use our old rules for figuring out the truth value of compounds formed from these atomic sentences using '&', 'v', '~', '⊃', and '≡'. For example, in this novel 'Ba & Lae' is true because both the components are true.

What about the truth value of '(∃x)Bx'? Intuitively, '(∃x)Bx' should be true in the novel because in the novel there is someone, namely Adam, who is blond. As another example, consider '(∃x)Lxa'. In this novel '(∃x)Lxa' is false because Eve does not love Adam and Adam does not love Adam. And in this novel there isn't anyone (or anything) else. So no one loves Adam. In other words, in this novel it is false that there is someone who loves Adam.

Let's move on and consider the sentence '(∀x)Lxe'. In our novel this sentence is true, because Adam loves Eve, and Eve loves herself, and that's all the people there are in this novel. If this novel were true, it would be true that everyone loves Eve. Finally, '(∀x)Bx' is false in the novel, for in this novel Eve is not blond. So in this novel it is false that everyone is blond.

Remember what we had set out to do: We wanted to give a precise account of the meaning of the quantifiers very like the precise account which truth table definitions gave to '&' and the other sentence logic connectives. In sentence logic we did this by giving precise rules which told us when a compound sentence is true, given the truth value of the compound's components.

We now have really done the same thing for '(∀x)' and '(∃x)' in one special case. For a line of a truth table (a "novel") that gives a truth value for all atomic sentences using 'B', 'L', 'a', and 'e', we can say whether a universally quantified or an existentially quantified sentence is true or false. For example, the universally quantified sentence '(∀x)Lxe' is true just in case 'Lxe' is true for all values of 'x' in the novel. At the moment we are considering a novel in which the only existing things are Adam and Eve. In such a novel '(∀x)Lxe' is true if **both** 'Lxe' is true when we take 'x' to refer to Adam **and** 'Lxe' is also true when we take 'x' to refer to Eve. Similarly, '(∃x)Bx' is true in such a novel just in case 'Bx' is true for some value of 'x' in the novel. As long as we continue to restrict attention to a novel with only Adam and Eve as characters, '(∃x)Bx' is true in the novel if **either** 'Bx' is true when we take 'x' to refer to Adam **or** 'Bx' is true if we take 'x' to refer to Eve.

If the example seems a bit complicated, try to focus on this thought: All we are really doing is following the intuitive meaning of "all x" and "some x" in application to our little example. If you got lost in the previous paragraph, go back over it with this thought in mind.

Now comes a new twist, which might not seem very significant, but which will make predicate logic more interesting (and much more complicated) than sentence logic. In sentence logic we always had truth tables with a finite number of lines. Starting with a fixed stock of atomic sentence letters, we could always, at least in principle, write out all possible cases to consider, all possible assignments of truth values to sentence letters. The list might be too long to write out in practice, but we could at least understand everything in terms of such a finite list of cases.

Can we do the same thing when we build up sentences with predicates and names? If, for example, we start with just 'B', 'L', 'a', and 'e', we can form six atomic sentences. We can write out a 64-line truth table which will give us the truth value for any compound built up from these six atomic sentences, for any assignment of truth values to the atomic sentences. But the fact that we are using quantifiers means that we must also consider further possibilities.

Consider the sentence '(∀x)Bx'. We know this is false in the one case we used as an example (in which 'Ba' is true and 'Be' is false). You will immediately think of three alternative cases (three alternative "novels") which must be added to our list of relevant possible cases: the case in which Eve is blond and Adam is not, the case in which Adam and Eve are both blond, and the case in which both are not blond. But there are still more cases which we must include in our list of all possible cases! I can generate more cases by writing new novels with more characters. Suppose I write a new novel with Adam, Eve, and Cid. I now have eight possible ways of distributing hair color (blond or not blond) among my characters, which can be combined with 512 different possible combinations of who does or does not love whom! And, of course, this is just the beginning of an unending list of novels describing possible cases in which '(∀x)Bx' will have a truth value. I can always expand my list of novels by adding new characters. I can even describe novels with infinitely many characters, although I would not be able to write such a novel down.

How are we going to manage all this? In sentence logic we always had, for a given list of atomic sentence, a finite list of possible cases, the finite number of lines of the corresponding truth table. Now we have infinitely many possible cases. We can't list them all, but we can still say what any one of these possible cases looks like. Logicians call a possible case for a sentence of predicate logic an *Interpretation* of the sentence. The example with which we started this chapter is an example of an interpretation, so actually you have already seen and understood an example of an interpretation. We need only say more generally what interpretations are.

We give an interpretation, first, by specifying a collection of objects which the interpretation will be about, called the *Domain* of the interpretation. A domain always has at least one object. Then we give names to the objects in the domain, to help us in talking about them. Next, we must say which predicates will be involved. Finally, we must go through the predicates and objects and say which predicates are true of which objects. If we are concerned with a one place predicate, the interpretation specifies a list of objects of which the object is true. If the predicate is a two place predicate, then the interpretation specifies a list of **pairs** of objects between which the two place relation is supposed to hold, that is, pairs of objects of which the two place relation is true. Of course, order is important. The pair a-followed-by-b counts as a different pair from the pair b-followed-by-a. Also, we must consider objects paired with themselves. For example, we must specify whether Adam loves himself or does not love himself. The interpretation deals similarly with three and more place predicates.

In practice, we often specify the domain of an interpretation simply by giving the interpretation's names for those objects. I should mention that in a fully developed predicate logic, logicians consider interpretations which have unnamed objects. In more advanced work, interpretations of this kind become very important. But domains with unnamed objects would make it more difficult to introduce basic ideas and would gain us nothing for the work we will do in part I of this volume. So we won't consider interpretations with unnamed objects until part II.

The following gives a summary and formal definition of an interpretation:

An *Interpretation* consists of

   a)   A collection of objects, called the interpretation's *Domain*. The domain always has at least one object.
   b)   A name for each object in the domain. An object may have just one name or more than one name. (In part II we will expand the definition to allow domains with unnamed objects.)

c) A list of predicates.

d) A specification of the objects of which each predicate is true and the objects of which each predicate is false—that is, which one place predicates apply to which individual objects, which two place predicates apply to which pairs of objects, and so on. In this way every atomic sentence formed from predicates and names gets a truth value.

e) An interpretation may also include atomic sentence letters. The interpretation specifies a truth value for any included atomic sentence letter.

By an *Interpretation of a Sentence*, we mean an interpretation which is sure to have enough information to determine whether or not the sentence is true or false in the interpretation:

> An *Interpretation of a Sentence* is an interpretation which includes all the names and predicates which occur in the sentence and includes truth values for any atomic sentence letters which occur in the sentence.

For example, the interpretation of figure 2–1 is an interpretation of 'Ba' and of '(∀x)Lxx'. In this interpretation 'Ba' is true and '(∀x)Lxx' is false. Note that for each of these sentences, the interpretation contains more information than is needed to determine whether the sentence is true or false. This same interpretation is not an interpretation of 'Bc' or of '(∃x)Txe'. This is because the interpretation does not include the name 'c' or the two place predicate 'T', and so can't tell us whether sentences which use these terms are true or false.

EXERCISES

2–1. I am going to ask you to give an interpretation for some sentences. You should use the following format. Suppose you are describing an interpretation with a domain of three objects named 'a', 'b', and 'c'. Specify the domain in this way: D = {a,b,c}. That is, specify the domain by giving a list of the names of the objects in the domain. Then specify what is true about the objects in the domain by using a sentence of predicate logic. Simply conjoin all the atomic and negated atomic sentences which say which predicates are true of which objects and which are false. Here is an example. The following is an interpretation of the sentence 'Tb & Kbd':

D = {b,d}; Tb & Td & Kbb & Kbd & Kdb & Kdd.

In this interpretation all objects have property T and everything stands in the relation K to itself and to everything else. Here is another interpretation of the same sentence:

D = {b,d}; ~Tb & Td & Kbb & ~Kbd & ~Kdb & Kdd.

Sometimes students have trouble understanding what I want in this exercise. They ask, How am I supposed to decide which interpretation to write down? You can write down any interpretation you want as long as it is **an** interpretation of the sentence I give you. In every case you have infinitely many interpretations to choose from because you can always get more interpretations by throwing in more objects and then saying what is true for the new objects. Choose any you like. Just make sure you are writing down an interpretation of the sentence I give you.

a) Lab

b) Lab ⊃ Ta

c) Lab ∨ ~Lba

d) (∀x)(Fx≡Rxb)

e) Ga & (∃x)(Lxb ∨ Rax)

f) (Kx & (∀x)Rax) ⊃ (∃x)(Mx ∨ Rcx)

2–2. TRUTH IN AN INTERPRETATION

Just like a line of a truth table, an interpretation tells us whether each atomic sentence formed from predicates and names is true or false. What about compound sentences? If the main connective of a compound sentence does not involve a quantifier, we simply use the old rules for the connectives of sentence logic. We have only one more piece of work to complete: We must make more exact our informal description of the conditions under which a quantified sentence is true or is false in an interpretation.

Intuitively, a universally quantified sentence is going to be true in an interpretation if it is true in the interpretation for **every**thing to which the variable could refer in the interpretation. (Logicians say, "For **every** value of the universally quantified variable.") An existentially quantified sentence will be true in an interpretation if it is true for **some**thing to which the variable could refer in the interpretation (that is, "for **some** value of the existentially quantified variable.") What we still need to do is to make precise what it is for a quantified sentence to be true for a value of a variable. Let's illustrate with the same example we have been using, the interpretation given in figure 2–1.

Consider the sentence '(∀x)Bx'. In the interpretation we are considering, there are exactly two objects, a, and e. '(∀x)Bx' will be true in the interpretation just in case, roughly speaking, it is true both for the case of 'x' referring to a and the case of 'x' referring to e. But when 'x' refers to a, we have the sentence 'Ba'. And when 'x' refers to 'e', we have the sentence 'Be'. Thus '(∀x)Bx' is true in this interpretation just in case both 'Ba' and 'Be' are true. We call 'Ba' the *Substitution Instance* of '(∀x)Bx' formed by substituting 'a' for 'x'. Likewise, we call 'Be' the substitution instance of '(∀x)Bx' formed by substituting 'e' for 'x'. Our strategy is to explain the meaning of universal quantification by defining this notion of substitution instance and then specifying that a universally quantified sentence is true in an interpretation just in case it is true for all substitution instances in the interpretation:

> (Incomplete Definition) For any universally quantified sentence (∀**u**)(. . . **u** . . .), the *Substitution Instance* of the sentence with the name **s** substituted for the variable **u** is (. . . **s** . . .), the sentence formed by dropping the initial universal quantifier and writing **s** wherever **u** had occurred.

A word of warning: This definition is not yet quite right. It works only as long as we don't have multiple quantification, that is, as long as we don't have sentences which stack one quantifier on top of other quantifiers. But until chapter 3 we are going to keep things simple and consider only simple sentences which do not have one quantifier applying to a sentence with another quantifier inside. When we have the basic concepts we will come back and give a definition which is completely general.

Now we can easily use this definition of substitution instance to characterize truth of a universally quantified sentence in an interpretation:

> (Incomplete Definition) A *universally quantified sentence is true in an interpretation* just in case **all** of the sentence's substitution instances, formed with names in the interpretation, are true in the interpretation.

Another word of warning: As with the definition of substitution instance, this definition is not quite right. Again, chapter 3 will straighten out the details.

To practice, let's see whether '(∀x)(Bx ⊃ Lxe)' is true in the interpretation of figure 2–1. First we form the substitution instances with the names of the interpretation, 'a', and 'e'. We get the first substitution instance by dropping the quantifier and writing in 'a' everywhere we see 'x'. This gives

Ba ⊃ Lae.

Note that because 'Ba' and 'Lae' are both true in the interpretation, this first substitution instance is true in the interpretation. Next we form the second substitution instance by dropping the quantifier and writing in 'e' wherever we see 'x':

Be ⊃ Lee.

Because 'Be' is false and 'Lee' is true in the interpretation, the conditional 'Be ⊃ Lee' is true in the interpretation. We see that all the substitution instances of '(∀x)(Bx ⊃ Lxe)' are true in the interpretation. So this universally quantified sentence is true in the interpretation.

To illustrate further our condition for truth of a universally quantified sentence, consider the sentence '(∀x)(Bx ⊃ Lxa)'. This has the substitution instance 'Ba ⊃ Laa'. In this interpretation 'Ba' is true and 'Laa' is false, so 'Ba ⊃ Laa' is false in the interpretation. Because '(∀x)(Bx ⊃ Lxa)' has a false substitution instance in the interpretation, it is false in the interpretation.

You may have noticed the following fact about the truth of a universally quantified sentence and the truth of its substitution instances. By definition '(∀x)(Bx ⊃ Lxe)' is true in the interpretation just in case all of its instances are true in the interpretation. But its instances are all true just in case the **conjunction** of the instances is true. That is, '(∀x)(Bx ⊃ Lxe)' is true in the interpretation just in case the conjunction

(Ba ⊃ Lae) & (Be ⊃ Lee)

is true in the interpretation. If you think about it, you will see that this will hold in general. In the interpretation we have been discussing (or any interpretation with two objects named 'a' and 'e'), any universally quantified sentence, '(∀x)(. . . x . . .)', will be true just in case the conjunction of its substitution instance, '(. . . a . . .)&(. . . e . . .)', is true in the interpretation.

It's looking like we can make conjunctions do the same work that the universal quantifier does. A universally quantified sentence is true in an interpretation just in case the conjunction of all its substitution instances is true in the interpretation. Why, then, do we need the universal quantifier at all?

To answer this question, ask yourself what happens when we shift to a new interpretation with fewer or more things in its domain. In the new interpretation, what conjunction will have the same truth value as a given universally quantified sentence? If the new interpretation has a larger domain, our conjunction will have more conjuncts. If the new interpretation has a smaller domain, our conjunction will have fewer conjuncts. In other words, when we are looking for a conjunction of instances to give us the truth value of a universally quantified sentence, the conjunction will change from interpretation to interpretation. You can see in this way that the universal quantifier really does add something new. It acts rather like a variable conjunction sign. It has the effect of forming a long conjunction, with one conjunct for each of the objects in an interpretation's domain. If an interpretation's domain has infinitely many objects, a universally quantified sentence has the effect of an infinitely long conjunction!

What about existentially quantified sentences? All the work is really done. We repeat everything we said for universal quantification, replacing the word 'all' with 'some':

(Incomplete Definition) For any existentially quantified sentence (∃)(. . . **u**. . .), the *Substitution Instance* of the sentence, with the name **s** substituted for the variable **u** is (. . . **s** . . .), the sentence formed by dropping the initial existential quantifier and writing **s** wherever **u** had occurred.

(Incomplete Definition) An *existentially quantified sentence is true in an interpretation* just in case **some** (i.e., one or more) of the sentence's substitution instances, formed with names in the interpretation, are true in the interpretation.

As with the parallel definitions for universally quantified sentences, these definitions will have to be refined when we get to chapter 3.

To illustrate, let's see whether the sentence '(∃x)(Bx & Lxe)' is true in the interpretation of figure 2–1. We will need the sentence's substitution instances. We drop the quantifier and write in 'a' wherever we see 'x', giving 'Ba & Lae', the instance with 'a' substituted for 'x'. In the same way, we form the instance with 'e' substituted for 'x', namely, 'Be & Lee'. '(∃x)(Bx &Lxe)' is true in the interpretation just in case one or more of its substitution instances are true in the interpretation. Because 'Ba' and 'Lae' are true in the interpretation, the first instance, 'Ba & Lae', is true, and so '(∃x)(Bx & Lxe)' is true.

Have you noticed that, just as we have a connection between universal quantification and conjunction, we have the same connection between existential quantification and **disjunction**: '(∃x)(Bx & Lxe)' is true in our interpretation just in case one or more of its instances are true. But one or more of its instances are true just in case their disjunction

(Ba & Lae) ∨ (Be & Lee)

is true. In a longer or shorter interpretation we will have the same thing with a longer or shorter disjunction. Ask yourself, when is an existentially quantified sentence true in an interpretation? It is true just in case the disjunction of all its substitution instances in that interpretation is true in the interpretation. Just as the universal quantifier acted like a variable conjunction sign, the existential quantifier acts like a variable disjunction sign. In an interpretation with an infinite domain, an existentially quantified sentence even has the effect of an infinite disjunction.

I hope that by now you have a pretty good idea of how to determine whether a quantified sentence is true or false in an interpretation. In understanding this you also come to understand everything there is to know about the meaning of the quantifiers. Remember that we explained the meaning of the sentence logic connectives '~', '&', '∨', '⊃', and '≡' by giving their truth table definitions. For example, explaining how to determine whether or not a conjunction is true in a line of a truth table tells you everything there is to know about the meaning of '&'. In the same way, our characterization of truth of a quantified sentence in an interpretation does the same kind of work in explaining the meaning of the quantifiers.

This point about the meaning of the quantifiers illustrates a more general fact. By a "case" in sentence logic we mean a line of a truth table, that is, an assignment of truth values to sentence letters. The interpretations of predicate logic generalize this idea of a case. Keep in mind that interpretations do the same kind of work in predicate logic that assignments of truth values to sentence letters do in sentence logic, and you will easily extend what you already know to understand validity, logical truth, contradictions, and other concepts in predicate logic.

By now you have also seen how to determine the truth value which an interpretation gives to any sentence, not just to quantified sentences. An interpretation itself tells you which atomic sentences are true and which are false. You can then use the rules of valuation for sentence logic connectives together with our two new rules for the truth of universally and existentially quantified sentences to determine the truth of any compound sentence in terms of the truth of shorter sentences. Multiple quantification still calls for some refinements, but in outline you have the basic ideas.

EXERCISES

2–2. Consider the interpretation

D = {a,b}; ~Ba & Bb & Laa & ~Lab & Lba & ~Lbb.

For each of the following sentences, give all of the sentence's substitution instances in this interpretation, and for each substitution instance say whether the instance is true or false in the interpretation. For example, for the sentence '(∀x)Bx', your answer should look like this:

GIVEN SENTENCE   SUBSTITUTION INSTANCES
(∀x)Bx   Ba, false in the interpretation
                  Bb, true

   a) (∃x)Bx   b) (∃x)~Lxa   c) (∀x)Lxa

   d) (∃x)Lbx   e) (∀)(Bx v Lax) f) (∃x)(Lxa & Lbx)

   g) (∀x)(Bx ⊃ Lbx) h) (∃x)[(Lbx & Bb) v Bx]

   i) (∀x)[Bx ⊃ (Lxx ⊃ Lxa)]

j) (∀x)[(Bx ∨ Lax) ⊃ (Lxb ∨ ~Bx)]

k) (∃x)[(Lax & Lxa) ≡ (Bx ∨ Lxb)]

2–3. For each of the sentences in exercise 2–2, say whether the sentence is true or false in the interpretation of exercise 2–2.

2–4. For each of the following sentences, determine whether the sentence is true or false in the interpretation of exercise 2–2. In this exercise, you must carefully determine the main connective of a sentence before applying the rules to determine its truth in an interpretation. Remember that a quantifier is a connective which applies to the **shortest** full sentence which follows it. Remember that the main connective of a sentence is the **last** connective that gets used in building the sentence up from its parts. To determine whether a sentence is true in an interpretation, first determine the sentence's main connective. If the connective is '&', 'v', '~', '⊃', or '≡', you must first determine the truth value of the components, and then apply the rules for the main connective (a conjunction is true just in case both conjuncts are true, and so on). If the main connective is a quantifier, you have to determine the truth value of the substitution instances and then apply the rule for the quantifier, just as you did in the last exercise.

a) (∃x)Lxx ⊃ (∀x)(Bx ∨ Lbx)
b) ~(∃x)(Lxx ⊃ Bx) & (∀x)(Bx ⊃ Lxx)
c) (∃x)[Bx ≡ (Lax ∨ Lxb)]
d) (∃x)(Lxb ∨ Bx) ⊃ (Lab ∨ ~Ba)
e) ~(∀x)(~Lxx ∨ Lxb) ⊃ (Lab ∨ ~Lba)
f) (∃x)[(Lbx ∨ Bx) ⊃ (Lxb & ~Bx)]
g) (∀x)~[(~Lxx ≡ Bx) ⊃ (Lax ≡ Lxa)]
h) (∀x)(Lax ∨ Lxb) ∨ (∃x)(Lax ∨ Lxb)
i) (∃x)[Lxx & (Bx ⊃ Laa)] & (∃x)~(Lab ≡ Lxx)
j) (∀x){[Bx ∨ (Lax & ~Lxb)] ⊃ (Bx ⊃ Lxx)}

2–5. In the past exercises we have given interpretations by explicitly listing objects in the domain and explicitly saying which predicates apply to which things. We can also describe an interpretation in more general terms. For example, consider the interpretation given by

i)   Domain: All U.S. citizens over the age of 21.
ii) Names: Each person in the domain is named by 'a' subscripted by his or her social security number.
iii) Predicates: Mx: x is a millionaire.
              Hx: x is happy.

(That is, a one place predicate 'Mx' which holds of someone just in case that person is a millionaire and a one place predicate 'Hx' which holds of someone just in case that person is happy.)

a) Determine the truth value of the following sentences in this interpretation. In each case explain your answer. Since you can't write out all the substitution instances, you will have to give an informal general statement to explain your answer, using general facts you know about being a millionaire, being happy, and the connection (or lack of connection) between these.

a1) (∃x)Mx   a2) (∀x)Hx   a3) (∀x)(Hx ⊃ Mx)   a4) (∃x)(Mx & ~Hx)

a5) (∀x)[(Mx ⊃ Hx) & (~Mx ⊃ ~Hx)]

a6) (∃x)[(Hx & Mx) ∨ (~Hx & ~Mx)]

a7) (∃x)(Mx & Hx) & (∃x)(Mx & ~Hx)

a8) (∀x)(Hx ⊃ Mx) ⊃ ~ (∃x)Mx

Here is another example:

    i) Domain: All integers, 1, 2, 3, 4, . . .
    ii) Names: Each integer is named by 'a' subscripted by that integer's numeral. For example, 17 is named by 'a_{17}'.
    iii) Predicates: Ox: x is odd.
                 Kxy: x is equal to or greater than y.

b) Again, figure out the truth value of the following sentences, and explain informally how you arrived at your answer.

b1) (∃x)Ox   b2) (∀x)~Ox   b3) (∃x)(Ox & Kxx)

b4) (∀x)Kxa$_{17}$ b5) (∀x)(Ox ∨ ~Ox)

b6) (∃x)(Ox & Kxa$_{17}$)

b7) (∀x)[Ox ≡ (~Kxa$_{18}$ & Kxa$_{17}$)]

b8) (∃x)(Kxa$_{17}$ ⊃ Kxa$_{18}$) & (∀x)(~Kxa$_{17}$ ∨ Kxa$_{18}$)

b9) (∀x)(Ox ⊃ Kxa$_{17}$) & (∀x)(~Ox ⊃ ~ Kxa$_{17}$)

2–3. VALIDITY IN PREDICATE LOGIC

In sentence logic, we said that an argument is valid if and only if, for all possible cases in which all the premises are true, the conclusion is true also. In predicate logic, the intuitive notion of validity remains the same. We change things only by generalizing the notion of possible case. Where before we meant that all lines in the truth table which made all premises true also make the conclusion true, now we mean that all interpretations which make all the premises true also make the conclusion true:

> An argument expressed with sentences in predicate logic is valid if and only if the conclusion is true in every interpretation in which all the premises are true.

You may remember that we got started on predicate logic at the beginning of chapter 1 because we had two arguments which seemed valid but which sentence logic characterized as invalid. To test whether predicate logic is doing the job it is supposed to do, let us see whether predicate logic gives us the right answer for these arguments;

Everyone loves Eve.	$(\forall x)Lxe$
Adam loves Eve.	Lae

Suppose we have an interpretation in which '$(\forall x)Lxe$' is true. Will 'Lae' have to be true in this interpretation also? Notice that 'Lae' is a substitution instance of '$(\forall x)Lxe$'. A universally quantified sentence is true in an interpretation just in case all its substitution instances are true in the interpretation. So in any interpretation in which '$(\forall x)Lxe$' is true, the instance 'Lae' will be true also. And this is just what we mean by the argument being valid.

Let's examine the other argument:

Adam loves Eve.	Lae
Someone loves Eve.	$(\exists x)Lxe$

Suppose we have an interpretation in which 'Lae' is true. Does '$(\exists x)Lxe$' have to be true in this interpretation? Notice that 'Lae' is an instance of '$(\exists x)Lxe$'. We know that '$(\exists x)Lxe$' is true in an interpretation if even one of its instances is true in the interpretation. Thus, if 'Lae' is true in an interpretation, '$(\exists x)Lxe$' will also be true in that interpretation. Once again, the argument is valid.

Along with validity, all our ideas about counterexamples carry over from sentence logic. When we talked about the validity of a sentence logic argument, we first defined it in this way: An argument is valid just in case any line of the truth table which makes all the premises true makes the conclusion true also. Then we reexpressed this by saying: An argument is valid just in case it has no counterexamples; that is, no lines of the truth table make all the premises true and the conclusion false. For predicate logic, all the ideas are the same. The only thing that has changed is that we now talk about interpretations where before we talked about lines of the truth table:

A *Counterexample* to a predicate logic argument is an interpretation in which the premises are all true and the conclusion is false.

A predicate logic argument is *Valid* if and only if it has no counterexamples.

Let's illustrate the idea of counterexamples in examining the validity of

Lae
———
(∃x)Lxe

Is there a counterexample to this argument? A counterexample would be an interpretation with 'Lae' true and '(∃x)Lxe' false. But there can be no such interpretation. 'Lae' is an instance of '(∃x)Lxe', and '(∃x)Lxe' is true in an interpretation if even one of its instances is true in the interpretation. Thus, if 'Lae' is true in an interpretation, '(∃x)Lxe' will also be true in that interpretation. In other words, there can be no interpretation in which 'Lae' is true and '(∃x)Lxe' is false, which is to say that the argument has no counterexamples. And that is just another way of saying that the argument is valid.

For comparison, contrast the last case with the argument

(∃x)Bx
———
Ba

It's easy to construct a counterexample to this argument. Any case in which someone other than Adam is blond and Adam is not blond will do the trick. So an interpretation with Adam and Eve in the domain and in which Eve is blond and Adam is not blond gives us a counterexample, showing the argument to be invalid.

This chapter has been hard work. But your sweat will be repaid. The concepts of interpretation, substitution instance, and truth in an interpretation provide **the** essential concepts you need to understand quantification. In particular, once you understand these concepts, you will find proof techniques for predicate logic to be relatively easy.

EXERCISES

2–6. For each of the following arguments, determine whether the argument is valid or invalid. If it is invalid, show this by giving a counterexample. If it is valid, explain your reasoning which shows it to be valid. Use the kind of informal reasoning which I used in discussing the arguments in this section.

You may find it hard to do these problems because I haven't given you any very specific strategies for figuring out whether an argument is valid. But don't give up! If you can't do one argument, try another first. Try to think of some specific, simple interpretation of the sentences in an argument, and ask yourself—"Are the premise and conclusion both true in that interpretation?" Can I change the interpretation so as to make the premise true and the conclusion false? If you succeed in doing that, you will have worked the problem because you will have constructed a counterexample and shown the argument to be invalid. If you can't seem to be able to construct a counterexample, try to understand why you can't. If you can see why you can't and put this into words, you will have succeeded in showing that the argument is valid. Even if you might not succeed in working many of these problems, playing around in this way with interpretations, truth in interpretations, and counterexamples will strengthen your grasp of these concepts and make the next chapter easier.

a) (∀x)Lxe   b) Lae   c) (∃x)Lxe

   ─────────   ─────────   ─────────

   (∃x)Lxe   (∀x)Lxe   Lae

d) (∀x)(Bx & Lxe)   e) (∀x)(Bx ⊃ Lxe)

   ─────────────────   ─────────────────

   (∀x)Bx   (∃x)Bx

f) (∃x)Bx & (∃x)Lxa   g) (∀x)(Bx ⊃ Lxe) & (∀x)(~Bx ⊃ Lxa)

   ─────────────────   ─────────────────────────────────

   (∃x)(Bx & Lxa)   (∀x)[(Bx ⊃ Lxe) & (~Bx ⊃ Lxa)]

CHAPTER SUMMARY EXERCISES

Provide short explanations for each of the following, checking against the text to make sure you understand each term clearly and saving your answers in your notebook for reference and review.

a) Interpretation
b) Interpretation of a Sentence
c) Substitution Instance
d) Truth in an Interpretation
e) Validity of a Predicate Logic Argument

More about Quantifiers 3

3–1. SOME EXAMPLES OF MULTIPLE QUANTIFICATION

All of the following are sentences of predicate logic:

    (1) $(\forall x)(\forall y)Lxy$
    (2) $(\exists x)(\exists y)Lxy$
    (3) $(\exists x)(\forall y)Lxy$
    (4) $(\exists x)(\forall y)Lyx$
    (5) $(\forall x)(\exists y)Lxy$
    (6) $(\forall x)(\exists y)Lyx$

Let's suppose that 'L' stands for the relation of loving. What do these sentences mean?

Sentence (1) says that everybody loves everybody (including themselves). (2) says that somebody loves somebody. (The somebody can be oneself or someone else.) Sentences (3) to (6) are a little more tricky. (3) says that there is one person who is such that he or she loves everyone. (There is one person who is such that, for all persons, the first loves the second—think of God as an example.) We get (4) from (3) by reversing the order of the 'x' and 'y' as arguments of 'L'. As a result, (4) says that there is one person who is loved by everyone. Notice what a big difference the order of the 'x' and 'y' makes.

Next, (5) says that everyone loves someone: Every person is such that there is one person such that the first loves the second. In a world in which (5) is true, each person has an object of their affection. Finally we get (6) out of (5) by again reversing the order of 'x' and 'y'. As a result, (6) says that everyone is loved by someone or other. In a world in which (6) is true no one goes unloved. But (6) says something significantly weaker than (3). (3) say that there is **one** person who loves everyone. (6) says that each person gets loved, but Adam might be loved by one person, Eve by another, and so on.

Can we say still other things by further switching around the order of the quantifiers and arguments in sentences (3) to (6)? For example, switching the order of the quantifiers in (6) gives

(7) $(\exists y)(\forall x)Lyx$

Strictly speaking, (7) is a new sentence, but it does not say anything new because it is logically equivalent to (3). It is important to see why this is so:

These diagrams will help you to see that (7) and (3) say exactly the same thing. The point is that there is nothing special about the variable 'x' or the variable 'y'. Either one can do the job of the other. What matters is the pattern of quantifiers and variables. These diagrams show that the pattern is the same. All that counts is that the variable marked at position 1 in the existential quantifier is tied to, or, in logicians' terminology, *Binds* the variable at position 3; and the variable at position 2 in the universal quantifier binds the variable at position 4. Indeed, we could do without the variables altogether and indicate what we want with the third diagram. This diagram gives the pattern of variable binding which (7) and (3) share.

3–2. QUANTIFIER SCOPE, BOUND VARIABLES, AND FREE VARIABLES

In the last example we saw that the variable at 3 is bound by the quantifier at 1 and the variable at 4 is bound by the quantifier at 2. This case contrasts with that of a variable which is not bound by any quantifier, for example

(8)   Lxa ⊃ (∃x)Lxb
       1   2 3

(9)   (∃x)Lxb ⊃ Lxa
       1 2   3

In (8), the occurrence of 'x' at 3 is bound by the quantifier at 2. However, the occurrence of 'x' at 1 is not bound by any quantifier. Logicians say that the occurrence of 'x' at 1 is *Free*. In (9), the occurrence of 'x' at 3 is free because the quantifier at 1 binds only variables in the shortest full sentence which follows it. Logicians call the shortest full sentence following a quantifier the quantifier's *Scope*. In (9), the 'x' at 3 is not in the scope of the quantifier at 1. Consequently, the quantifier does not bind 'x' at 3.

All the important ideas of this section have now been presented. We need these ideas to understand clearly how to apply the methods of derivations and truth trees when quantifiers get stacked on top of each other. All we need do to complete the job is to give the ideas an exact statement and make sure you know how to apply them in more complicated situations.

Everything can be stated in terms of the simple idea of scope. A quantifier is a connective. We use a quantifier to build longer sentences out of shorter ones. In building up sentences, a quantifier works just like the negation sign: It apples to the shortest full sentence which follows it. This shortest full following sentence is the quantifier's scope:

> The *Scope* of a quantifier is the shortest full sentence which follows it. Everything inside this shortest full following sentence is said to be in the scope of the quantifier.

We can now define 'bound' and 'free' in terms of scope:

> A variable, **u,** is *Bound* just in case it occurs in the scope of a quantifier, (∀u) or (∃u).

> A variable, **u,** is *Free* just in case it is not bound; that is, just in case it does not occur in the scope of any quantifier, (∀u) or (∃u).

Clearly, a variable gets bound only by using a quantifier expressed with the same variable. 'x' can never be bound by quantifiers such as '(∀y)' or '(∃z)'.

Occasionally, students ask about the variables that occur within the quantifiers—the 'x' in '(∃x)' and in '(∀x)'. Are they bound? Are they free? The answer to this question is merely a matter of convention on which nothing important turns. I think the most sensible thing to say is that the variable within a quantifier is part of the quantifier symbol and so does not count as either bound or free. Only variables outside a quantifier can be either bound or free. Some logicians prefer to deal with this question by defining the scope of a quantifier to include the quantifier itself as well as the shortest full sentence which follows it. On this convention one would say that a variable within a quantifier always binds itself.

These definitions leave one fine point unclear. What happens if the variable **u** is in the scope of **two** quantifiers that use **u**? For example, consider

(10) $(\exists x)[(\forall x)Lxa \supset Lxb]$
          1   2 3   4

The occurrence of 'x' at 3 is in the scope of both the 'x' quantifiers. Which quantifier binds 'x' at 3?

To get straight about this, think through how we build (10) up from atomic constituents. We start with the atomic sentences 'Lxa' and 'Lxb'. Because atomic sentences have no quantifiers, 'x' is free in both of these atomic sentences. Next we apply '$(\forall x)$' to 'Lxa', forming '$(\forall x)Lxa$', which we use as the antecedent in the conditional

(11) $(\forall x)Lxa \supset Lxb$
          2 3   4

In (11), the occurrence of 'x' at 3 is bound by the quantifier at 2. The occurrence of 'x' at 4 is free in (11).

Finally, we can clearly describe the effect of '$(\exists x)$' when we apply it to (11). '$(\exists x)$' binds just the **free** occurrences of 'x' in (11). The occurrence at 4 is free and so gets bound by the new quantifier. The occurrence at 3 is already bound, so the new quantifier can't touch it. The following diagram describes the overall effect:

(10) $(\exists x)[(\forall x)Lxa \supset Lxb]$
          1   2 3   4

First, the occurrence at 3 is bound by the quantifier at 2. Then the occurrence at 4 is bound by the quantifier at 1. The job being done by the 2–3 link is completely independent of the job being done by the 1–4 link.

Let's give a general statement to the facts we have uncovered:

> A quantifier $(\forall u)$ or $(\exists u)$ binds all and only all **free** occurrences of **u** in its scope. Such a quantifier does not bind an occurrence of **u** in its scope which is already bound by some other quantifier in its scope.

We can make any given case even clearer by using different variables where we have occurrences of a variable bound by different quantifiers. So, for example, (10) is equivalent to

(12) $(\exists x)[(\forall z)Lza \supset Lxb]$

In (12), there can be no confusion about which quantifier binds which variable—we keep track of everything by using different variables. Why, then, didn't we just resolve to use different variables from the beginning and save ourselves a lot of trouble? We could have done that, but then the definition of the sentences of predicate logic would have been much more complicated. Either way, we have work to do. Besides, the formulation I have presented here is the one traditionally used by logicians and so the one you will need to know if you study more logic.

Let's look at another, slightly more complicated, example to make sure you have put this all together. Draw in the lines which show which quantifier binds which variable in the following:

    (13) (∃x)[(∃x)(Bx ∨ Lxa) ⊃ (Bx & Lxb)]

If you are having trouble, think through how (13) gets built up from its parts. In

    (14) (∃x)(Bx ∨ Lxa) ⊃ (Bx & Lxb)
           2 3   4   5   6

the quantifier at 2 applies only to the shortest full sentence which follows it, which ends before the '⊃'. So the occurrences of 'x' at 3 and 4 are both bound by the quantifier at 2. The two occurrences of 'x' at 5 and 6 are not in the scope of a quantifier and are both free. So when we apply the second '(∃x)' to all of (14), the new '(∃x)' binds only the 'x's which are still free in (14), namely, the 'x's which occur at 5 and 6. In sum, the pattern of binding is

    (13) (∃x)[(∃x)(Bx ∨ Lxa) ⊃ (Bx & Lxb)]
         1 2 3 4   5 6

We can make this pattern even clearer by writing the sentence equivalent to (13):

    (15) (∃x)[(∃z)(Bz ∨ Lza) ⊃ (Bx & Lxb)]

In practice, of course, it is much better to use sentences such as (15) and (12) instead of the equivalent (13) and (10), which are more difficult to interpret.

EXERCISES

3–1. In the following sentences draw link lines to show which quantifiers bind which variables and say which occurrences of the variables are bound and which are free:

a) L zz   b) $(\forall y)(\forall z)Lzy$ c) $(\forall z)(Bz \supset Lxz)$
     12   12   1   23

d) $(\exists x)[Lxz\ \&\ (\forall y)(Lxy \lor Lzx)]$
     12   34   56

e) $(\forall x)(Lax\ \&\ Bx) \equiv (Lxx \supset (\exists x)Bx)$
     1   2   34   5

f) $(\forall x)[Lyx \supset (Bx \supset (\exists x)Lyx)]$
    12   3   45

3–3. CORRECT DEFINITIONS OF SUBSTITUTION INSTANCE AND TRUTH IN AN INTERPRETATION

In chapter 2 I gave an incorrect definition of 'substitution instance.' I said that we get the substitution instance of $(\forall u)$ (. . . **u** . . .) with s substituted for **u** by simply dropping the initial (**u**) and writing in **s** wherever we find **u** in (. . . **u** . . .). This is correct as long as neither a second $(\forall u)$ nor a $(\exists u)$ occurs within the scope of the initial $(\forall u)$, that is, within the sentence (. . . **u** . . .). Since I used only this kind of simple sentence in chapter 2, there we could get away with the simple but incorrect definition. But now we must correct our definition so that it will apply to any sentence. Before reading on, can you see how multiple quantification can make trouble for the simple definition of substitution instance, and can you see how to state the definition correctly?

To correct the definition of substitution instance, all we have to do is to add the qualification that the substituted occurrences of the variable be **free**:

For any universally quantified sentence $(\forall u)$ (. . . **u** . . .), the *Substitution Instance* of the sentence, with the name **s** substituted for the variable **u,** is (. . . **s** . . .), the sentence formed by dropping the initial universal quantifier and writing **s** for all **free** occurrences of **u** in (. . . **u** . . .).

For any existentially quantified sentence $(\exists u)$ (. . . **u** . . .), the *Substitution Instance* of the sentence, with the name **s** substituted for the variable **u,** is (. . . **s** . . .), the sentence formed by dropping the initial existential quantifier and writing **s** for all **free** occurrences of **u** in (. . . **u** . . .).

For example, look back at (13). Its substitution instance with 'c' substituted for 'x' is

(16) $(\exists x)(Bx \lor Lxa) \supset (Bc\ \&\ Lcb)$
      2   3   4   5   6

The occurrences of 'x' at 3 and 4 are not free in the sentence which results from (13) by dropping the initial quantifier. So we don't substitute 'c' for 'x' at 3 and 4. We substitute 'c' only at the free occurrences, which were at 5 and 6.

Can you see why, when we form substitution instances, we pay attention only to the occurrences which are free after dropping the outermost quantifier? The occurrences at 3 and 4, bound by the '(∃x)' quantifier at 2, have nothing to do with the outermost quantification. When forming substitution instances of a quantified sentence, we are concerned only with the outermost quantifier and the occurrences which it binds.

To help make this clear, once again consider (15), which is equivalent to (13). In (15), we have no temptation to substitute 'c' for 'z' when forming the 'c'-substitution instance for the sentence at a whole. (15) says that there is some x such that so on and so forth about x. In making this true for some specific x, say c, we do not touch the occurrences of 'z'. The internal 'z'-quantified sentence is just part of the so on and so forth which is asserted about x in the quantified form of the sentence, that is, in (15). So the internal 'z'-quantified sentence is just part of the so on and so forth which is asserted about c in the substitution instance of the sentence. Finally, (13) says exactly what (15) says. So we treat (13) in the same way.

Now let's straighten out the definition of truth of a sentence in an interpretation. Can you guess what the problem is with our old definition? I'll give you a clue. Try to determine the truth value of 'Lxe' in the interpretation of figure 2–1. You can't do it! Nothing in our definition of an interpretation gives us a truth value for an atomic sentence with a free variable. An interpretation only gives truth values for atomic sentences which use no variables. You will have just as much trouble trying to determine the truth value of '(∀x)Lxy' in any interpretation. A substitution instance of '(∀x)Lxy' will still have the free variable 'y', and no interpretation will assign such a substitution instance a truth value.

Two technical terms (mentioned in passing in chapter 1) will help us in talking about our new problem:

> A sentence with one or more free variables is called an *Open Sentence*.
>
> A sentence which is not open (i.e., a sentence with no free variables) is called a *Closed Sentence*.

In a nutshell, our problem is that our definitions of truth in an interpretation do not specify truth values for open sentences. Some logicians deal with this problem by treating all free variables in an open sentence as if they were universally quantified. Others do what I will do here: We simply say that open sentences have no truth value.

If you think about it, this is really very natural. What, anyway, is the truth value of the English "sentence" 'He is blond.', when nothing has been said or done to give you even a clue as to who 'he' refers to? In such a situation you can't assign any truth value to 'He is blond.' 'He is blond.' functions syntactically as a sentence—it has the form of a sentence. But there is still something very problematic about it. In predicate logic we allow such open sentences to function syntactically as sentences. Doing this is very useful in making clear how longer sentences get built up from shorter ones. But open sentences never get assigned a truth value, and in this way they fail to be full-fledged sentences of predicate logic.

It may seem that I am dealing with the problem of no truth value for open sentences by simply ignoring the problem. In fact, as long as we acknowledge up-front that this is what we are doing, saying that open sentences have no truth value is a completely adequate way to proceed.

We have only one small detail to take care of. As I stated the definitions of truth of quantified sentences in an interpretation, the definitions were said to apply to any quantified sentences. But they apply only to **closed** sentences. So we must write in this restriction:

> A universally quantified closed sentence is true in an interpretation just in case all of the sentence's substitution instances, formed with names in the interpretation, are true in the interpretation.

> An existentially quantified closed sentence is true in an interpretation just in case some (i.e., one or more) of the sentence's substitution instances, formed with names in the interpretation, are true in the interpretation.

These two definitions, together with the rules of valuation given in chapters 1 and 4 of volume I for the sentence logic connectives, specify a truth value for any **closed** sentence in any of our interpretations.

You may remember that in chapter 1 in volume I we agreed that sentences of logic would always be true or false. Sticking by that agreement now means stipulating that only the closed sentences of predicate logic are real sentences. As I mentioned in chapter 1 in this volume, some logicians use the phrase *Formulas,* or *Propositional Functions* for predicate logic open sentences, to make the distinction clear. I prefer to stick with the word 'sentence' for both open and closed sentences, both to keep terminology to a minimum and to help us keep in mind how longer (open and closed) sentences get built up from shorter (open and closed) sentences. But you must keep in mind that only the closed sentences are full-fledged sentences with truth values.

EXERCISES

3-2. Write a substitution instance using 'a' for each of the following sentences:

a) $(\forall y)(\exists x)Lxy$ b) $(\exists z)[(\forall x)Bx \lor Bz]$
c) $(\exists x)[Bx \equiv (\forall x)(Lax \lor Bx)]$
d) $(\forall y)[(\exists x)(Bx \supset By) \& (\forall x)(By \supset Bx)]$
e) $(\forall y)\{(\exists x)Bx \lor [(\exists y)By \supset Lyy]\}$

f) $(\forall y)(\exists x)[(Rxy \supset Dy) \supset Ryx]$

g) $(\forall x)(\forall y)(\forall z)\{[Sxy \lor (Hz \supset Lxz)] \equiv (Scx \& Hy)\}$

h) $(\exists x)(\forall z)\{(Pxa \supset Kz) \& (\exists y)[(Pxy \lor Kc) \& Pxx]\}$

i) $(\exists z)(\forall y)\{[(\exists x)Mzx \lor (\exists x)(Mxy \supset Myz)] \& (\exists x)Mzx\}$

j) $(\forall x)\{[(\forall x)Rxa \supset Rxb] \lor [(\exists x)(Rcx \lor Rxa) \supset Rxx]\}$

3–3. If **u** does not occur free in **X**, the quantifiers $(\forall u)$ and $(\exists u)$ are said to occur *Vacuously* in $(\forall u)X$ and $(\exists u)X$. Vacuous quantifiers have no effect. Let's restrict our attention to the special case in which **X** is closed, so that it has a truth value in any of its interpretations. The problem I want to raise is how to apply the definitions for interpreting quantifiers to vacuously occurring quantifiers. Because truth of a quantified sentence is defined in terms of substitution instances of $(\forall u)X$ and $(\exists u)X$, when **u** does not occur free in **X**, we most naturally treat this vacuous case by saying that **X** counts as a substitution instance of $(\forall u)(X)$ and $(\exists u)(X)$. (If you look back at my definitions of 'substitution instance', you will see that they really say this if by 'for all free occurrences of **u**' you understand 'for no occurrences of **u**' when **u** does not occur free in **X** at all. In any case, this is the way you should understand these definitions when **u** does not occur free in **X**.) With this understanding, show that $(\forall u)X$, $(\exists u)X$, and **X** all have the same truth value in any interpretation of **X**.

3–4. a)   As I have defined interpretation, every object in an interpretation has a name. Explain why this chapter's definitions of truth of existentially and universally quantified sentences would not work as intended if interpretations were allowed to have unnamed objects.

b)   Explain why one might want to consider interpretations with unnamed objects.

In part II we will consider interpretations with unnamed objects and revise the definitions of truth of quantified sentences accordingly.

3–4. SOME LOGICAL EQUIVALENCES

The idea of logical equivalence transfers from sentence logic to predicate logic in the obvious way. In sentence logic two sentences are logically equivalent if and only if in all possible cases the sentences have the same truth value, where a possible case is just a line of the truth table for the sentence, that is, an assignment of truth values to sentence letters. All we have to do is to redescribe possible cases as interpretations:

Two closed predicate logic sentences are *Logically Equivalent* if and only if in each of their interpretations the two sentences are either both true or both false.

Notice that I have stated the definition only for closed sentences. Indeed, the definition would not make any sense for open sentences because open sentences don't have truth values in interpretations. Nonetheless, one can extend the idea of logical equivalence to apply to open sentences. That's a good thing, because otherwise the law of substitution of logical equivalents would break down in predicate logic. We won't be making much use of these further ideas in this book, so I won't hold things up with the details. But you might amuse yourself by trying to extend the definition of logical equivalence to open sentences in a way which will make the law of substitution of logical equivalents work in just the way you would expect.

Let us immediately take note of two equivalences which will prove very useful later on. By way of example, consider the sentence, 'No one loves Eve', which we transcribe as '$\sim(\exists x)Lxe$', that is, as 'It is not the case that someone loves Eve'. How could this unromantic situation arise? Only if **everyone didn't** love Eve. In fact, saying '$\sim(\exists x)Lxe$' comes to the same thing as saying '$(\forall x)\sim Lxe$'. If there is not a single person who does love Eve, then it has to be that everyone does not love Eve. And conversely, if positively everyone does not love Eve, then not even one person does love Eve.

There is nothing special about the example I have chosen. If our sentence is of the form $\sim(\exists u)(\ldots u \ldots)$, this says that there is not a single **u** such that so on and so forth about **u.** But this comes to the same as saying about each and every **u** that so on and so forth is not true about **u,** that is, that $(\forall u)\sim(\ldots u \ldots)$.

We can easily prove the equivalence of $\sim(\exists u)(\ldots u \ldots)$ and $(\forall u)\sim(\ldots u \ldots)$ by appealing to De Morgan's laws. We have to prove that these two sentences have the same truth value in each and every interpretation. In any one interpretation, $\sim(\exists u)(\ldots u \ldots)$ is true just in case the negation of the disjunction of the instances

$$\sim[(\ldots a \ldots) \vee (\ldots b \ldots) \vee (\ldots c \ldots) \vee \ldots]$$

is true in the interpretation, where we have included in the disjunction all the instances formed using names which name things in the interpretation. By De Morgan's laws, this is equivalent to the conjunction of the negation of the instances

$$\sim(\ldots a \ldots) \& \sim(\ldots b \ldots) \& \sim(\ldots c \ldots) \& \ldots$$

which is true in the interpretation just in case $(\forall u)\sim(\ldots u \ldots)$ is true in the interpretation. Because this is true in all interpretations, we see that

Rule $\sim\exists$: $\sim(\exists u)(\ldots u \ldots)$ is logically equivalent to $(\forall u)\sim(\ldots u \ldots)$.

Now consider the sentence 'Not everyone loves Eve,' which we transcribe as '$\sim(\forall x)Lxe$'. If not everyone loves Eve, then there must be someone who does not love Eve. And if there is someone who does not love Eve, then not everyone loves Eve. So '~(∀x)Lxe' is logically equivalent to '(∃x)~Lxe'.

Pretty clearly, again there is nothing special about the example. ~(∀u)(. . . u . . .) is logically equivalent to (∃u)~(. . . u . . .). If it is not the case that, for all **u,** so on and so forth about **u,** then there must be some **u** such that not so on and so forth about **u.** And, conversely, if there is some **u** such that not so on and so forth about **u,** then it is not the case that for all **u,** so on and so forth about **u.** In summary

Rule ~∀: ~(∀u)(. . . u . . .) is logically equivalent to (∃u)~(. . . u . . .).

You can easily give a proof of this rule by imitating the proof of the rule ~∃. But I will let you write out the new proof as an exercise.

EXERCISES

3–5. a) Give a proof of the rule of logical equivalence, ~∀. Your proof will be very similar to the proof given in the text for the rule ~∃.

b) The proof for the rule ~∃ is flawed! It assumes that all interpretations have finitely many things in their domain. But not all interpretations are finite in this way. (Exercise 2–5 gives an example of an infinite interpretation.) The problem is that the proof tries to talk about the disjunction of all the substitution instances of a quantified sentence. But if an interpretation is infinite, there are infinitely many substitution instances, and no sentence can be infinitely long. Since I instructed you, in part (a) of this problem, to imitate the proof in the text, probably your proof has the same problem as mine.

Your task is to correct this mistake in the proofs. Give informal arguments for the rules ~∃ and ~∀ which take account of the fact that some interpretations have infinitely many things in their domain.

3–6. In the text I defined logical equivalence for closed sentences of predicate logic. However, this definition is not broad enough to enable us to state a sensible law of substitution of logical equivalents for predicate logic. Let me explain the problem with an example. The following two sentences are logically equivalent:

(1)   ~(∀x)(∀y)Lxy

(2)   (∃x)(∃y)~Lxy

But we cannot prove that (1) and (2) are logically equivalent with the rule ~∀ as I have stated it. Here is the difficulty. The rule ~∀ tells us that (1) is logically equivalent to

(3)   (∃x)~(∀y)Lxy

What we would like to say is that ~(∀y)Lxy is logically equivalent to (∃y)~Lxy, again by the rule ~∀. But the rule ~∀ does not license this because I have defined logical equivalence only for closed sentences and '~(∀y)Lxy' and '(∃y)~Lxy' are open sentences. (Strictly speaking, I should have restricted the ~∀ and ~∃ rules to closed sentences. I didn't because I anticipated the results of this exercise.) Since open sentences are never true or false, the idea of logical equivalence for open sentences does not make any sense, at least not on the basis of the definitions I have so far introduced.

Here is your task:

a) Extend the definition of logical equivalence for predicate logic sentences so that it applies to open as well as closed sentences. Do this in such a way that the law of substitution of logical equivalents will be correct when one open sentence is substituted for another when the two open sentences are logically equivalent according to your extended definition.

b) Show that the law of substitution of logical equivalents works when used with open sentences which are logically equivalent according to your extended definition.

CHAPTER SUMMARY EXERCISES

Here are this chapter's important terms. Check your understanding by writing short explanations for each, saving your results in your notebook for reference and review.

- a) Bound Variables
- b) Free Variables
- c) Scope
- d) Closed Sentence
- e) Open Sentence
- f) Truth of a Sentence in an Interpretation
- g) Rule ~∃
- h) Rule ~∀

Transcription

$$\overline{4}$$

4–1. RESTRICTED QUANTIFIERS

For three chapters now I have been merrily transcribing '(∃x)' both as 'something' and 'someone', and I have been transcribing '(∀x)' both as 'everything' and 'everyone.' I justified this by saying that when we talked only about people we would restrict the variables 'x', 'y', etc. to refer only to people, and when we talked about everything, we would let the variables be unrestricted. It is actually very easy to make precise this idea of restricting the universe of discourse. If we want the universe of discourse to be restricted to people, we simply declare that all the objects in our interpretations must be people. If we want a universe of discourse consisting only of cats, we declare that all the objects in our interpretations must be cats. And so on.

As I mentioned, this common practice is not fully satisfactory. What if we want to talk about people and things, as when we assert, 'Everyone likes sweet things.'? Restricted quantifiers will help us out here. They also have the advantage of getting what we need explicitly stated in the predicate logic sentences themselves.

We could proceed by using '(∃x)' and '(∀x)' to mean 'something' and 'everything' and introduce new quantifiers for 'someone' and 'everyone'. To see how to do this, let's use the predicate 'P' to stand for 'is a person.'

Then we can introduce the new quantifier '$(\exists x)_P$' to stand for some x chosen from among the things that are P, that is, chosen from among people. We call this a restricted quantifier. You should think of a restricted quantifier as saying exactly what an unrestricted quantifier says except that the variable is restricted to the things of which the subscripted predicate is true. With 'P' standing for 'is a person', '$(\exists x)_P$' has the effect of 'someone' or 'somebody'. We can play the same game with the universal quantifier. '$(\forall x)_P$' will mean all x chosen from among the things that are P. With 'P' standing for 'is a person', '$(\forall x)_P$' means, not absolutely everything, but all people, that is, everyone or everybody or anyone or anybody.

This notion of a restricted quantifier can be useful for other things. Suppose we want to transcribe 'somewhere' and 'everywhere' or 'sometimes' and 'always'. Let's use 'N' stand for 'is a place' or 'is a location'. 'Somewhere' means 'at some place' or 'at some location'. So we can transcribe 'somewhere' as '$(\exists x)_N$' and 'everywhere' as '$(\forall x)_N$'. For example, to transcribe 'There is water everywhere', I would introduce the predicate 'Wx' to stand for 'there is water at x'. Then '$(\forall x)_N Wx$' says that there is water everywhere. Continuing the same strategy, let's use 'Q' to stand for 'is a time'. Then '$(\exists x)_Q$' stands for 'sometime(s)' and '$(\forall x)_Q$' stands for 'always' ('at all times').

In fact, we can also use the same trick when English has no special word corresponding to the restricted quantifier. Suppose I want to say something about all cats, for example, that all cats are furry. Let 'Cx' stand for 'x is a cat' and 'Fx' stand for 'x is furry'. Then '$(\forall x)_C Fx$' says that all things which are cats are furry; that is, all cats are furry. Suppose I want to say that some animals have tails. Using 'Ax' for 'x is an animal' and 'Txy' for 'x is a tail of y', I write '$(\exists x)_A(\exists y)Tyx$': There is an animal, x, and there is a thing, y, such that y is a tail of x.

As you will see, restricted quantifiers are very useful in figuring out transcriptions, but there is a disadvantage in introducing them as a new kind of quantifier in our system of logic. If we have many different kinds of quantifiers, we will have to specify a new rule for each of them to tell us the conditions under which a sentence formed with the quantifier is true. And when we get to checking the validity of arguments, we will have to have a new rule of inference to deal with each new quantifier. We could state the resulting mass of new rules in a systematic way. But the whole business would still require a lot more work. Fortunately, we don't have to do any of that, for we can get the full effect of restricted quantifiers with the tools we already have.

Let's see how to rewrite subscripted quantifiers. Consider the restricted quantifier '$(\exists x)_C$', which says that there is cat such that, or there are cats such that, or some cats are such that. We say 'some cats are furry' (or 'there is a furry cat' or the like) with '$(\exists x)_C Fx$'. Now what has to be true for it to be true that some cats are furry, or that there is a furry cat? There has to be one or more things that is both a cat and is furry. If there is not something which is both a cat and is furry, it is false that there is a furry cat. So we can say that some cats are furry by writing '$(\exists x)(Cx$ & $Fx)$'. In short, we can faithfully rewrite '$(\exists x)_C Fx$' as '$(\exists x)(Cx$ & $Fx)$'. This strategy will work generally:

> Rule for rewriting *Subscripted Existential Quantifiers:* For any predicate **S**, any sentence of the form $(\exists u)_S(.\ .\ .\ \mathbf{u}.\ .\ .)$ is shorthand for $(\exists u)[\mathbf{S}u$ & $(.\ .\ .\ \mathbf{u}\ .\ .\ .)]$.

Here are some examples:

Some cats are blond.	$(\exists x)_C Bx$	$(\exists x)(Cx$ & $Bx)$
Eve loves a cat.	$(\exists x)_C Lex$	$(\exists x)(Cx$ & $Lex)$
Eve loves a furry cat.	$(\exists x)_C(Fx$ & $Lex)$	$(\exists x)[Cx$ & $(Fx$ & $Lex)]$

Clearly, we can proceed in the same way with 'someone' and 'somebody':

Someone loves Eve.	$(\exists x)_P Lxe$	$(\exists x)(Px$ & $Lxe)$
Somebody loves Eve or Adam.	$(\exists x)_P(Lxe \vee Lxa)$	$(\exists x)[Px$ &$(Lxe \vee Lxa)]$
If somebody loves Eve, then Eve loves somebody.		
	$(\exists x)_P Lxe \supset$	$(\exists x)(Px$ & $Lxe) \supset (\exists x)(Px$ & $Lex)$
	$(\exists x)_P Lex$	

Notice that in the last example I used the rule for rewriting the subscript on each of two sentences **X** and **Y, inside** a compound sentence, **X** $\supset$ **Y**.

How should we proceed with restricted universal quantifiers? This is a little tricky. Let's work on '$(\forall x)_C Fx$'—that is, 'All cats are furry'. Under what conditions is this sentence true? To answer the question, imagine that everything in the world is lined up in front of you: All the cats, dogs, people, stones, basketballs, everything. You go down the line and examine the items, one by one, to determine whether all cats are furry. If the first thing in line is a dog, you don't have to determine whether or not it is furry. If the second thing is a basketball, you don't have to worry about it either. But as soon as you come to a cat you must examine it further to find out if it is furry. When you finally come to the end of the line, you will have established that all cats are furry if you have found of each thing that, if it is a cat, then it is furry. In short, to say that all cats are furry is to say '$(\forall x)(Cx \supset Fx)$'.

At this point, many students balk. Why, they want to know, should we rewrite a restricted universal quantifier with the '$\supset$' when we rewrite a restricted existential quantifier with the '&'? Shouldn't '&' work also for restricted universal quantifiers? Well, I'm sorry. It doesn't. That is just not what restricted universal quantifiers mean.

You can prove this for yourself by trying to use '&' in rewriting the subscripted 'C' in our transcription of 'All cats are furry.' You get

(1) $(\forall x)(Cx \ \& \ Fx)$

What does (1) say? It says that everything is a furry cat, and in particular that everything is a cat! That's much too strong. All cats could be furry even though there are lots of things which are not cats. Thus 'All cats are furry' could be true even when (1) is false, so that (1) cannot be the right way to rewrite '$(\forall x)_C Fx$'.

What has gone wrong? The unrestricted universal quantifier applies to everything. So we can use conjunction in expressing the restriction of cats only if we somehow disallow or except the cases of noncats. We can do this by saying that everything is either not a cat or is a cat and is furry:

(2) $(\forall x)[\sim Cx \lor (Cx \ \& \ Fx)]$

(2) does indeed say what 'All cats are furry' says. So (2) should satisfy your feeling that an '&' also comes into the restricted universal quantifier in some way. But you can easily show that (2) is logically equivalent to '$(\forall x)(Cx \supset Fx)$'! As the formulation with the '$\supset$' is more compact, and is also traditional, it is the one we will use.

In general, we rewrite restricted universal quantifiers according to the rule

> Rule for rewriting *Subscripted Universal Quantifiers:* For any predicate **S**, any sentence of the form $(\forall u)_S(. . . \ u \ . . .)$ is shorthand for $(\forall u)[Su \supset (. . . \ u \ . . .)]$.

Here are some examples to make sure you see how this rule applies:

Eve loves all cats.	$(\forall x)_C(Lex)$	$(\forall x)(Cx \supset Lex)$
Everybody loves Eve.	$(\forall x)_P Lxe$	$(\forall x)(Px \supset Lxe)$
Everyone loves either Adam or Eve.		
	$(\forall x)_P(Lxa \lor Lxe)$	$(\forall x)[Px \supset (Lxa \lor Lxe)]$
Not everyone loves both Adam and Eve.		
	$\sim(\forall x)_P(Lxa \ \& \ Lxe)$	$\sim(\forall x)[Px \supset (Lxa \ \& \ Lxe)]$

In the last example, I used the rewriting rule on a sentence, **X, inside** a negated sentence of the form $\sim$**X.**

If you are still feeling doubtful about using the '$\supset$' to rewrite restricted universal quantifiers, I have yet another way to show you that this way of rewriting must be right. I am assuming that you agree that our way of rewriting restricted existential quantifiers is right. And I will use a new rule of logical equivalence. This rule tells us that the same equivalences that hold for negated unrestricted universal quantifiers hold for negated restricted universal quantifiers. In particular, saying that not all cats are furry is clearly the same as saying that some cat is not furry. In general

Rule ~∀$_S$: A sentence of the form ~(∀**u**)$_S$(. . . **u** . . .) is logically equivalent to (∃**u**)$_S$~(. . . **u** . . .).

You can prove this new rule along the same lines we used in proving the rule ~∀.

Now, watch the following chain of logical equivalents:

1 (∀**u**)$_S$(. . . **u** . . .)
2 ~~(∀**u**)$_S$(. . . **u** . . .)   DN
3 ~(∃**u**)$_S$~(. . . **u** . . .)   ~∀$_S$
4 ~(∃**u**)[**Su** & ~(. . . **u** . . .)]   Rule for rewriting (∃**u**)$_S$
5 ~(∃**u**)~~[**Su** & ~(. . . **u** . . .)]   DN
6 ~(∃**u**)~[~**Su** ∨ (. . . **u** . . .)]   DM, DN
7 ~(∃**u**)~[**Su** ⊃ (. . . **u** . . .)]   C
8 ~~(∀**u**)[**Su** ⊃ (. . . **u** . . .)]   ~∃
9 (∀**u**)[**Su** ⊃ (. . . **u** . . .)]   DN

Since the last line is logically equivalent to the first, it must be a correct way of rewriting the first.

If you are having a hard time following this chain of equivalents, let me explain the strategy. Starting with a restricted universal quantifier, I turn it into a restricted existential quantifier in lines 2 and 3 by using double denial and pushing one of the two negation signs through the restricted quantifier. I then get line 4 by using the rule we have agreed on for rewriting restricted existential quantifiers. Notice that I am applying this rule inside a negated sentence, so that here (and below) I am really using substitution of logical equivalents. In lines 5, 6, and 7 I use rules of logical equivalence to transform a conjunction into a conditional. These steps are pure sentence logic. They involve no quantifiers. Line 8 comes from line 7 by pushing the negation sign back out through what is now an unrestricted existential quantifier, changing it into an unrestricted universal quantifier. Finally, in line 9, I drop the double negation. It's almost like magic!

EXERCISES

4–1. Give an argument which shows that the rule ~∀$_S$ is correct. Similarly, show that

Rule ~∃$_X$: a sentence of the form ~(∃**u**)$_S$(. . . **u** . . .) is logically equivalent to (∀**u**)$_S$~(. . . **u** . . .).

is also correct.

4–2. Use the rule $\sim\exists_S$ to show that, starting from the rule for rewriting subscripted universal quantifiers, you can derive the rule for rewriting subscripted existential quantifiers. Your argument will closely follow the one given in the text for arguing the rule for rewriting subscripted universal quantifiers from the rule for rewriting subscripted existential quantifiers.

4–3. Transcribe the following English sentences into the language of predicate logic. Use this procedure: In a first step, transcribe into a sentence using one or more subscripted quantifiers. Then rewrite the resulting sentence using the rules for rewriting subscripted quantifiers. Show both your first and second steps. Here are two examples of sentences to transcribe and the two sentences to present in presenting the problem:

Someone loves Eve.   All cats love Eve.
   $(\exists x)_P Lxe$ $(\forall x)_C Lxe$
   $(\exists x)(Px \ \& \ Lxe)$ $(\forall x)(Cx \supset Lxe)$

Transcription Guide
   e: Eve   Dx: x is a dog
 Px: x is a person   Bx: x is blond
 Cx: x is a cat   Lxy: x loves y

   a)   Everyone loves Eve.
   b)   Eve loves somebody.
   c)   Eve loves everyone.
   d)   Some cat loves some dog.
   e)   Somebody is neither a cat nor a dog.
   f)   Someone blond loves Eve.
   g)   Some cat is blond.
   h)   Somebody loves all cats.
   i)   No cat is a dog.
   j)   Someone loves someone.
   k)   Everybody loves everyone.
   l)   Someone loves everyone.
   m)   Someone is loved by everyone.
   n)   Everyone loves someone.
   o)   Everyone is loved by somebody.

4–2. TRANSCRIBING FROM ENGLISH INTO LOGIC

Transcribing into the language of predicate logic can be extremely difficult. Actually, one can do logic perfectly well without getting very good at transcription. But transcriptions into logic provide one of predicate logic's important uses. This is because, when it comes to quantification, English is often extremely confusing, ambiguous, and even downright obscure. Often we can become clearer about what is being said if we put a statement into logic. Sometimes transcribing into logic is a must for clarity and precision. For example, how do you understand the highly ambiguous sentence, 'All of the boys didn't kiss all of the girls.'? I, for one, am lost unless I transcribe into logic.

Before we get started, I should mention a general point. Just as in the case of sentence logic, if two predicate logic sentences are logically equivalent they are both equally good (or equally bad!) transcriptions of an English sentence. Two logically equivalent sentences share the same truth value in all possible cases (understood as all interpretations), and in this sense two logically equivalent sentences "say the same thing." But if two predicate logic sentences say the same thing, then to the extent that one of them says what an English sentence says, then so does the other.

We are going to be looking at quite a few examples, so let's agree on a transcription guide:

Transcription Guide

a:	Adam	Px:	x is a person
J:	The lights will be on	Rx:	x is a registered voter
Ax:	x is an adult	Vx:	x has the right to vote
Bx:	x is a boy	Kxy:	x kissed y
Cx:	x is a cat	Lxy:	x loves y
Dx:	x is a dog	Mxy:	x is married to y
Fx:	x can run a 3:45 mile	Oxy:	x owns y
Gx:	x is a girl	Txy:	x is a tail of y
Hx:	x is at home		

Take note of the fact that in giving you a transcription guide, I have been using open sentences to indicate predicates. For example, I am using the open sentence 'Px' to indicate the predicate 'is a person.' The idea of using an open sentence to indicate a predicate will soon become very useful.

To keep us focused on the new ideas, I will often use subscripts on restricted quantifiers. However, you should keep in mind that complete transcriptions require you to rewrite the subscripts, as explained in the last section.

Now let's go back and start with the basics. '$(\forall x)(Cx \supset Fx)$' transcribes 'all cats are furry,' 'Every cat is furry,' 'Any cat is furry,' and 'Each cat is furry.' This indicates that

Usually, the words 'all', 'every', 'any', and 'each' signal a universal quantifier.

Let's make a similar list for the existential quantifier. '(∃x)(Cx & Fx)' transcribes 'Some cat is furry', 'Some cats are furry,' 'At least one cat is furry', 'There is a furry cat,' and 'There are furry cats':

> Usually, the expressions 'some', 'at least one', 'there is', and 'there are' signal an existential quantifier.

These lists make a good beginning, but you must use care. There are no hard and fast rules for transcribing English quantifier words into predicate logic. For starters, 'a' can easily function as a universal or an existential quantifier. For example, 'A car can go very fast.' is ambiguous. It can be used to say either that any car can go very fast or that some car can go very fast.

To make it clearer that 'a' can function both ways, consider the following examples. You probably understand 'A man is wise.' to mean that some man is wise. But most likely you understand 'A dog has four legs.' to mean that all dogs have four legs. Actually, both of these sentences are ambiguous. In both sentences, 'a' can correspond to 'all' or 'some'. You probably didn't notice that fact because when we hear an ambiguous sentence we tend to notice only one of the possible meanings. If a sentence is obviously true when understood with one of its meanings and obviously false when understood with the other, we usually hear the sentence only as making the true statement. So if all the men in the world were wise, we would take 'A man is wise.' to mean that all men are wise, and if only one dog in the world had four legs we would take 'A dog has four legs.' to mean that some dog has four legs.

It is a little easier to hear 'A car can go very fast.' either way. This is because we interpret this sentence one way or the other, depending on how fast we take 'fast' to be. If 'fast' means 30 miles an hour (which is very fast by horse and buggy standards), it is easy to hear 'A car can go very fast.' as meaning that all cars can go very fast. If "fast' means 180 miles an hour it is easy to hear 'a car can go very fast.' as meaning that some car can go very fast.

'A' is not the only treacherous English quantifier word. 'Anyone' usually gets transcribed with a universal quantifier. But not always. Consider

(3)   If anyone is at home, the lights will be on.

(4)   If anyone can run a 3:45 mile, Adam can.

We naturally hear (3), not as saying that if everyone is at home the lights will be on, but as saying that if **someone** is at home the lights will be on. So a correct transcription is

(3a) $(∃x)_PHx ⊃ J$

Likewise, by (4), we do not ordinarily mean that if everyone can run a 3:43 mile, Adam can. We mean that if **someone** can run that fast, Adam can:

(4a) $(\exists x)_P Fx \supset Fa$

At least that's what one would ordinarily mean by (4). However, I think that (4) actually is ambiguous. I think 'anyone' in (4) **could** be understood as 'everyone'. This becomes more plausible if you change the '3:45 mile' to '10-minute mile'. And it becomes still more plausible after you consider the following example: 'Anyone can tie their own shoe laces. And if anyone can, Adam can.'

Going back to (3), one would think that if (4) is ambiguous, (3) should be ambiguous in the same way. I just can't hear an ambiguity in (3). Can you?

'Someone' can play the reverse trick on us. Usually, we transcribe it with an existential quantifier. But consider

(5)   Someone who is a registered voter has the right to vote.

We naturally hear this as the generalization stating that anyone who is a registered voter has the right to vote. Thus we transcribe it as

(5a) $(\forall x)_P(Rx \supset Vx)$

As in the case of (4), which uses 'anyone', we can have ambiguity in sentences such as (5), which uses 'someone'. If you don't believe me, imagine that you live in a totalitarian state, called Totalitarania. In Totalitarania, everyone is a registered voter. But voter registration is a sham. In fact, only one person, **the boss,** has the right to vote. As a citizen of Totalitarania, you can still truthfully say that someone who is a registered voter (namely, **the boss**) has the right to vote. (You can make this even clearer by emphasizing the word 'someone: '**someone** who is a registered voter has the right to vote.') In this context we hear the sentence as saying

(5b) $(\exists x)_P(Rx \ \& \ Vx)$

Ambiguity can plague transcription in all sorts of ways. Consider an example traditional among linguists:

(6)   All the boys kissed all the girls

This can easily mean that each and every one of the boys kissed each and every one of the girls:

(6a) $(\forall x)_B(\forall y)_G Kxy$

But it can also mean that each of the boys kissed some girls so that, finally, each and every girl got kissed by some boy:

(6b) $(\forall x)_B(\exists y)_G Kxy \ \& \ (\forall y)_G(\exists x)_B Kxy$

If you think that was bad, things get much worse when multiple quantifiers get tangled up with negations. Consider

(7) All the boys didn't kiss all the girls.

Everytime I try to think this one through, I blow a circuit. Perhaps the most natural transcription is to take the logical form of the English at face value and take the sentence to assert that of each and every boy it is true that he did not kiss all the girls; that is, for each and every boy there is at least one girl not kissed by that boy:

(7a) $(\forall x)_B \sim (\forall y)_G Kxy,$ or $(\forall x)_B(\exists y)_G \sim Kxy$

But one can also take the sentence to mean that each and every boy refrained from kissing each and every girl, that is, didn't kiss the first girl and didn't kiss the second girl and not the third, and so on. In yet other words, this says that for each and every boy there was no girl whom he kissed, so that nobody kissed anybody:

(7b) $(\forall x)_B(\forall y)_G \sim Kxy,$ or $(\forall x)_B \sim (\exists y)_G Kxy$, or $\sim (\exists x)_B(\exists y)_G Kxy$

We are still not done with this example, for one can **also** use (7) to mean that not all the boys kissed every single girl—that is, that some boy did not kiss all the girls, in other words that at least one of the boys didn't kiss at least one of the girls:

(7c) $\sim (\forall x)_B(\forall y)_G Kxy,$ or $(\exists x)_B \sim (\forall y)_G Kxy$, or $(\exists x)_B(\exists y)_G \sim Kxy$

It's worth an aside to indicate how it can happen that an innocent-looking sentence such as (7) can turn out to be so horribly ambiguous. Modern linguistics postulates that our minds carry around more than one representation of a given sentence. There is one kind of structure that represents the logical form of a sentence. Another kind of structure represents sentences as we speak and write them. Our minds connect these (and other) representations of a given sentence by making all sorts of complicated transformations. These transformations can turn representations of **different** logical forms into the **same** representation of a spoken or written sentence. Thus one sentence which you speak or write can correspond to two, three, or sometimes quite a few different structures that carry very different meanings. In particular, the written sentence (7) corresponds to (at least!) three different logical forms. (7a), (7b), and (7c) don't give all the details of the different, hidden structures that can be transformed into (7). But they do describe the differences which show up in the language of predicate logic.

You can see hints of all this if you look closely at (7), (7a), (7b), and (7c). In (7) we have two universal quantifier words and a negation. But since the quantifier words appear on either side of 'kissed', it's really not all that clear where the negation is meant to go in relation to the universal quantifiers. We must consider three possibilities. We could have the negation between the two universal quantifiers. Indeed, that is what you see in (7a), in the first of its logically equivalent forms. Or we could have the negation coming after the two universal quantifiers, which is what you find in the first of the logically equivalent sentences in (7b). Finally, we could have the negation preceding both universal quantifiers. You see this option in (7c). In sum, we have three similar, but importantly different, structures. Their logical forms all have two universal quantifiers and a negation, but the three differ, with the negation coming before, between, or after the two quantifiers. The linguistic transformations in our minds connect all three of these structures with the same, highly ambiguous English sentence, (7).

Let's get back to logic and consider some other words which you may find especially difficult to transcribe. I am always getting mixed up by sentences which use 'only', such as 'Only cats are furry.' So I use the strategy of first transcribing a clear case (it helps to use a sentence I know is true) and then using the clear case to figure out a formula. I proceed in this way: Transcribe

(8)   Only adults can vote.

This means that anyone who is not an adult can't vote, or equivalently (using the law of contraposition), anyone who can vote is an adult. So either of the following equivalent sentences provides a correct transcription:

(8a) $(\forall x)_P(\sim Ax \supset \sim Vx)$

(8b) $(\forall x)_P(Vx \supset Ax)$

This works in general. (In the following I used boldface capital **P** and **Q** to stand for arbitrary predicates.) Transcribe

(9)   Only **P**s are **Q**s.

either as

(9a) $(\forall x)(\sim \mathbf{P}x \supset \sim \mathbf{Q}x)$

or as

(9b) (∀x)(Qx ⊃ **P**X)

Thus 'Only cats are furry' becomes (∀x)(Fx ⊃ Cx).

'Nothing' and 'not everything' often confuse me also. We must carefully distinguish

(10) Nothing is furry: (∀x)~Fx, or ~(∃x)Fx

and

(11) Not everything is furry: ~(∀x)Fx, or (∃x)~Fx

(The alternative transcriptions given in (10) and (11) are logically equivalent, by the rules ~(∀x) and ~(∃x) for logical equivalence introduced in section 3–4.) 'Not everything' can be transcribed literally as 'not all x . . . .'. 'Nothing' means something different and much stronger. 'Nothing' means 'everything is not . . . .' Be careful not to confuse 'nothing' with 'not everything.' If the distinction is not yet clear, make up some more examples and carefully think them through.

'None' and 'none but' can also cause confusion:

(12) None but adults can vote: (∀x)(~Ax ⊃ ~Vx)

(13) None love Adam: (∀x)~Lxe

'None but' simply transcribes as 'only.' When 'none' without the 'but' fits in grammatically in English you will usually be able to treat it as you do 'nothing'. 'Nothing' and 'none' differ in that we tend to use 'none' when there has been a stated or implied restriction of domain: "How many cats does Adam love? He loves none." In this context a really faithful transcription of the sentence 'Adam loves none.' would be '(∀x)_C~Lax', or, rewriting the subscript, '(∀x)(Cx ⊃ ~Lax).

Perhaps the most important negative quantifier expression in English is 'no', as in

(14) No cats are furry.

To say that no cats are furry is to say that absolutely all cats are not furry, so that we transcribe (18) as

(15) (∀x)_C~Fx, that is, (∀x)(Cx ⊃ ~Fx)

In general, transcribe

(16) No **P**s are **Q**x.

as

(17) $(\forall x)_P \sim Q$, that is, $(\forall x)(P \supset \sim Q)$

EXERCISES

4–4. Transcribe the following English sentences into the language of predicate logic. Use subscripts if you find them helpful in figuring out your answers, but no subscripts should appear in your final answers.

Transcription Guide

a:	Adam	Fx:	x is furry
e:	Eve	Px:	x is a person
Ax:	x is an animal	Qx:	x purrs
Bx:	x is blond	Lxy:	x loves y
Cx:	x is a cat	Sxy:	x is a son of y
Dx:	x is a dog	Txy:	x is tickling y

    a) Anything furry loves Eve.
    b) No cat is furry.
    c) If anyone loves Adam, Eve does.
    d) Eve does not love anyone.
    e) Nothing is furry.
    f) Adam, if anyone, is blond.
    g) Not all cats are furry.
    h) Some cats are not furry.
    i) No one is a cat.
    j) No cat is a dog.
    k) If something purrs, it is a cat.
    l) Not everything blond is a cat.
    m) A dog is not an animal. (Ambiguous)
    n) Not all animals are dogs.
    o) Only cats purr.
    p) Not only cats are furry.
    q) Any dog is not a cat.
    r) No blonds love Adam.
    s) None but blonds love Adam.
    t) Some dog is not a cat.
    u) Nothing furry loves anyone.
    v) Only cat lovers love dogs. (Ambiguous?)
    w) If someone is a son of Adam, he is blond.
    x) No son of Adam is a son of Eve.

y) Someone who is a son of Adam is no son of Eve. (Ambiguous)

z) Each cat which loves Adam also loves Eve.

aa) Not everyone who loves Adam also loves Eve.

bb) Anyone who is tickling Eve is tickling Adam.

cc) None but those who love Adam also love Eve.

4–5. Give alternative transcriptions which show the ways in which the following sentences are ambiguous. In this problem you do not have to eliminate subscripts. (It is sometimes easier to study the ambiguity if we write these sentences in the compact subscript notation.)

a) Everyone loves someone.

b) Someone loves everyone.

c) Something is a cat if and only if Adam loves it.

d) All cats are not furry.

e) Not anyone loves Adam.

4–6. In this section I discussed ambiguities connected with words such as 'a', 'someone', and 'anyone.' In fact, English has a great many sorts of ambiguity arising from the ways in which words are connected with each other. For example, 'I won't stay at home to please you.' can mean that if I stay at home, I won't do it in order to please you. But it can also mean that I will go out because going out will please you. 'Eve asked Adam to stay in the house.' can mean that Eve asked Adam to remain in a certain location, and that location is the house. It can also mean that Eve asked Adam to remain in some unspecified location, and that she made her request in the house.

For the following English sentences, provide alternative transcripts showing how the sentences are ambiguous. Use the transcription guides given for each sentence.

a) Flying planes can be dangerous. (Px: x is a plane. Fx: x is flying. Dx: x can be dangerous. Ax: x is an act of flying a plane.)

b) All wild animal keepers are blond. (Kxy: x keeps y. Wx: x is wild. Ax: x is an animal. Bx: x is blond.)

c) Adam only relaxes on Sundays. (a: Adam. Rxy: x relaxes on day y. Lxy: x relaxes ("is lazy") all day long on day y. Sx: x is Sunday.)

d) Eve dressed and walked all the dogs. (e: Eve. Cxy: x dressed y. Dx: x is a dog. Wxy: x walked y.)

Linguists use the expression *Structural Ambiguity* for the kind of ambiguity in these examples. This is because the ambiguities have to do with alternative ways in which the grammatical structure of the sentences can be correctly analyzed. Structural ambiguity contrasts with *Lexical Ambiguity,* which has to do with the ambiguity in the meaning of isolated words. Thus the most obvious ambiguity of 'I took my brother's picture yesterday.' turns on the ambiguity of the meaning of 'took' (stole vs. produced a picture). The ambiguity involved with quantifier words such as 'a', 'someone', and 'anyone' is actually structural ambiguity, not lexical ambiguity. We can see a hint of this in the fact that '(∃x)Hx ⊃ J' is logically equivalent to '(∀x)(Hx ⊃ J)' and the fact that '(∀x)Hx ⊃ J' is logically equivalent to (∃x)(Hx ⊃ J), as you will prove later on in the course.

4–3. TRANSCRIPTION STRATEGIES

I'm going to turn now from particularly hard cases to general strategy. If you are transcribing anything but the shortest of sentences, don't try to do it all at once. Transcribe parts into logic, writing down things which are part logic and part English. Bit by bit, transcribe the parts still in English into logic until all of the English is gone.

Let's do an example. Suppose we want to transcribe

(18) Any boy who loves Eve is not a furry cat.

(18) says of any boy who loves Eve that he is not a furry cat; that is, it says of all things, x, of which a first thing is true (that x is a boy who loves Eve) that a second thing is true (x is not a furry cat). So the sentence has the form (∀x)(**P**x ⊃ **Q**):

(18a) (∀x)(x is a boy who loves Eve ⊃ x is not a furry cat)

Now all you have to do is to fashion transcriptions of 'x is a boy who loves Eve' and of 'x is not a furry cat' and plug them into (18a):

(18b) x is a boy who loves Eve: Bx & Lxe

(18c) x is not a furry cat: ~(Fx & Cx)

(Something which is not a furry cat is not both furry and a cat. Such a thing could be furry, or a cat, but not both.) Now we plug (18b) and (18c) into (18a), getting our final answer:

(18d) (∀x)[(Bx & Lxe) ⊃ ~(∃x & Cx)]

Here is another way you could go about the same problem. Think of the open sentence 'Bx & Lxe' as indicating a complex one place predicate. The open sentence 'Bx & Lxe' presents something which might be true of an object or person such as Adam. For example, if the complex predicate is true of Adam, we would express that fact by writing in 'a' for 'x' in 'Bx & Lxe', giving 'Ba & Lae'. Now, thinking of 'Bx & Lxe' as a predicate, we can use the method of quantifier subscripts which we discussed in section 4-1. (18) is somewhat like a sentence which asserts that everything is not a furry cat. But (18) asserts this, not about absolutely everything, but just about all those things which have the complex property Bx & Lxe. So we can write (18) as a universally quantified sentence with the universal quantifier restricted by the predicate 'Bx & Lxe':

(18e) $(\forall x)_{(Bx\ \&\ Lxe)} \sim (Fx\ \&\ Cx)$

Now you simply use the rule for rewriting subscripts on universal quantifiers, giving (18d).

In yet a third way of working on (18), you could first use the method of subscripting quantifiers before transcribing the complex predicates into logic. Following this route you would first write.

(18f) $(\forall x)_{(x\ is\ a\ boy\ who\ loves\ Eve)}(x\ is\ not\ a\ furry\ cat)$

Now transcribe the English complex predicates as in (18b) and (18c), plug the results into (18f), giving (18e). Then you rewrite the subscript, giving (18d) as before. You have many alternative ways of proceeding.

Generally, it is very useful to think of complex descriptions as complex predicates. In particular, this enables us to use two place predicates to construct one place predicates. We really took advantage of this technique in the last example. 'Lxy' is a two place predicate. By substituting a name for 'y', we form a one place predicate, for example, 'Lxe'. 'Lxe' is a one place predicate which is true of anything which loves Eve.

Here is another useful way of constructing one place predicates from two place predicates. Suppose we need the one place predicate 'is married', but our transcription guide only gives us the two place predicate 'Mxy', meaning that x is married to y. To see how to proceed, consider what it means to say that Adam, for example, is married. This is to say that there is someone to whom Adam is married. So we can say Adam is married with the sentence '$(\exists y)May$'. We could proceed in the same way to say that Eve, or anyone else, is married. In short, the open sentence '$(\exists y)Mxy$' expresses the predicate 'x is married'.

Here's another strategy point: When 'who' or 'which' comes after a predicate they generally transcribe as 'and'. As you saw in (18), the complex predicate 'x is a boy who loves Eve' becomes 'Bx & Lxe'. The complex predicate 'x is a dog which is not furry but has a tail' becomes 'Dx & ($\sim$Fx & $(\exists y)Tyx$)'.

When 'who' or 'which' comes after a quantifier word, they indicate a subscript on the quantifier: 'Anything which is not furry but has a tail' should be rendered as $(\forall x)_{(\sim Fx\ \&\ (\exists y)Tyx)}$. When the quantifier word itself calls for a subscript, as does 'someone', you need to combine both these ideas for treating 'who': 'Someone who loves Eve' is the subscripted quantifier '$(\exists x)_{Px\ \&\ Lxe}$'.

Let's apply these ideas in another example. Before reading on, see if you can use only 'Cx' for 'x is a cat', 'Lxy' for 'x loves y', and 'Oxy' for 'x owns y' and transcribe

(19)   Some cat owner loves everyone who loves themselves.

Let's see how you did. (19) says that there is something, taken from among the cat owners, and that thing loves everyone who loves themselves. Using a subscript and the predicates 'x is a cat owner' and 'x loves everyone who loves themselves', (19) becomes

(19a) $(\exists x)_{(x\ is\ a\ cat\ owner)}$(x loves everyone who loves themselves)

Now we have to fashion transcriptions for the two complex English predicates used in (19a). Someone (or something) is a cat owner just in case there is a cat which they own:

(19b)   . x is a cat owner: $(\exists y)(Cy\ \&\ Oxy)$

To say that x loves everyone who loves themselves is to say that x loves, not absolutely everyone, but everyone taken from among those that are, first of all people, and second, things which love themselves. So we want to say that x loves all y, where y is restricted to be a person, Py, and restricted to be a self-lover, Lyy:

(19c)   x loves everyone who loves themselves: $(\forall y)_{(Py\ \&\ Lyy)}Lxy$

Putting the results of (19b) and (19c) into (19a), we get

(19d) $(\exists x)_{(\exists y)(Cy\ \&\ Oxy)}[(\forall y)_{(Py\ \&\ Lyy)}Lxy]$

Discharging first the subscript of '$(\exists x)$' with an '&' and then the subscript of '$(\forall y)$' with a '⊃', we get

(19e) $(\exists x)\{(\exists y)(Cy\ \&\ Oxy)\ \&\ (\forall y)_{(Py\ \&\ Lyy)}Lxy\}$

(19f) $(\exists x)\{(\exists y)(Cy\ \&\ Oxy)\ \&\ (\forall y)[(Py\ \&\ Lyy)\supset Lxy]\}$

This looks like a lot of work, but as you practice, you will find that you can do more and more of this in your head and it will start to go quite quickly.

I'm going to give you one more piece of advice on transcribing. Suppose you start with an English sentence and you have tried to transcribe it into logic. In many cases you can catch mistakes by transcribing your logic sentence back into English and comparing your retranscription with the original sentence. This check works best if you are fairly literal minded in retranscribing. Often the original and the retranscribed English sentences will be worded differently. But look to see if they still seem to say the same thing. If not, you have almost certainly made a mistake in transcribing from English into logic.

Here is an illustration. Suppose I have transcribed

(20) If something is a cat, it is not a dog.

as

(20a) $(\exists x)(Cx \supset \sim Dx)$

To check, I transcribe back into English, getting

(20b) There is something such that if it is a cat, then it is not a dog.

Now compare (20b) with (20). To make (20b) true it is enough for there to be **one** thing which, if a cat, is not a dog. The truth of (20b) is consistent with there being a million cat-dogs. But (20) is not consistent with there being any cat-dogs. I conclude that (20a) is a wrong transcription. Having seen that (20) is stronger than (20a), I try

(20c) $(\forall x)(Cx \supset \sim Dx)$

Transcribing back into English this time gives me

(20d) Everything which is a cat is not a dog.

which does indeed seem to say what (20) says. This time I am confident that I have transcribed correctly.

(Is (20) ambiguous in the same way that (5) was? I don't think so!)

Here is another example. Suppose after some work I transcribe

(21) Cats and dogs have tails.

as

(21a) $(\forall x)[(Cx \& Dx) \supset (\exists y)Txy]$

To check, I transcribe back into English:

(21b) Everything is such that if it is both a cat and a dog, then it has a tail.

Obviously, something has gone wrong, for nothing is both a cat and a dog. Clearly, (21) is not supposed to be a generalization about such imaginary cat-dogs. Having noticed this, I see that (21) is saying one thing about cats and then the **same** thing about dogs. Thus, without further work, I try the transcription

(21c) $(\forall x)(Cx \supset (\exists y)Txy) \& (\forall x)(Dx \supset (\exists y)Txy)$

To check (21c), I again transcribe back into English, getting

(21d) If something is a cat, then it has a tail, and if something is a dog, then it has a tail.

which is just a long-winded way of saying that all cats and dogs have tails—in other words, (21). With this check, I can be very confident that (21c) is a correct transcription.

EXERCISES

Use this transcription guide for exercises 4–7 and 4–8:

a:	Adam	Fx:	x is furry
e:	Eve	Px:	x is a person
Ax:	x is an animal	Qx:	x purrs
Bx:	x is blond	Lxy:	x loves y
Cx:	x is a cat	Sxy:	x is a son of y
Dx:	x is a dog	Txy:	x is a tail of y
		Oxy:	x owns y

4–7. Transcribe the following sentences into English:

    a) $(\exists x)(\exists y)(Px \& Py \& Sxy)$

    b) $\sim(\exists x)(Px \& Ax)$

    c) $\sim(\forall x)[Qx \supset (Fx \& Cx)]$

    d) $(\exists x)[Qx \& \sim(Fx \& Cx)]$

    e) $(\forall x)\sim[Px \& (Lxa \& Lxe)]$

    f) $(\forall x)[Px \supset \sim(Lxa \& Lxe)]$

    g) $(\forall x)(\forall y)[(Dx \& Cy) \supset Lxy]$

    h) $(\forall x)(\forall y)[Dx \supset (Cy \supset Lxy)]$

    i) $(\exists x)[Px \& (\exists y)(\exists z)(Py \& Szy \& Lxz)]$

    j) $(\exists x)[Px \& (\exists y)(\exists z)(Pz \& Syz \& Lxz)]$

    k) $(\forall x)\{[Bx \& (\exists y)(Fy \& Txy)] \supset (\exists z)(Cz \& Txz\}$

    l) $(\forall x)\{(\exists y)Sxy \supset [(\exists z)(Cz \& Lxz) \equiv (\exists z)(Dz \& Lxz)]\}$

4–8. Transcribe the following sentences into predicate logic. I have included some easy problems as a review of previous sections along with some real brain twisters. I have marked the sentences which seem to me clearly ambiguous, and you should give different transcriptions for these showing the different ways of understanding the English. Do you think any of the sentences I haven't marked are also ambiguous? You should have fun arguing out your intuitions about ambiguous cases with your classmates and instructor.

   a)   All furry cats purr.

   b)   Any furry cat purrs.

   c)   No furry cats purr.

   d)   None of the furry cats purr.

   e)   None but the furry cats purr. (Ambiguous?)

   f)   Some furry cats purr.

   g)   Some furry cats do not purr.

   h)   Some cats and dogs love Adam.

   i)   Except for the furry ones, all cats purr.

   j)   Not all furry cats purr.

   k)   If a cat is furry, it purrs.

   l)   A furry cat purrs. (Ambiguous)

   m)   Only furry cats purr.

   n)   Adam is not a dog or a cat.

   o)   Someone is a son.

   p)   Some sons are blond.

   q)   Adam loves a blond cat, and Eve loves one too.

   r)   Adam loves a blond cat and so does Eve. (Ambiguous)

   s)   Eve does not love everyone.

   t)   Some but not all cats are furry.

   u)   Cats love neither Adam nor Eve.

   v)   Something furry loves Eve.

   w)   Only people love someone.

   x)   Some people have sons.

   y)   Any son of Adam is a son of Eve.

   z)   Adam is a son and everybody loves him.

  aa)   No animal is furry, but some have tails.

  bb)   Any furry animal has a tail.

  cc)   No one has a son.

  dd)   Not everyone has a son.

  ee)   Some blonds love Eve, some do not.

  ff)   Adam loves any furry cat.

  gg)   All blonds who love themselves love Eve.

  hh)   Eve loves someone who loves themself.

   ii)   Anyone who loves no cats loves no dogs.

   jj)   Cats love Eve if they love anyone. (Ambiguous)

  kk)   If anyone has a son, Eve loves Adam. (Ambiguous)

   ll)   If anyone has a son, that person loves Adam.

mm)   Anyone who has a son loves Eve.

nn)   If someone has a son, Adam loves Eve.

oo)   If someone has a son, that person loves Adam.

pp)   Someone who has a son loves Adam. (Ambiguous)

qq)   All the cats with sons, except the furry ones, love Eve.

rr)   Anyone who loves a cat loves an animal.

ss)   Anyone who loves a person loves no animal.

tt)   Adam has a son who is not furry.

uu)   If Adam's son has a furry son, so does Adam.

vv)   A son of Adam is a son of Eve. (Ambiguous)

ww)   If the only people who love Eve are blond, then nobody loves Eve.

xx)   No one loves anyone. (Ambiguous)

yy)   No one loves someone. (Ambiguous)

zz)   Everyone loves no one.

aaa)   Everyone doesn't love everyone. (Ambiguous!)

bbb)   Nobody loves nobody. (Ambiguous?)

ccc)   Except for the furry ones, every animal loves Adam.

ddd)   Everyone loves a lover. (Ambiguous)

eee)   None but those blonds who love Adam own cats and dogs.

fff)   No one who loves no son of Adam loves no son of Eve.

ggg)   Only owners of dogs with tails own cats which do not love Adam.

hhh)   None of Adam's sons are owners of furry animals with no tails.

iii)   Anyone who loves nothing without a tail owns nothing which is loved by an animal.

jjj)   Only those who love neither Adam nor Eve are sons of those who own none of the animals without tails.

kkk)   Anyone who loves all who Eve loves loves someone who is loved by all who love Eve.

4–9. Transcribe the following sentences into predicate logic, making up your own transcription guide for each sentence. Be sure to show as much of the logical form as possible.

a)   No one likes Professor Snarf.

b)   Any dog can hear better than any person.

c)   Neither all Republicans nor all Democrats are honest.

d)   Some movie stars are better looking than others.

e)   None of the students who read **A Modern Formal Logic Primer** failed the logic course.

f)   Only people who eat carrots can see well in the dark.

g)   Not only people who eat carrots can see as well as people who eat strawberries.

h)   Peter likes all movies except for scary ones.

i) Some large members of the cat family can run faster than any horse.

j) Not all people with red hair are more temperamental than those with blond hair.

k) Some penny on the table was minted before any dime on the table.

i) No pickle tastes better than any strawberry.

m) John is not as tall as anyone on the basketball team.

n) None of the pumpkins at Smith's fruit stand are as large as any of those on MacGreggor's farm.

o) Professors who don't prepare their lectures confuse their students.

p) Professor Snarf either teaches Larry or teaches someone who teaches Larry.

q) Not only logic teachers teach students at Up State U.

r) Anyone who lives in Boston likes clams more than anyone who lives in Denver. (Ambiguous)

s) Except for garage mechanics who fix cars, no one has greasy pants.

t) Only movies shown on channel 32 are older than movies shown on channel 42.

u) No logic text explains logic as well as some professors do.

v) The people who eat, drink, and are merry are more fun than those who neither smile nor laugh.

CHAPTER SUMMARY EXERCISES

In reviewing this chapter make a short summary of the following to ensure your grasp of these ideas:

a) Restricted Quantifiers

b) Rule $\sim\forall_s$

c) Rule $\sim\exists_s$

d) Transcription Guide

e) Words that generally transcribe with a universal quantifier

f) Word that generally transcribe with an existential quantifier

g) Negative Quantifier Words

h) Ambiguity

i) Give a summary of important transcription strategies

Natural Deduction
for Predicate Logic

5

Fundamentals

5–1. REVIEW AND OVERVIEW

Let's get back to the problem of demonstrating argument validity. You know how to construct derivations which demonstrate the validity of valid sentence logic arguments. Now that you have a basic understanding of quantified sentences and what they mean, you are ready to extend the system of sentence logic derivations to deal with quantified sentences.

Let's start with a short review of the fundamental concepts of natural deduction: To say that an argument is valid is to say that in every possible case in which the premises are true, the conclusion is true also. The natural deduction technique works by applying **truth preserving** rules. That is, we use rules which, when applied to one or two sentences, license us to draw certain conclusions. The rules are constructed so that in any case in which the first sentence or sentences are true, the conclusion drawn is guaranteed to be true also. Certain rules apply, not to sentences, but to subderivations. In the case of these rules, a conclusion which they license is guaranteed to be true if all the sentences reiterated into the subderivation are true.

A derivation begins with no premises or one or more premises. It may include subderivations, and any subderivation may itself include a subderivation. A new sentence, or conclusion, may be added to a derivation if one of the rules of inference licenses us to draw the conclusion from previous premises, assumptions, conclusions, or subderivations. Because these rules are truth preserving, if the original premises are true in a case, the first conclusion drawn will be true in that case also. And if this first conclusion is true, then so will the next. And so on. Thus, altogether, in any case in which the premises are all true, the final conclusion will be true.

The only further thing you need to remember to be able to write sentence logic derivations are the rules themselves. If you are feeling rusty, please refresh your memory by glancing at the inside front cover, and review chapters 5 and 7 of Volume I, if you need to.

Now we are ready to extend our system of natural deduction for sentence logic to the quantified sentences of predicate logic. Everything you have already learned will still apply without change. Indeed, the only fundamental conceptual change is that we now must think in terms of an expanded idea of what constitutes a **case**. For sentence logic derivations, truth preserving rules guarantee that if the premises are true for an assignment of truth values to sentence letters, then conclusions drawn will be true for the same assignment. In predicate logic we use the same overall idea, except that for a "case" we use the more general idea of an **interpretation** instead of an assignment of truth values to sentence letters. Now we must say that if the premises are true in an interpretation, the conclusions drawn will be true in the same interpretation.

Since interpretations include assignment of truth values to any sentence letters that might occur in a sentence, everything from sentence logic applies as before. But our thinking for quantified sentences now has to extend to include the idea of interpretations as representations of the case in which quantified sentences have a truth value.

You will remember each of our new rules more easily if you understand why they work. You should understand why they are truth preserving by thinking in terms of interpretations. That is, you should try to understand why, if the premises are true in a given interpretation, the conclusion licensed by the rule will inevitably also be true in that interpretation.

Predicate logic adds two new connectives to sentence logic: the universal and existential quantifiers. So we will have four new rules, an introduction and elimination rule for each quantifier. Two of these rules are easy and two are hard. Yes, you guessed it! I'm going to introduce the easy rules first.

5–2. THE UNIVERSAL ELIMINATION RULE

Consider the argument

Everyone is blond.	$(\forall x)Bx$
Adam is blond.	Ba

Intuitively, if everyone is blond, this must include Adam. So if the premise is true, the conclusion is going to have to be true also. In terms of interpretations, let's consider any interpretation you like which is an interpretation of the argument's sentences and in which the premise, '(∀x)Bx', is true. The definition of truth of a universally quantified sentence tells us that '(∀x)Bx' is true in an interpretation just in case all of its substitution instances are true in the interpretation. Observe that 'Ba' is a substitution instance of '(∀x)Bx'. So in our arbitrarily chosen interpretation in which '(∀x)Bx' is true, 'Ba' will be true also. Since 'Ba' is true in any interpretation in which '(∀x)Bx' is true, the argument is valid.

(In this and succeeding chapters I am going to pass over the distinction between some**one** and some**thing**, as this complication is irrelevant to the material we now need to learn. I could give examples of things instead of people, but that makes learning very dull.)

The reasoning works perfectly generally:

> *Universal Elimination Rule:* If **X** is a universally quantified sentence, then you are licensed to conclude any of its substitution instances below it. Expressed with a diagram, for any name, **s,** and any variable, **u,**

```
┌─────────────────────
│  ┌─────────────────┐
│  │ (∀u)(. . . u . . .) │
│  └─────────────────┘
│  .
│  .
│  .
│  (. . . s . . .)        ∀E
```

Remember what the box and the circle mean: If on a derivation you encounter something with the form of what you find in the box, the rule licenses you to conclude something of the form of what you find in the circle.

Here is another example:

Everyone loves Eve.	(∀x)Lxe	1	(∀x)Lxe	P
Adam loves Eve.	Lae	2	Lae	1, ∀E

In forming the substitution instance of a universally quantified sentence, you must be careful always to put the same name everywhere for the substituted variable. Substituting 'a' for 'x' in '(∀x)Lxx', we get 'Laa', **not** 'Lxa'. Also, be sure that you substitute your name only for the occurrences of the variable which are **free** after deleting the initial quantifier. Using the name 'a' again, the substitution instance of '(∀x)(Bx ⊃ (∀x)Lxe)' is 'Ba ⊃ (∀x)Lxe'. The occurrence of 'x' in 'Lxe' is bound by the second

'(∀x)', and so is still bound after we drop the first '(∀x)'. If you don't understand this example, you need to review bound and free variables and substitution instances, discussed in chapter 3.

When you feel confident that you understand the last example, look at one more:

(∀x)(Gx ⊃ Kx)	1	(∀x)(Gx ⊃ Kx)	P
Gf	2	Gf	P
Kf	3	Gf ⊃ Kf	1, ∀E
	4	Kf	2, 3, ⊃E

EXERCISES

5–1. Provide derivations which demonstrate the validity of these arguments. Remember to work from the conclusion backward, seeing what you will need to get your final conclusions, as well as from the premises forward. In problem (d) be sure you recognize that the premise is a universal quantification of a conditional, while the conclusion is the very different conditional with a universally quantified antecedent.

a)
(∀x)(Px & Dx)
_____
Pk

b)
(∀x)(Px & Dx)
_____
Pd & Dk

c)
(∀x)(Dx ⊃ Kx)
(∀x)Dx
_____
Ka

d)
(∀x)(Mx ⊃ A)
_____
(∀x)Mx ⊃ A

e)
(∀x)(Fx v Hx)
(∀x)(Fx ⊃ Dx)
(∀x)(Hx ⊃ Dx)
_____
Dp & Db

f)
(∀x)(~Bx v Lcx)
_____
(∀x)Bx ⊃ Lcd

g)
(∀x)(Lxx ⊃ Lxh)
~Lmh
_____
~(∀x)Lxx

h)
(∀x)(Rxx v Rxk)
(∀y)~Ryk
_____
Rcc & Rff

5–3. THE EXISTENTIAL INTRODUCTION RULE

Consider the argument

Adam is blond.	Ba
Someone is blond.	(∃x)Bx

Intuitively, this argument is valid. If Adam is blond, there is no help for it: Someone is blond. Thinking in terms of interpretations, we see that this argument is valid according to our new way of making the idea of validity precise. Remember how we defined the truth of an existentially quantified sentence in an interpretation: '(∃x)Bx' is true in an interpretation if and only if at least one of its substitution instances is true in the interpretation. But 'Ba' **is** a substitution instance of '(∃x)Bx'. So, in any interpretation in which 'Ba' is true, '(∃x)Bx' is true also, which is just what we mean by saying that the argument "Ba. Therefore (∃x)Bx." is valid.

You can probably see the form of reasoning which is at play here: From a sentence with a name we can infer what we will call an *Existential Generalization* of that sentence. '(∃x)Bx' is an existential generalization of 'Ba'. We do have to be a little careful in making this notion precise because we can get tripped up again by problems with free and bound variables. What would you say is a correct existential generalization of '(∀x)Lax'? In English: If Adam loves everyone, then we know that someone loves everyone. But we have to use two different variables to transcribe 'Someone loves everyone': '(∃y)(∀x)Lyx'. If I start with '(∀x)Lax', and replace the 'a' with 'x', my new occurrence of 'x' is bound by that universal quantifier. I will have failed to generalize **existentially** on 'a'.

Here is another example for you to try: Existentially generalize

(i)   Ba ⊃ (∀x) Lax

    2   3   45

If I drop the 'a' at 2 and 4, write in 'x', and preface the whole with '(∃x)', I get

(ii)   (∃x)(Bx ⊃ (∀x)Lxx)   **Wrong**

     1   2   3 45

The 'x' at 4, which replaced one of the 'a's, is bound by the universally quantified 'x' at 3, not by the existentially quantified 'x' at 1, as we intend in forming an **existential** generalization. We have to use a new variable. A correct existential generalization of 'Ba ⊃ (∀x)Lax' is

(iii)   (∃y)(By ⊃ (∀x) Lyx)

     1   2   3 45

as are

(iv)   (∃y)(By ⊃ (∀x)Lax)

     1   2   3 45

and

(v) (∃y)(Ba⊃(∀x)Lyx)

     1   2   3 45

Here is how you should think about this problem: Starting with a closed sentence, (. . . **s** . . .), which uses a name, **s**, take out one or more of the occurrences of the name **s**. For example, take out the 'a' at 4 in (i). Then look to see if the vacated spot is already in the scope of one (or more) quantifiers. In (i) to (v), the place marked by 4 is in the scope of the '(∀x)' at 3. So you can't use 'x'. You must perform your existential generalization with some variable which is not already bound at the places at which you replace the name. After taking out one or more occurrences of the name, **s**, in (. . . **s** . . .), replace the vacated spots with a variable (the **same** variable at each spot) which is not bound by some quantifier already in the sentence.

Continuing our example, at this point you will have turned (i) into

(vi) Ba ⊃ (∀x)Lya

You will have something of the form (. . . **u** . . .) in which **u** is **free**: 'y' is free in (vi). At this point you must have an **open sentence**. Now, at last, you can apply your existential quantifier to the resulting open sentence to get the closed sentence (∃**u**)(. . . **u** . . .).

To summarize more compactly:

> (∃**u**)(. . . **u** . . .) is an *Existential Generalization* of (. . . **s** . . .) with respect to the name **s** if and only if (∃**u**)(. . . **u** . . .) results from (. . . **s** . . .) by
>
> a)   Deleting any number of occurrences of **s** in (. . . **s** . . .),
> b)   Replacing these occurrences with a variable, **u**, which is **free** at these occurrences, and
> c)   Applying (∃**u**) to the result.

(In practice you should read (a) in this definition as "Deleting one or more occurrences of **s** in (. . . **s** . . .)." I have expressed (a) with "any number of" so that it will correctly treat the odd case of vacuous quantifiers, which in practice you will not need to worry about. But if you are interested, you can figure out what is going on by studying exercise 3–3.)

It has taken quite a few words to set this matter straight, but once you see the point you will no longer need the words.

With the idea of an existential generalization, we can accurately state the rule for existential introduction:

> *Existential Introduction Rule:*   From any sentence, **X**, you are licensed to conclude any existential generalization of **X** anywhere below. Expressed with a diagram,

$$\boxed{(.\;.\;.\;\textbf{s}\;.\;.\;.)}$$

.
.
.

$\overline{(\exists \textbf{u})(.\;.\;.\;\textbf{u}\;.\;.\;.)}\;\; \exists \textbf{I}$

Where $(\exists \textbf{u})(.\;.\;.\;\textbf{u}\;.\;.\;.)$ is an existential generalization of $(.\;.\;.\;\textbf{s}\;.\;.\;.)$.

Let's look at a new example, complicated only by the feature that it involves a second name which occurs in both the premise and the conclusion:

Adam loves Eve.	Lae
Adam loves someone.	$(\exists x)Lax$

'$(\exists x)Lax$' is an existential generalizaton of 'Lae'. So $\exists I$ applies to make the following a correct derivation:

1	Lae	P
2	$(\exists x)Lax$	1, $\exists I$

To make sure you have the hang of rule $\exists I$, we'll do one more example. Notice that in this example, the second premise has an atomic sentence letter as its consequent. Remember that predicate logic is perfectly free to use atomic sentence letters as components in building up sentences.

Ka
$(\exists x)Kx \supset P$
___
P

1	Ka	P
2	$(\exists x)Kx \supset P$	P
3	$(\exists x)Kx$	1, $\exists I$
4	P	2, 3, $\supset E$

In line 4 I applied $\supset E$ to lines 2 and 3. $\supset E$ applies here in exactly the same way as it did in sentence logic. In particular $\supset E$ and the other sentence logic rules apply to sentences the components of which may be quantified sentences as well as sentence logic sentences.

Now let's try an example which applies both our new rules:

$(\forall x)Lxx$
___
$(\exists x)Lxx$

1	$(\forall x)Lxx$	P
2	Laa	1, $\forall E$
3	$(\exists x)Lxx$	2, $\exists I$

In addition to illustrating both new rules working together, this example illustrates something else we have not yet seen. In past examples, when I applied $\forall E$ I instantiated a universally quantified sentence with a name which already occurred somewhere in the argument. In this case no name occurs in the argument. But if a universally quantified sentence is true in an interpretation, all of its substitution instances must be true in the interpretation. And every interpretation must have at least one object in it. So a universally quantified sentence must always have at least one substitution instance true in an interpretation. Since a universally quantified sentence always has at least one substitution instance, I can introduce a name into the situation with which to write that substitution instance, if no name already occurs.

To put the point another way, because every interpretation always has at least one object in it, I can always introduce a name to refer to some object in an interpretation and then use this name to form my substitution instance of the universally quantified sentence.

Good. Let's try yet another example:

(∀x)(Cx ⊃ Mx)	1	(∀x)(Cx ⊃ Mx)	P
Cd	2	Cd	P
——————	3	Cd ⊃ Md	1, ∀E
(∃x)Mx	4	Md	2, 3, ⊃E
	5	(∃x)Mx	4, ∃I

Notice that although the rules permit me to apply ∃I to line 2, doing so would not have gotten me anywhere. To see how I came up with this derivation, look at the final conclusion. You know that it is an existentially quantified sentence, and you know that ∃I permits you to derive such a sentence from an instance, such as 'Md'. So you must ask yourself: Can I derive such an instance from the premises? Yes, because the first premise says about everything that if it is C, then it is M. And the second premise says that d, in particular, is C. So applying ∀E to 1 you can get 3, which, together with 2, gives 4 by ⊃E.

EXERCISES

5–2. Provide derivations which demonstrate the validity of the following arguments:

a)
$$\frac{Na}{(∃x)(Nx \lor Gx)}$$

b)
$$\frac{(∀x)(Kx \& Px)}{(∃x)Kx \& (∃x)Px}$$

c)
$$\frac{(∀x)(Hx ⊃ \sim Dx)}{Dg}$$
$$(∃x)\sim Hx$$

d)
$$\frac{(∀x)Ax \& (∀x)Txd}{(∃x)(Ax \& Txd)}$$

e)
$$\frac{Fa \lor Nh}{(∃x)Fx \lor (∃x)Nx}$$

f)
$$\frac{(∀x)(Sx \lor Jx)}{(∃x)Sx \lor (∃x)Jx}$$

g) $(\exists x)Rxa \supset (\forall x)Rax$
Rea
_____
$(\exists x)Rax$

h) $Lae \lor Lea$
$(\exists x)Lax \supset A$
$(\exists x)Lxa \supset A$
_____
A

i) $(\exists x)Jx \supset Q$
$(\forall x)Jx$
_____
Q

j) $(\forall x)(Max \lor Mex)$
$\sim(\exists x)Max \lor Bg$
$\sim(\exists x)Mex \lor Bg$
_____
$(\exists x)Bx$

k) $(\forall x)(Kxx \equiv Px)$
$(\forall x)[Kjx \,\&\, (Px \supset Sx)]$
_____
$(\exists x)Sx$

l) $(\forall x)(\sim Oxx \lor Ix)$
$(\forall x)(Ix \supset Rxm)$
_____
$(\forall x)Oxx \supset (\exists x)Rxm$

5–4. THE EXISTENTIAL ELIMINATION AND UNIVERSAL INTRODUCTION RULES: BACKGROUND IN INFORMAL ARGUMENT

Now let's go to work on the two harder rules. To understand these rules, it is especially important to see how they are motivated. Let us begin by looking at some examples of informal deductive arguments which present the kind of reasoning which our new rules will make exact. Let's start with this argument:

> Everyone likes either rock music or country/western.
> Someone does not like rock.
> _____
> Someone likes country/western.

Perhaps this example is not quite as trivial as our previous examples. How can we see that the conclusion follows from the premises? We commonly argue in the following way. We are given the premise that someone does not like rock. To facilitate our argument, let us suppose that this person (or one of them if there are more than one) is called Doe. (Since I don't know this person's name, I'm using 'Doe' as the police do when they book a man with an unknown name as 'John Doe.') Now, since according to the first premise, everyone likes either rock or country/western, this must be true, in particular, of Doe. That is, either Doe likes rock, or he or she likes country/western. But we had already agreed that Doe does not like rock. So Doe must like country/western. Finally, since Doe likes country/western, we see that someone likes country/western. But that was just the conclusion we were trying to derive.

What you need to focus on in this example is how I used the name 'Doe'. The second premise gives me the assumption that someone does not like rock. So that I can talk about this someone, I give him or her a name: 'Doe'. I don't know anything more that applies to just this person, but I do have a fact, the first premise, which applies to everyone. So I can use this fact in arguing about Doe, even though I really don't know who Doe is. I use this general fact to conclude that Doe, whoever he or she might be, does like country/western. Finally, before I am done, I acknowledge that I really don't know who Doe is, in essence by saying: Whoever this person Doe might be, I know that he or she likes country/western. That is, what I really can conclude is that there is someone who likes country/western.

Now let's compare this argument with another:

(1) Everyone either likes rock or country/western.
(2) Anyone who likes country/western likes soft music.

(3) Anyone who doesn't like rock likes soft music.

This time I have deliberately chosen an example which might not be completely obvious so that you can see the pattern of reasoning doing its work.

The two premises say something about absolutely everyone. But it's hard to argue about 'everyone'. So let us think of an arbitrary example of a person, named 'Arb', to whom these premises will then apply. My strategy is to carry the argument forward in application to this arbitrarily chosen individual. I have made up the name 'Arb' to emphasize the fact that I have chosen this person (and likewise the name) perfectly arbitrarily. We could just as well have chosen any person named by any name.

To begin the argument, the first premise tells us that

(4) Either Arb likes rock, or Arb likes country/western.

The second premise tells us that

(5) If Arb does like country/western, then Arb likes soft music.

Now, let us make a further assumption about Arb:

(6) (Further Assumption): Arb doesn't like rock.

From (6) and (4), it follows that

(7) Arb likes country/western.

And from (7) and (5), it follows that

(8) Arb likes soft music.

Altogether we see that Arb's liking soft music, (8), follows from the further assumption, (6), with the help of the original premises (1) and (2) (as applied through this application to Arb, in (4) and (5)). Consequently, from the original premises it follows that

(9)   If Arb doesn't like rock, then Arb likes soft music.

All this is old hat. Now comes the new step. The whole argument to this point has been conducted in terms of the person, Arb. But Arb could have been anyone, or equally, we could have conducted the argument with the name of anyone at all. So the argument is perfectly general. What (9) says about Arb will be true of anyone. That is, we can legitimately conclude that

(3)   Anyone who doesn't like rock likes soft music.

which is exactly the conclusion we were trying to reach.

We have now seen two arguments which use "stand-in" names, that is, names that are somehow doing the work of "someone" or of "anyone". Insofar as both arguments use stand-in names, they seem to be similar. But they are importantly different, and understanding our new rules turns on understanding how the two arguments are different. In the second argument, Arb could be anyone—absolutely anyone at all. But in the first argument, Doe could not be anyone. Doe could only be the person, or one of the people, who does not like rock. 'Doe' is "partially arbitrary" because we are careful not to assume anything we don't know about Doe. But we do know that Doe is a rock hater and so is not just anyone at all. Arb, however, could have been anyone.

We must be very careful not to conflate these two ways of using stand-in names in arguments. Watch what happens if you do conflate the ways:

Someone does not like rock.
$\overline{\text{Everyone does not like rock.}}$ (Invalid)

The argument is just silly. But confusing the two functions of stand-in names could seem to legitimate the argument, if one were to argue as follows: Someone does not like rock. Let's call this person 'Arb'. So Arb does not like rock. But Arb could be anyone, so everyone does not like rock. In such a simple case, no one is going to blunder in this way. But in more complicated arguments it can happen easily.

To avoid this kind of mistake, we must find some way to clearly mark the difference between the two kinds of argument. I have tried to bring out the distinction by using one kind of stand-in name, 'Doe', when we are talking about the existence of some particular person, and another kind of stand-in name, 'Arb', when we are talking about absolutely any arbitrary individual. This device works well in explaining that a stand-in name can function in two very different ways. Unfortunately, we cannot incorporate this device in natural deduction in a straightforward way simply by using two different kinds of names to do the two different jobs.

Let me try to explain the problem. (You don't need to understand the problem in detail right now; detailed understanding will come later. All you need at this point is just a glimmer of what the problem is.) At the beginning of a derivation a name can be arbitrary. But then we might start a subderivation in which the name occurs, and although arbitrary from the point of view of the outer derivation, the name might **not** be arbitrary from the point of view of the subderivation. This can happen because in the original derivation nothing special, such as hating rock, is assumed about the individual. But inside the subderivation we might make such a further assumption about the individual. **While the further assumption is in effect, the name is not arbitrary,** although it can become arbitrary again when we discharge the further assumption of the subderivation. In fact, exactly these things happened in our last example. If, while the further assumption (6) was in effect, I had tried to generalize on statements about Arb, saying that what was true of Arb was true of anyone, I could have drawn all sorts of crazy conclusions. Look back at the example and see if you can figure out for yourself what some of these conclusions might be.

Natural deduction has the job of accurately representing valid reasoning which uses stand-in names, but in a way which won't allow the sort of mistake or confusion I have been pointing out. Because the confusion can be subtle, the natural deduction rules are a little complicated. The better you understand what I have said in this section, the quicker you will grasp the natural deduction rules which set all this straight.

EXERCISES

5-3. For each of the two different uses of stand-in names discussed in this section, give a valid argument of your own, expressed in English, which illustrates the use.

5-5. THE UNIVERSAL INTRODUCTION RULE

Here is the intuitive idea for universal introduction, as I used this rule in the soft music example: If a name, as it occurs in a sentence, is completely arbitrary, you can *Universally Generalize* on the name. This means that you rewrite the sentence with a variable written in for all occurrences of the arbitrary name, and you put a universal quantifier, written with the same variable, in front. To make this intuition exact, we have to say exactly when a name is arbitrary and what is involved in universal generalization. We must take special care because universal generalization differs importantly from existential generalizaton.

Let's tackle arbitrariness first. When does a name **not** occur arbitrarily? Certainly not if some assumption is made about (the object referred to by) the name. If some assumption is made using a name, then the name can't refer to absolutely anything. If a name occurs in a premise or assumption, the name can refer only to things which satisfy that premise or assumption. So a name does not occur arbitrarily when the name appears in a premise or an assumption, and it does not occur arbitrarily as long as such a premise or assumption is in effect.

The soft music example shows these facts at work. I'll use 'Rx' for 'x likes rock.', 'Cx' for 'x likes country/western.', and 'Sx' for 'x likes soft music.' Here are the formalized argument and derivation which I am going to use to explain these ideas:

$$
\begin{array}{ll}
(\forall x)(Rx \lor Cx) \\
(\forall x)(Cx \supset Sx) \\
\hline
(\forall x)(\sim Rx \supset Sx)
\end{array}
$$

1	$(\forall x)(Rx \lor Cx)$	P
2	$(\forall x)(Cx \supset Sx)$	P
3	Ra ∨ Ca	1, ∀E
4	Ca ⊃ Sa	2, ∀E
5	∼Ra	A
6	Ra ∨ Ca	3, R
7	Ca	5, 6, ∨E
8	Ca ⊃ Sa	4, R
9	Sa	7, 8, ⊃E
10	∼Ra ⊃ Sa	5–9, ⊃I
11	$(\forall x)(\sim Rx \supset Sx)$	10, ∀I

Where does 'a' occur arbitrarily in this example? It occurs arbitrarily in lines 3 and 4, because at these lines no premise or assumption using 'a' is in effect. We say that these lines are *Not Governed* by any premise or assumption in which 'a' occurs. In lines 5 through 9, however, 'a' does not occur arbitrarily. Line 5 is an assumption using 'a'. In lines 5 through 9, the assumption of line 5 is in effect, so these lines are governed by the assumption of line 5. (We are going to need to say that a premise or assumption always governs itself.) In all these lines something special is being assumed about the thing named by 'a', namely, that it has the property named by '∼R'. So in these lines the thing named by 'a' is not just any old thing. However, in line 10 we discharge the assumption of line 5. So in line 10 'a' again occurs arbitrarily. Line 10 is only governed by the premises 1 and 2, in which 'a' does not occur. Line 10 is not governed by the assumption of line 5.

I am going to introduce a device to mark the arbitrary occurrences of a name. If a name occurs arbitrarily we will put a hat on it, so it looks like this: â. Marking all the arbitrary occurrences of 'a' in the last derivation makes the derivation look like this:

1	(∀x)(Rx ∨ Cx)	P
2	(∀x)(Cx ⊃ Sx)	P
3	Râ ∨ Câ	1, ∀E
4	Câ ⊃ Sâ	2, ∀E
5	~Ra	A
6	Ra ∨ Ca	3, R
7	Ca	5, 6, ∨E
8	Ca ⊃ Sa	4, R
9	Sa	7, 8, ⊃E
10	~Râ ⊃ Sâ	5–9, ⊃I
11	(∀x)(~Rx ⊃ Sx)	10, ∀I

Read through this copy of the derivation and make sure you understand why the hat occurs where it does and why it does not occur where it doesn't. If you have a question, reread the previous paragraph, remembering that a hat on a name just means that the name occurs arbitrarily at that place.

I want to be sure that you do not misunderstand what the hat means. A name with a hat on it is not a new kind of name. A name is a name is a name, and two occurrences of the same name, one with and one without a hat, are two occurrences of the same name. A hat on a name is a kind of flag to remind us that at that point the name is occurring arbitrarily. Whether or not a name occurs arbitrarily is not really a fact just about the name. It is a fact about the relation of the name to the derivation in which it occurs. If, at an occurrence of a name, the name is governed by a premise or assumption which uses the same name, the name does not occur there arbitrarily. It is not arbitrary there because the thing it refers to has to satisfy the premise or assumption. Only if a name is not governed by any premise or assumption using the same name is the name arbitrary, in which case we mark it by dressing it with a hat.

Before continuing, let's summarize the discussion of arbitrary occurrence with an exact statement:

> Suppose that a sentence, **X**, occurs in a derivation or subderivation. That occurrence of **X** is *Governed* by a premise or assumption, **Y**, if and only if **Y** is a premise or assumption of **X**'s derivation, or of any outer derivation of **X**'s derivation (an outer derivation, or outer-outer derivation, and so on). In particular, a premise or assumption is always governed by itself.

A name *Occurs Arbitrarily* in a sentence of a derivation if that occurrence of the sentence is not governed by any premise or assumption in which the name occurs. To help us remember, we mark an arbitrary occurrence of a name by writing it with a hat.

The idea for the universal introduction rule was that we would *Universally Generalize* on a name that occurs arbitrarily. We have discussed arbitrary occurrence. Now on to universal generalization.

The idea of a universal generalization differs in one important respect from the idea of an existential generalization. To see the difference, you must be clear about what we want out of a generalization: We want a new quantified sentence which follows from a sentence with a name.

For the existential quantifier, '(∃x)Lxx', '(∃x)Lax', and '(∃x)Lxa' all follow from 'Laa'. From the fact that Adam loves himself, it follows that Adam loves someone, someone loves Adam, and someone loves themself.

Now suppose that the name 'â' occurs arbitrarily in 'Lââ'. We know that "Adam" loves himself, where Adam now could be just anybody at all. What universal fact follows? **Only** that '(∀x)Lxx', that everyone loves themself. It does **not** follow that '(∀x)Lâx' or '(∀x)Lxâ'. That is, it does not follow that Adam loves everyone or everyone loves Adam. Even though 'Adam' occurs arbitrarily, '(∀x)Lâx' and '(∀x)Lxâ' make it sound as if someone ("Adam") loves everyone and as if someone ("Adam") is loved by everyone. These surely do not follow from 'Lââ'. But ∃I would license us to infer these sentences, respectively, from '(∀x)Lâx' and from '(∀x)Lxâ'.

Worse, â is still arbitrary in '(∀x)Lâx'. So if we could infer '(∀x)Lâx' from 'Lââ', we could then argue that in '(∀x)Lâx', 'â' could be anyone. We would then be able to infer '(∀y)(∀x)Lyx', that everyone loves everyone! But from 'Lââ' we should only be able to infer '(∀x)Lxx', that everyone loves themself, not '(∀y)(∀x)Lyx', that everyone loves everyone.

We want to use the idea of existential and universal generalizations to express valid rules of inference. The last example shows that, to achieve this goal, we have to be a little careful with sentences in which the same name occurs more than once. If **s** occurs more than once in (. . . **s** . . .), we may form an **existential** generalization by generalizing on any number of the occurrences of **s**. But, to avoid the problem I have just described and to get a valid rule of inference, we must insist that a **universal** generalization of (. . . **s** . . .), with respect to the name, **s**, must leave no instance of **s** in (. . . **s** . . .).

In other respects the idea of universal generalization works just like existential generalization. In particular, we must carefully avoid the trap of trying to replace a name by a variable already bound by a quantifier. This idea works exactly as before, so I will proceed immediately to an exact statement:

The sentence (∀**u**)(. . . **u** . . .) results by *Universally Generalizing* on the name **s** in (. . . **s** . . .) if and only if one obtains (∀**u**)(. . . **u** . . .) from (. . . **s** . . .) by

  a) Deleting **all** occurrences of **s** in (. . . **s** . . .),
  b) Replacing these occurrences with a variable, **u**, which is **free** at these occurrences, and
  c) Applying (∀**u**) to the result.

(∀**u**)(. . . **u** . . .) is then said to be the *Universal Generalization of* (. . . **s** . . .) *with Respect to the Name* **s**.

With these definitions, we are at last ready for an exact statement of the universal introduction rule:

Universal Introduction Rule: If a sentence, **X**, appears in a derivation, and if at the place where it appears a name, ŝ, occurs arbitrarily in **X**, then you are licensed to conclude, anywhere below, the sentence which results by universally generalizing on the name ŝ in **X**. Expressed with a diagram:

$$\boxed{\begin{array}{|l}\fbox{(. . . ŝ . . .)}\\ \hline \text{(∀u)(. . u . . .)} \end{array}}\quad ∀\text{I}$$

Where ŝ occurs arbitrarily in (. . . ŝ . . .) and (∀u)(. . u . . .) is the universal generalization of (. . . ŝ . . .) with respect to ŝ.

Let's look at two simple examples to illustrate what can go wrong if you do not follow the rule correctly. The first example is the one we used to illustrate the difference between existential and universal generalization:

Everyone loves themself.
———————————————
Everyone loves Adam. **(Invalid!)**

1	(∀x)Lxx	*P*
2	Lââ	1, ∀E
3	(∀x)Lxâ	**Mistaken attempt to apply ∀I to 2. 3 is not a universal generalization of 2.**

The second example will make sure you understand the requirement that ∀I applies only to an arbitrary occurrence of a name:

Adam is blond.
——————————— **(Invalid!)**
Everyone is blond.

1	Ba	*P*
2	(∀x)Bx	**Mistaken attempt to apply ∀I to 1. 'a' is not arbitrary at 1.**

The problem here is that the premise assumes something special about the thing referred to by 'a', that it has the property referred to by 'B'. We can universally generalize on a name—that is, apply ∀I—**only** when nothing special is assumed in this way, that is, when the name is arbitrary. You will see this even more clearly if you go back to our last formalization of the soft music example and see what sorts of crazy conclusions you could draw if you were to allow yourself to generalize on occurrences of names without hats.

Let's consolidate our understanding of ∀I by working through one more example. Before reading on, try your own hand at providing a derivation for

$$\frac{(\forall x)(Lax \ \& \ Lxa)}{(\forall x)(Lax \equiv Lxa)}$$

If you don't see how to begin, use the same overall strategy we developed in chapter 6 of volume I. Write a skeleton derivation with its premise and final conclusion and ask what you need in order to get the final, or target, conclusion.

1 | (∀x)(Lax & Lxa)   *P*
  | ?
  | ?
  | (∀x)(Lax ≡ Lxa)

We could get our target conclusion by ∀I if we had a sentence of the form 'Lab̂ ≡ Lb̂a'. Let's write that in to see if we can make headway in this manner:

1 | (∀x)(Lax & Lxa)   *P*
  | ?
  | ?
  | Lab̂ ≡ Lb̂a
  | (∀x)(Lax ≡ Lxa)   ∀I

'Lab̂ ≡ Lb̂a' is now our target conclusion. As a biconditional, our best bet is to get it by ≡I from 'Lab ⊃ Lba' and 'Lba ⊃ Lab'. (I didn't write hats on any names because, as I haven't written the sentences as part of the derivation, I am not yet sure which sentences will govern these two conditionals.) The conditionals, in turn, I hope to get from two subderivations, one each starting from one of the antecedents of the two conditionals:

```
1 │ (∀x)(Lax & Lxa)      P
  ├─────────────────
  │ ?
  │       ┌─ Lab          A
  │       ├──
  │       │  ?
  │       │
  │       └─ Lba
  │
  │ Lab̂ ⊃ Lb̂a             ⊃I
  │
  │ ?
  │       ┌─ Lba          A
  │       ├──
  │       │  ?
  │       │
  │       └─ Lab
  │
  │ Lb̂a ⊃ Lab̂             ⊃I
  │ Lab̂ ≡ Lb̂a             ≡I
  │ (∀x)(Lax ≡ Lxa)       ∀I
  └─
```

Notice that 'b' gets a hat wherever it appears in the main derivation. There, 'b' is not governed by any assumption in which 'b' occurs. But 'b' occurs in the assumptions of both subderivations. So in the subderivations 'b' gets no hat. Finally, 'a' occurs in the original premise. That by itself rules out putting a hat on 'a' anywhere in the whole derivation, which includes all of its subderivations.

Back to the question of how we will fill in the subderivations. We need to derive 'Lba' in the first and 'Lab' in the second. Notice that if we apply ∀E to the premise, using 'b' to instantiate 'x', we get a conjunction with exactly the two new target sentences as conjuncts. We will be able to apply &E to the conjunction and then simply reiterate the conjuncts in the subderivations. Our completed derivation will look like this:

1	(∀x)(Lax & Lxa)	P
2	Lab̂ & L̂ba	1, ∀E
3	Lab̂	2, &E
4	L̂ba	2, &E
5	⌐ Lab	A
6	└ Lba	4, R
7	Lab̂ ⊃ L̂ba	5–6, ⊃I
8	⌐ Lba	A
9	└ Lab	3, R
10	L̂ba ⊃ Lab̂	8–9, ⊃I
11	Lab̂ ≡ L̂ba	7, 10, ≡I
12	(∀x)(Lax ≡ Lxa)	11, ∀I

Once more, notice that 'b' gets a hat in lines 2, 3, and 4. In these lines no premise or assumption using 'b' is operative. But in lines 5, 6, 8, and 9, 'b' gets no hat, even though exactly the same sentences appeared earlier (lines 3 and 4) with hats on 'b'. This is because when we move into the subderivations an assumption goes into effect which says something special about 'b'. So in the subderivations, off comes the hat. As soon as this special assumption about 'b' is discharged, and we move back out of the subderivation, no special assumption using 'b' is in effect, and the hat goes back on 'b'.

You may well wonder why I bother with the hats in lines like 2, 3, 4, 7, and 10, on which I am never going to universally generalize. The point is that, so far as the rules go, I am permitted to universally generalize on 'b' in these lines. In this problem I don't bother, because applying ∀I to these lines will not help me get my target conclusion. But you need to develop awareness of just when the formal statement of the ∀I rule allows you to apply it. Hence you need to learn to mark those places at which the rule legitimately could apply.

Students often have two more questions about hats. First, ∀I permits you to universally generalize on a name with a hat. But you can **also** apply ∃I to a name with a hat. Now that I have introduced the hats, the last example in section 5–3 should really look like this:

1	(∀x)Lxx	P
2	Lâ â	1, ∀E
3	(∃x)Lxx	2, ∃I

If everyone loves themself, then Arb loves him or herself, whoever Arb may be. But then someone loves themself. When a name occurs arbitrarily, the name can refer to anything. But then it **also** refers to something. You can apply **either ∀I or ∃I** to a hatted name.

It is also easy to be puzzled by the fact that a name which is introduced in the assumption of a subderivation, and thus does not occur arbitrarily there, can occur arbitrarily after the assumption of the subderivation has been discharged. Consider this example:

1	(∃x)Px ⊃ (∀x)Qx	P
2	Pa	A
3	(∃x)Px	2, ∃I
4	(∃x)Px ⊃ (∀x)Qx	1, R
5	(∀x)Qx	3, 4, ⊃E
6	Qa	5, ∀E
7	Pâ ⊃ Qâ	2–6, ⊃I
8	(∀x)(Px ⊃ Qx)	7, ∀I

In the subderivation something is assumed about 'a', namely, that it has the property P. So, from the point of view of the subderivation, 'a' is not arbitrary. As long as the assumption of the subderivation is in effect, 'a' cannot refer to just anything. It can only refer to something which is P. But after the subderivation's assumption has been discharged, 'a' is arbitrary. Why? The rules tell us that 'a' is arbitrary in line 7 because line 7 is not governed by any premises or assumptions in which 'a' occurs. But to make this more intuitive, notice that I could have just as well constructed the same subderivation using the name 'b' instead of 'a', using ⊃E to write 'Pb̂ ⊃ Qb̂' on line 7. Or I could have used 'c', 'd', or any other name. This is why 'a' is arbitrary in line 7. I could have arrived at a conditional in line 7 using any name I liked instead of using 'a'.

Some students get annoyed and frustrated by having to learn when to put a hat on a name and when to leave it off. But it's worth the effort to learn. Once you master the hat trick, ∀I is simple: You can apply ∀I whenever you have a name with a hat. Not otherwise.

EXERCISES

5-4. There is a mistake in the following derivation. Put on hats where they belong, and write in the justification for those steps which are justified. Identify and explain the mistake.

$$
\begin{array}{l|ll}
1 & (\forall x)(Bx \supset Cx) & P \\
2 & Be \supset Ce & \\
\\
3 & \quad \underline{Be} & A \\
4 & \quad Be \supset Ce & \\
5 & \quad Ce & \\
6 & \quad (\forall x)Ce & \\
\\
7 & Be \supset (\forall x)Cx &
\end{array}
$$

5–5. Provide derivations which establish the validity of the following arguments. Be sure you don't mix up sentences which are a quantification of a sentence formed with a '&', a 'v', or a '⊃' with compounds formed with a '&', a 'v', or a '⊃', the components of which are quantified sentences. For example, '(∀x)(Px & Qa)' is a universally quantified sentence to which you may apply ∀E. '(∀x)Px & Qa' is a conjunction to which you may apply &E but not ∀E.

a) $\dfrac{(\forall x)(Fx \ \& \ Gx)}{(\forall x)Fx}$ b) $\dfrac{(\forall x)(Mx \supset Nx)}{(\forall x)Mx}$ c) $\dfrac{A}{(\forall x)(A \lor Nx)}$
$\qquad\qquad\qquad\qquad\quad (\forall x)Nx$

d) $\dfrac{(\forall x)Hx \ \& \ (\forall x)Qx}{(\forall x)(Hx \ \& \ Qx)}$ e) $\dfrac{(\forall x)(Kxm \ \& \ Kmx)}{(\forall x)Kxm \ \& \ (\forall x)Kmx}$ f) $\dfrac{(\forall x)(Fx \lor Gx)}{(\forall x)(Fx \supset Gx)}$
$\qquad\qquad\qquad\qquad\qquad\qquad\qquad\qquad\qquad\qquad (\forall x)Gx$

g) $\dfrac{(\forall x)\sim Px \lor C}{(\forall x)(\sim Px \lor C)}$ h) $\dfrac{(\forall x)(Rxb \supset Rax)}{(\forall x)Rxb \supset (\forall x)Rax}$ i) $\dfrac{(\forall x)(Gxh \supset Gxm)}{(\forall x)(\sim Gxm \supset \sim Gxh)}$

j) $\dfrac{\begin{array}{l}(\forall x)(Mx \supset Nx) \\ (\forall x)(Nx \supset Ox)\end{array}}{(\forall x)(Mx \supset Ox)}$ k) $\dfrac{T \supset (\forall x)Mdx}{(\forall x)(T \supset Mdx)}$ l) $\dfrac{(\forall x)(Hff \supset Lxx)}{Hff \supset (\forall x)Lxx}$

m) $\dfrac{(\forall x)Px \lor (\forall x)Qx}{(\forall x)(Px \lor Qx)}$ n) $\dfrac{(\forall x)Hx}{(\forall x)Jx}\ \ \dfrac{(\exists x)Hx \supset (\forall x)(Hx \supset Jx)}{}$ o) $\dfrac{(\forall x)(Sx \equiv Ox)}{(\forall x)Sx \equiv (\forall x)Ox}$

p) $\dfrac{(\exists x)Px \supset A}{(\forall x)(Px \supset A)}$ q) $\dfrac{\sim(\exists x)Px}{(\forall x)\sim Px}$ r) $\dfrac{\sim(\forall x)Px}{(\exists x)\sim Px}$ s) $\dfrac{(\forall x)Px \supset A}{(\exists x)(Px \supset A)}$

t) $\dfrac{\sim(\forall x)(Jx \supset \sim Kx)}{(\exists x)(Jx \ \& \ Kx)}$ u) $\dfrac{\sim(\exists x)Qx \lor H}{(\forall x)(\sim Qx \lor H)}$ v) $\dfrac{\sim(\exists x)Dx}{(\forall x)(Dx \supset Kx)}$

5–6. THE EXISTENTIAL ELIMINATION RULE

∀I and ∃E are difficult rules. Many of you will have to work patiently over this material a number of times before you understand them clearly. But if you have at least a fair understanding of ∀I, we can proceed to ∃E because ultimately these two rules need to be understood together.

Let's go back to the first example in section 5–4: Everyone likes either rock music or country/western. Someone does not like rock. So someone likes country/western. I will symbolize this as

$$(\forall x)(Rx \lor Cx)$$
$$(\exists x)\!\sim\! Rx$$
$$\overline{(\exists x)Cx}$$

In informally showing this argument's validity, I used 'Doe', which I will now write just as 'd', as a stand-in name for the unknown "someone" who does not like rock. But I must be careful in at least two respects:

i) I must not allow myself to apply ∀I to the stand-in name, 'd'. Otherwise, I could argue from '(∃x)~Rx' to '~Rd' to '(∀x)~Rx'. In short, I have to make sure that such a name never gets a hat.

ii) When I introduce the stand-in name, 'd', I must not be assuming anything else about the thing to which 'd' refers other than that '~R' is true of it.

It's going to take a few paragraphs to explain how we will meet these two requirements. To help you follow these paragraphs, I'll begin by writing down our example's derivation, which you should not expect to understand until you have read the explanation. Refer back to this example as you read:

$(\forall x)(Rx \lor Cx)$	1	$(\forall x)(Rx \lor Cx)$	P
$(\exists x)\!\sim\! Rx$	2	$(\exists x)\!\sim\! Rx$	P
$(\exists x)Cx$	3	d $\sim$Rd	A
	4	$(\forall x)(Rx \lor Cx)$	1, R
	5	Rd $\lor$ Cd	4, ∀E
	6	Cd	3, 5, ∨E
	7	$(\exists x)Cx$	6, ∃I
	8	$(\exists x)Cx$	2, 3–7, ∃E

I propose to argue from the premise, '(∃x)~Rx', by using the stand-in name, 'd'. I will say about the thing named by 'd' what '(∃x)~Rx' says about "someone". But I must be sure that 'd' never gets a hat. How can I guarantee that? Well, names that occur in assumptions can't get hats anywhere in the subderivation governed by the assumption. So we can guarantee that 'd' won't get a hat by introducing it as an assumption of a subderivation and insisting that 'd' **never occur outside** that subderivation. This is what I did in line 3. '~Rd' appears as the subderivation's assumption, and the 'd' written just to the left of the scope line signals the requirement that 'd' be an *Isolated Name*. That is to say, 'd' is isolated in the subderivation the scope line of which is marked with the 'd'. An isolated name may never appear outside its subderivation.

Introducing 'd' in the assumption of a subderivation might seem a little strange. I encounter the sentence, '(∃x)~Rx', on a derivation. I reason: Let's assume that this thing of which '~R' is true is called 'd', and let's record this assumption by starting a subderivation with '~Rd' as its assumption, and see what we can derive. Why could this seem strange? Because if I already know '(∃x)~Rx', no further assumption is involved in assuming that there is something of which '~R' is true. But, in a sense, I do make a new assumption in assuming that this thing is called 'd'. It turns out that this sense of making a special assumption is just what we need.

By making 'd' occur in the assumption of a subderivation, and insisting that 'd' be isolated, that it appear **only** in the subderivation, I guarantee that 'd' never gets a hat. But this move also accomplishes our other requirement: If 'd' occurs only in the subderivation, 'd' cannot occur in any outer premise or assumption.

Now let's see how the overall strategy works. Look at the argument's subderivation, steps 3–7. You see that, with the help of reiterated premise 1, from '~Rd' I have derived '(∃x)Cx'. But neither 1 nor the conclusion '(∃x)Cx' uses the name 'd'. Thus, in this subderivation, the fact that I used the name 'd' was immaterial. I could have used any other name not appearing in the outer derivation. The real force of the assumption '~Rd' is that **there exists something of which '~R' is true** (there is someone who does not like rock). But that there exists something of which '~R' is true has already been given to me in line 2! Since the real force of the assumption of line 3 is that there exists something of which '~R' is true, and since I am already given this fact in line 2, I don't really need the assumption 3. I can discharge it. In other words, if I am given the truth of lines 1 and 2, I know that the conclusion of the subderivation, 7, must also be true, and I can enter 7 as a further conclusion of the outer derivation.

It is essential, however, that 'd' not appear in line 7. If 'd' appeared in the final conclusion of the subderivation, then I would not be allowed to discharge the assumption and enter this final conclusion in the outer derivation. For if 'd' appeared in the subderivation's final conclusion, I would be relying, not just on the assumption that '~R' was true of something, but on the assumption that this thing was named by 'd'.

The example's pattern of reasoning works perfectly generally. Here is how we make it precise:

A name is *Isolated in a Subderivation* if it does not occur outside the subderivation. We mark the isolation of a name by writing the name at the top left of the scope line of its subderivation. In applying this definition, remember that a sub-sub-derivation of a subderivation counts as part of the subderivation.

Existential Elimination Rule: Suppose a sentence of the form (∃u)(. . . u. . . .) appears in a derivation, as does a subderivation with assumption (. . . s . . .), a substitution instance of (∃u)(. . . u . . .). Also suppose that s is isolated in this subderivation. If **X** is any of the subderivation's conclusions in which s does not occur, you are licensed to draw **X** as a further conclusion in the outer derivation, anywhere below the sentence (∃u)(. . . u . . .) and below the subderivation. Expressed with a diagram:

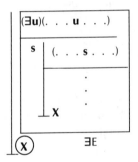

Where (. . . s . . .) is a
substitution instance of
(∃u) (. . . u . . .) and s
is isolated in the ~ '⊃-
derivation.

When you annotate your application of the ∃E rule, cite the line number of the existentially quantified sentence and the inclusive line numbers of the subderivation to which you appeal in applying the rule.

You should be absolutely clear about three facets of this rule. I will illustrate all three.

Suppose the ∃E rule has been applied, licensing the new conclusion, **X**, by appeal to a sentence of the form (∃u)(. . . u . . .) and a subderivation beginning with assumption (. . . s . . .):

1) **s** cannot occur in any premise or prior assumption governing the subderivation,
2) **s** cannot occur in (∃u)(. . . u . . .), and
3) **s** cannot occur in **X**.

All three restrictions are automatically enforced by requiring **s** to be isolated in the subderivation. (Make sure you understand why this is cor-

rect.) Some texts formulate the ∃E rule by imposing these three requirements separately instead of requiring that **s** be isolated. If you reach chapter 15, you will learn that these three restrictions are really all the work
that the isolation requirement needs to do. But, since it is always easy to
pick a name which is unique to a subderivation, I think it is easier simply
to require that **s** be isolated in the subderivation.

Let us see how things go wrong if we violate the isolation requirement
in any of these three ways. For the first, consider:

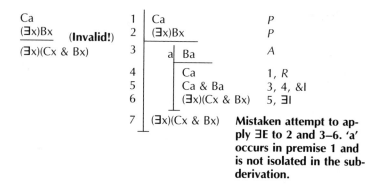

From the fact that Adam is clever and someone (it may well not be Adam)
is blond, it does not follow that any **one** person is both clever and blond.

Now let's see what happens if one violates the isolation requirement in
the second way:

1	(∀x)(∃y)Lxy	P
2	(∃y)Lây	1, ∀E
3	a⌐ Laa	A
4	⌐ (∃x)Lxx	3, ∃I
5	(∃x)Lxx	Mistaken attempt to ap-ply ∃E to 2 and 3–4. 'a' occurs in 2 and is not isolated in the subderi-vation.

(∀x)(∃y)Lxy
―――――― **(Invalid!)**
(∃x)Lxx

From the fact that everyone loves someone, it certainly does not follow
that someone loves themself.

And, for violation of the isolation requirement in the third way:

	(∃x)Bx			**(Invalid)**
	(∀x)Bx			

1	(∃x)Bx			*P*
2		a	Ba	*A*
3			Ba	2, *R*
4	Bâ			
5	(∀x)Bx			

Mistaken attempt to apply ∃E to 1 and 2–3. 'a' occurs in 4 and is not isolated in the sub-derivation.

From the fact that someone is blond, it will never follow that everyone is blond.

One more example will illustrate the point about a sub-sub-derivation being part of a subderivation. The following derivation is completely correct:

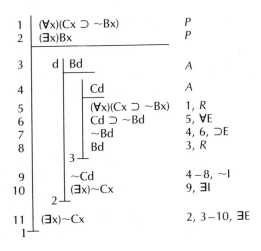

1	(∀x)(Cx ⊃ ~Bx)	*P*
2	(∃x)Bx	*P*
3	d | Bd	*A*
4	Cd	*A*
5	(∀x)(Cx ⊃ ~Bx)	1, *R*
6	Cd ⊃ ~Bd	5, ∀E
7	~Bd	4, 6, ⊃E
8	Bd	3, *R*
9	~Cd	4–8, ~I
10	(∃x)~Cx	9, ∃I
11	(∃x)~Cx	2, 3–10, ∃E

You might worry about this derivation: If 'd' is supposed to be isolated in subderivation 2, how can it legitimately get into sub-sub-derivation 3?

A subderivation is always **part** of the derivation in which it occurs, and the same holds between a sub-sub-derivation and the subderivation in which it occurs. We have already encountered this fact in noting that the premises and assumptions of a derivation or subderivation always apply to the derivation's subderivations, its sub-sub-derivations, and so on.

Now apply this idea about parts to the occurrence of 'd' in sub-sub-derivation 3 above: When I say that a name is isolated in a subderivation I mean that the name can occur in the subderivation **and all its parts,** but the name cannot occur outside the subderivation.

Here is another way to think about this issue: The 'd' at the scope line of the second derivation means that 'd' occurs to the right of the scope line and not to the left. But the scope line of subderivation 3 is not marked by any name. So the notation permits you to use 'd' to the right of this line also.

I hope that you are now beginning to understand the rules for quantifiers. If your grasp still feels shaky, the best way to understand the rules better is to go back and forth between reading the explanations and practicing with the problems. As you do so, try to keep in mind why the rules are supposed to work. Struggle to see why the rules are truth preserving. By striving to understand the rules, as opposed to merely learning them as cookbook recipes, you will learn them better, and you will also have more fun.

EXERCISES

5–6. There is one or more mistakes in the following derivation. Write the hats where they belong, justify the steps that can be justified, and identify and explain the mistake, or mistakes.

1	(∀y)(∃x)Lxy	P
2	(∃x)Lxb	
3	⎢ Lab	A
4	⎢ (∀y)Lay	
5	⎢ (∃x)(∀y)Lxy	
6	(∃x)(∀y)Lxy	

5–7. Provide derivations which establish the validity of the following arguments:

a) $\dfrac{(∃x)Ix \quad (∀x)(Ix ⊃ Jx)}{(∃x)Jx}$

b) $\dfrac{(∃x)(A ⊃ Px)}{A ⊃ (∃x)Px}$

c) $\dfrac{(∃x)Hmx \quad (∀x)(\sim Hmx ∨ Gxn)}{(∃x)Gxn}$

d) $\dfrac{(∃x)(Cfx \& Cxf)}{(∃x)Cfx \& (∃x)Cxf}$

e) $\dfrac{(∃x)(Px ∨ Qx)}{(∃x)Px ∨ (∃x)Qx}$

f) $\dfrac{(∃x)Px ∨ (∃x)Qx}{(∃x)(Px ∨ Qx)}$

g) $\dfrac{(\exists x)(Px \supset A)}{(\forall x)Px \supset A}$ h) $\dfrac{(\forall x)(Px \supset A)}{(\exists x)Px \supset A}$ i) $(\exists x)(Lxa \equiv Lex)$
                                                                   $\dfrac{(\forall x)Lxa}{(\exists x)Lex}$

j) $\dfrac{(\forall x)(Gsx \supset \sim Gxs)}{(\exists x)Gsx \supset (\exists x)\sim Gsx}$

k) $(\exists x)(Px \lor Qx)$ l) $(\exists x)(\sim Mxt \lor Mtx)$ m) $(\exists x)Hxg \lor (\exists x)Nxf$
     $(\forall x)(Px \supset Kx)$ $\dfrac{(\exists x)(Mtx \supset Axx)}{(\exists x)(\sim Mxt \lor Axx)}$ $(\forall x)(Hxg \supset Cx)$
     $\dfrac{(\forall x)(Qx \supset Kx)}{(\exists x)Kx}$ $\dfrac{(\forall x)(Nxf \supset Cx)}{(\exists x)Cx}$

n) $(\forall x)[(Fx \lor Gx) \supset Lxx]$ o) $(\forall x)[Fx \supset (Rxa \lor Rax)]$
     $\dfrac{(\exists x)\sim Lxx}{(\exists x)\sim Fx \,\&\, (\exists x)\sim Gx}$ $\dfrac{(\exists x)\sim Rxa}{(\forall x)\sim Rax \supset (\exists x)\sim Fx}$

p) $(\exists x)Qxj$ q) $\dfrac{(\forall x)\sim Fx}{\sim(\exists x)Fx}$ r) $\dfrac{(\exists x)\sim Fx}{\sim(\forall x)Fx}$
     $\dfrac{(\exists x)(Qxj \lor Dgx) \supset (\forall x)Dgx}{(\forall x)(Dgx \lor Qjx)}$

s) $\dfrac{(\forall x)(Jxx \supset \sim Jxf)}{\sim(\exists x)(Jxx \,\&\, Jxf)}$ t) $(\exists x)Px \lor Qa$ u) $\dfrac{A \supset (\exists x)Px}{(\exists x)(A \supset Px)}$
                                                                                             $\dfrac{(\forall x)\sim Px}{(\exists x)Qx}$

5–8. Are you bothered by the fact that ∃E requires use of a subderivation with an instance of the existentially quantified sentence as its assumption? Good news! Here is an alternate version of ∃E which does not require starting a subderivation:

| $(\exists u)(.\ .\ .\ \mathbf{u}\ .\ .\ .)$ |
| $(\forall u)[(.\ .\ .\ \mathbf{u}\ .\ .\ .) \supset \mathbf{X}]$ |

Ⓧ   ∃E

Show that, in the presence of the other rules, this version is exchangeable with the ∃E rule given in the text. That is, show that the above is a derived rule if we start with the rules given in the text. And show that if we start with all the rules in the text except for ∃E, and if we use the above rule for ∃E, then the ∃E of the text is a derived rule.

CHAPTER SUMMARY EXERCISES

Here is a list of important terms from this chapter. Explain them briefly and record your explanations in your notebook:

a) Truth Preserving Rule of Inference
b) Sound
c) Complete
d) Stand-in Name
e) Govern
f) Arbitrary Occurrence
g) Existential Generalization
h) Universal Generalization
i) Isolated Name
j) Existential Introduction Rule
k) Existential Elimination Rule
l) Universal Introduction Rule
m) Universal Elimination Rule

More on Natural Deduction for Predicate Logic

6

6–1. MULTIPLE QUANTIFICATION AND HARDER PROBLEMS

In chapter 5 I wanted you to focus on understanding the basic rules for quantifiers. So there I avoided the complications that arise when we have sentences, such as '(∀x)(∀y)(Px & Py)', which stack one quantifier on top of another. Such sentences involve no new principles. It's just a matter of keeping track of the main connective. For example, '(∀x)(∀y)(Px & Qy)' is a universally quantified sentence, with '(∀x)' as the main connective. You practiced forming substitution instances of such sentences in chapter 3. The substitution instance of '(∀x)(∀y)(Px & Qy)' formed with 'a' (a sentence you could write when applying ∀E) is '(∀y)(Pa & Qy)'.

You will see how to deal with such sentences most quickly by just looking at a few examples. So let's write a derivation to establish the validity of

(∀x)(∀y)(Px & Qy)	1	(∀x)(∀y)(Px & Qy)	P
(∀x)Px & (∀x)Qx	2	(∀y)(Pâ & Qy)	1, ∀E
	3	Pâ & Qb̂	2, ∀E
	4	Pâ	3, &E
	5	Qb̂	3, &E
	6	(∀x)Px	4, ∀I
	7	(∀x)Qx	5, ∀I
	8	(∀x)Px & (∀x)Qx	6, 7, &I

In line 2 I applied ∀E by forming the substitution instance of 1 using the name 'a'. Then in line 3 I formed a substitution instance of the universally quantified line 2.

Let's look at an example of multiple existential quantification. The basic ideas are the same. But observe that in order to treat the second existential quantifier, we must start a sub-sub-derivation:

(∃x)(∃y)(Px & Qy)
―――――――――――――
(∃x)Px & (∃x)Qx

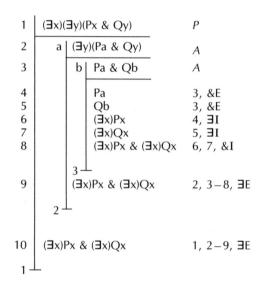

In line 2 I wrote down '(∃y)(Pa & Qy)', a substitution instance of line 1, formed with 'a', substituted for 'x', which is the variable in the main connective, '(∃x)', of line 1. Since I plan to appeal to ∃E in application to line 1, I make '(∃y)(Pa & Qy)' the assumption of a subderivation with 'a' an isolated name. I then do the same thing with '(∃y)(Pa & Qy)', but because this is again an existentially quantified sentence to which I will want to apply ∃E, I must make my new substitution instance, 'Pa & Qb', the assumption of a sub-sub-derivation, this time with 'b' the isolated name.

In the previous example, I would have been allowed to use 'a' for the second as well as the first substitution instance, since I was applying ∀E. But, in the present example, when setting up to use two applications of ∃E, I must use a new name in each assumption. To see why, let's review what conditions must be satisfied to correctly apply ∃E to get line 9. I must have an existentially quantified sentence (line 2) and a subderivation (sub-sub-derivation 3), the assumption of which is a substitution instance of the existentially quantified sentence. Furthermore, the name used in forming the substitution instance must be isolated to the subderivation. Thus, in forming line 3 as a substitution instance of line 2, I can't use 'a'. I use the name 'b' instead. The 'a' following 'P' in line 3 does not violate the requirement. 'a' got into the picture when we formed line 2, the substitution instance of line 1, and you will note that 'a' is indeed isolated to subderivation 2, as required, since sub-sub-derivation 3 is **part** of subderivation 2.

Here's another way to see the point. I write line 3 as a substitution instance of line 2. Since I will want to apply ∃E, the name I use must be isolated to subderivation 3. If I tried to use 'a' in forming the substitution instance of line 2, I would have had to put an 'a' (the "isolation flag") to the left of scope line 3. I would then immediately see that I had made a mistake. 'a' as an isolation flag means that 'a' can occur only to the right. But 'a' already occurs to the left, in line 2. Since I use 'b' as my new name in subderivation 3, I use 'b' as the isolation flag there. Then the 'a' in line 3 causes no problem: All occurrences of 'a' are to the right of scope line 2, which is the line flagged by 'a'.

All this is not really as hard to keep track of as it might seem. The scope lines with the names written at the top to the left (the isolation flags) do all the work for you. 'a' can only appear to the right of the scope line on which it occurs as an isolation flag. 'b' can only occur to the right of the scope line on which it occurs as an isolation flag. That's all you need to check.

Make sure you clearly understand the last two examples before continuing. They fully illustrate, in a simple setting, what you need to understand about applying the quantifier rules to multiply quantified sentences.

Once you have digested these examples, let's try a hard problem. The new example also differs from the last two in that it requires repeated use of a quantifier introduction rule instead of repeated use of a quantifier elimination rule. In reading over my derivation you might well be baffled as to how I figured out what to do at each step. Below the problem I explain the informal thinking I used in constructing this derivation, so that you will start to learn how to work such a problem for yourself.

(∀x)Px ⊃ (∃x)Qx
_____
(∃x)(∃y)(Px ⊃ Qy)

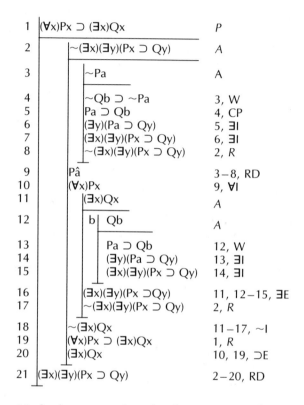

1	(∀x)Px ⊃ (∃x)Qx	P
2	~(∃x)(∃y)(Px ⊃ Qy)	A
3	~Pa	A
4	~Qb ⊃ ~Pa	3, W
5	Pa ⊃ Qb	4, CP
6	(∃y)(Pa ⊃ Qy)	5, ∃I
7	(∃x)(∃y)(Px ⊃ Qy)	6, ∃I
8	~(∃x)(∃y)(Px ⊃ Qy)	2, R
9	Pâ	3–8, RD
10	(∀x)Px	9, ∀I
11	(∃x)Qx	A
12	b| Qb	A
13	Pa ⊃ Qb	12, W
14	(∃y)(Pa ⊃ Qy)	13, ∃I
15	(∃x)(∃y)(Px ⊃ Qy)	14, ∃I
16	(∃x)(∃y)(Px ⊃Qy)	11, 12–15, ∃E
17	~(∃x)(∃y)(Px ⊃ Qy)	2, R
18	~(∃x)Qx	11–17, ~I
19	(∀x)Px ⊃ (∃x)Qx	1, R
20	(∃x)Qx	10, 19, ⊃E
21	(∃x)(∃y)(Px ⊃ Qy)	2–20, RD

My basic strategy is reductio, to assume the opposite of what I want to prove. From this I must get a contraction with the premise. The premise is a conditional, and a conditional is false only if its antecedent is true and its consequent is false. So I set out to contradict the original premise by deriving its antecedent and the negation of its consequent from my new assumption.

To derive (∀x)Px (line 10), the premise's antecedent, I need to derive Pâ. I do this by assuming ~Pa from which I derive line 7, which contradicts line 2. To derive ~(∃x)Qx (line 18), the negation of the premise's consequent, I assume (∃x)Qx (line 11), and derive a contradiction, so that I can use ~I. This proceeds by using ∃E, as you can see in lines 11 to 16.

Now it's your turn to try your hand at the following exercises. The problems start out with ones much easier than the last example—and gradually get harder!

EXERCISES

6–1. Provide derivations to establish the validity of the following argument:

a)   (∃x)Lxx

    (∃x)(∃y)Lxy

Note that the argument, $\dfrac{(\forall x)Lxx}{(\forall x)(\forall y)Lyx}$, is invalid. Prove that this argument is invalid by giving a counterexample to it (that is, an interpretation in which the premise is true and the conclusion is false). Explain why you can't get from (∀x)Lxx to (∀x)(∀y)Lxy by using ∀E and ∀I as you can get from (∃x)Lxx to (∃x)(∃y)Lxy by using ∃E and ∃I.

b)   (∀x)(∀y)Lxy

    (∀x)Lxx

Note that the argument, $\dfrac{(\exists x)(\exists y)Lxy}{(\exists x)Lxx}$, is invalid. Prove that this argument is invalid by giving a counterexample to it. Explain why you can't get from (∃x)(∃y)Lxy to (∃x)Lxx by using ∃E and ∃I as you can get from (∀x)(∀y)Lxy to (∀x)Lxx by using ∀E and ∀I.

c)   (∀x)(∀y)Lxy   d)   (∃x)(∃y)Lxy

    (∀y)(∀x)Lxy   (∃y)(∃x)Lxy

e)   (∃x)(∀y)Lxy

    (∀y)(∃x)Lxy

Note that the converse argument, $\dfrac{(\forall y)(\exists x)Lxy}{(\exists x)(\forall y)Lxy}$, is invalid. Prove this by providing a counterexample.

f)   (∀x)Px & (∀x)Qx   g)   (∃x)Px & (∃x)Qx   h)   (∀x)Px ∨ (∀x)Qx

    (∀x)(∀y)(Px & Qy)   (∃x)(∃y)(Px & Qy)   (∀x)(∀y)(Px ∨ Qy)

i)   (∃x)Px ∨ (∃x)Qx   j)   (∃x)(∃y)(Px ∨ Qy)   k)   (∀x)(∀y)(Lxy ⊃ ~Lxy)

    (∃x)(∃y)(Px ∨ Qy)   (∃x)Px ∨ (∃x)Qx   (∀x)~Lxx

l)   (∀x)(∀y)(Px ⊃ Qy)   m)   (∃x)(∃y)(Px ⊃ Qy)   n)   (∃x)(∀y)(Px ⊃ Qy)

    (∃x)Px ⊃ (∀x)Qx   (∀x)Px ⊃ (∃x)Qx   (∀x)Px ⊃ (∀x)Qx

o) $(\forall x)(\exists y)(Px \supset Qy)$ p) $(\forall x)Px \supset (\forall x)Qx$ q) $(\forall x)(\forall y)(Px \vee Qy)$
    ───────────────────────   ────────────────────   ────────────────────
    $(\exists x)Px \supset (\exists x)Qx$ $(\exists x)(\forall y)(Px \supset Qy)$ $(\forall x)Px \vee (\forall x)Qy$

r) $(\exists x)(\forall y)Jxy$
    $(\exists y)(\exists z))(Hzy \mathbin{\&} \sim Py)$
    $(\forall z)(\forall w)[(Jzw \mathbin{\&} \sim Pw) \supset Gz]$
    ────────────────────────────
    $(\exists z)Gz$

6–2. SOME DERIVED RULES

Problem 5–7(q) posed a special difficulty:

We would like to apply $\sim$I to derive $\sim(\exists x)Fx$. To do this, we need to get a contradiction in subderivation 2. But we can use the assumption of subderivation 2 only by using $\exists$E, which requires starting subderivation 3, which uses 'a' as an isolated name. We do get a sentence and its negation in subderivation 3, but these sentences use the isolated name 'a', so that we are not allowed to use $\exists$E to bring them out into subderivation 2 where we need the contradiction. What can we do?

We break this impasse by using the fact that from a contradiction you can prove **anything**. Be sure you understand this general fact before we apply it to resolving our special problem. Suppose that in a derivation you have already derived **X** and $\sim$**X**. Let **Y** be **any** sentence you like. You can then derive **Y**:

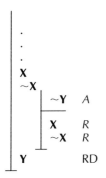

We can use this general fact to resolve our difficulty in the following way. Since anything follows from the contradiction of 'Pa' and '~Pa', we can use this contradiction to derive a **new** contradiction, 'A &~A', which does not use the name 'a'. ∃E then licenses us to write 'A &~A' in derivation 2 where we need the contradiction.

To streamline our work, we will introduce several new derived rules. The first is the one I have just proved, that any sentence, **Y**, follows from a contradiction:

Contradiction

In practice, I will always use a standard contradiction, 'A & ~A', for **Y**. I will also use a trivial reformulation of the rules ~I and Rd expressed in terms of a conjunction of a sentence and its negation where up to now these rules have, strictly speaking, been expressed only in terms of a sentence and the negation of the sentence on separate lines:

Negation Introduction   *Reductio*

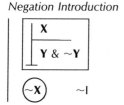   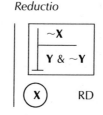

These derived rules enable us to deal efficiently with problem 5–7(q) and ones like it:

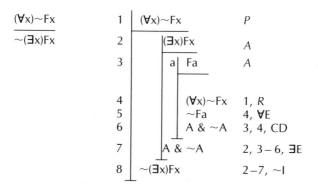

(∀x)~Fx	1	(∀x)~Fx	*P*
~(∃x)Fx	2	(∃x)Fx	*A*
	3	a‎ Fa	*A*
	4	(∀x)~Fx	1, *R*
	5	~Fa	4, ∀E
	6	A & ~A	3, 4, CD
	7	A & ~A	2, 3–6, ∃E
	8	~(∃x)Fx	2–7, ~I

Let's turn now to four more derived rules, ones which express the rules of logical equivalence, ~∀ and ~∃, which we discussed in chapter 3. There we proved that they are correct rules of logical equivalence. Formulated as derived rules, you have really done the work of proving them in problems 5–4(q) and (r) and 5–7(q) and (r). To prove these rules, all you need do is to copy the derivations you provided for those problems, using an arbitrary open sentence (. . . **u** . . .), with the free variable **u**, instead of the special case with the open sentence 'Px' or 'Fx' with the free variable 'x'.

Negated Quantifier Rules

~(∀u)(. . . u . . .)
(∃u)~(. . . u . . .) ~∀

(∃u)~(. . . u . . .)
~(∀u)(. . . u . . .) ∃~

~(∃u)(. . . u . . .)
(∀u)~(. . . u . . .) ~∃

(∀u)~(. . . u . . .)
~(∃u)(. . . u . . .) ∀~

A word of caution in using these negated quantifier rules: Students often rush to apply them whenever they see the opportunity. In many cases you may more easily see how to get a correct derivation by using these rules than if you try to make do without the rules. But often, if you work hard and are ingenious, you can produce more elegant derivations without using the quantifier negation rules. In the following exercises, use the rules so that you have some practice with them. But in later exercises, be on the lookout for clever ways to produce derivations without the quantifier negation rules. Instructors who are particularly keen on their students learning to do derivations ingeniously may require you to do later problems without the quantifier negation rules. (These comments do not apply to the derived contradiction rule and derived forms of ~I and RD rules. These rules just save work which is invariably boring, so you should use them whenever they will shorten your derivations.)

EXERCISES

6–2.

a) (∀x)Px
(∀x)~Qx

~(∃x)(Px ≡ Qx)

b) (∀x)(Fx ⊃ Gx)
(∀x)(Gx ⊃ Hx)
~(∃x)Hx

~(∃x)Fx

c) ~(∀x)(∀y)Lxy

(∃x)(∃y)~Lxy

d) ~(∃x)(∃y)Lxy

(∀x)(∀y)~Lxy

e) ~(∃x)(Px ∨ Qx)

(∀x)~Px & (∀x)~Qx

f) ~(∀x)(Px & Qx)

(∃x)~Px ∨ (∃x)~Qx

g) (∀x)[~(∃y)Rxy & ~(∃y)Ryx]

(∀x)(∀y)~Rxy

h) (∃x)[Px ⊃ (∀y)(Py ⊃ Qy)]
~(∃x)Qx

~(∀x)Px

i) (∃y)(∃z)[(∀x)~Rxy ∨ (∀x)~Rxz]

~(∀y)(∀z)(∃x)(Rxy & Rxz)

6–3. LOGICAL TRUTH, CONTRADICTIONS, INCONSISTENCY, AND LOGICAL EQUIVALENCE

This section straightforwardly applies concepts you have already learned for sentence logic. We said that a sentence of sentence logic is a logical truth if and only if it is true in all cases, that is, if and only if it comes out true for all assignments of truth values to sentence letters. The concept of logical truth is the same in predicate logic if we take our cases to be interpretations of a sentence:

> A closed predicate logic sentence is a *Logical Truth* if and only if it is true in all its interpretations.

Proof of logical truth also works just as it did for sentence logic, as we discussed in section 7–3 of Volume I. A derivation with no premises shows all its conclusions to be true in all cases (all assignments of truth values to sentence letters in sentence logic, all interpretations in predicate logic). A brief reminder of the reason: If we have a derivation with no premises we can always tack on unused premises at the beginning of the derivation. But any case which makes the premises of a derivation true makes all the derivation's conclusions true. For any case you like, tack on a premise in which that case is true. Then the derivation's conclusions will be true in that case also:

> A derivation with no premises shows all its conclusions to be logical truths.

Contradictions in predicate logic also follow the same story as in sentence logic. The whole discussion is the same as for logical truth, except that we replace "true" with "false":

> A closed predicate logic sentence is a *Contradiction* if and only if it is false in all its interpretations.

> To demonstrate a sentence, **X**, to be a contradiction, demonstrate its negation, ~**X**, to be a logical truth. That is, construct a derivation with no premises, with ~**X** as the final conclusion.

If you did exercise 7–5 (in volume I), you learned an alternative test for contradictions, which also works in exactly the same way in predicate logic:

> A derivation with a sentence, **X**, as its only premise and two sentences, **Y** and ~**Y**, as conclusions shows **X** to be a contradiction.

Exercise 7–8 (volume I) dealt with the concept of inconsistency. Once more, the idea carries directly over to predicate logic. I state it here, together with several related ideas which are important in more advanced work in logic:

> A collection of closed predicate logic sentences is *Consistent* if there is at least one interpretation which makes all of them true. Such an interpretation is called a *Model* for the consistent collection of sentences. If there is no inter-

pretation which makes all of the sentences in the collection true (if there is no model), the collection is *Inconsistent*.

A finite collection of sentences is inconsistent if and only if their conjunction is a contradiction.

To demonstrate that a finite collection of sentences is inconsistent, demonstrate their conjunction to be a contradiction. Equivalently, provide a derivation with all of the sentences in the collection as premises and a contradiction as the final conclusion.

Finally, in predicate logic, the idea of logical equivalence of closed sentences works just as it did in sentence logic. We have already discussed this in section 3–4:

Two closed predicate logic sentences are *Logically Equivalent* if and only if in each of their interpretations the two sentences are either both true or both false.

Exercise 4–3 (volume I) provides the key to showing logical equivalence, as you already saw if you did exercise 7–9 (volume I). Two sentences are logically equivalent if in any interpretation in which the first is true the second is true, and in any interpretation in which the second is true the first is true. (Be sure you understand why this characterization comes to the same thing as the definition of logical equivalence I just gave.) Consequently

To demonstrate that two sentences, **X** and **Y**, are logically equivalent, show that the two arguments, "**X**. Therefore **Y**." and "**Y**. Therefore **X**." are both valid. That is, provide two derivations, one with **X** as premise and **Y** as final conclusion and one with **Y** as premise and **X** as final conclusion.

EXERCISES

6–3. Provide derivations which show that the following sentences are logical truths:

a) $(\forall x)(\forall y)Lxy \supset (\exists x)(\exists y)Lxy$
b) $(\forall x)(Gx \lor \sim Gx)$
c) $(\forall x)(\exists y)(Ax \,\&\, By) \supset (\exists x)(Ax \,\&\, Bx)$
d) $(\exists y)[Ky \,\&\, (\forall x)(Dx \supset Rxy)] \supset (\forall x)[Dx \supset (\exists y)(Ky \,\&\, Rxy)]$
e) $(\exists x)(\forall y)(Fy \supset Fx)$
f) $(\forall x)(\exists y)(Fy \supset Fx)$
g) $(\exists x)(\forall y)(Fx \supset Fy)$

6–4. Provide derivations which show that the following sentences are contradictions:

   a) $(\forall x)(Ax \supset Bx)$ & $(\exists x)(\sim Bx$ & $(\forall y)Ay)$
   b) $(\forall x)(Rxb \supset \sim Rxb)$ & $(\exists x)Rxb$
   c) $(\forall x)[(\forall y)Lxy$ & $(\exists y)\sim Lyx]$
   d) $(\forall x)(\exists y)(Mx$ & $\sim My)$
   e) $(\forall x)(\exists y)(\forall w)(\exists z)(Lxw$ & $\sim Lyz)$

6–5. Provide derivations which show that the following collections of sentences are inconsistent:

   a) $(\forall x)Kx,$ $(\forall y)\sim(Ky \vee Lya)$
   b) $(\forall x)(\exists y)Rxy,$ $(\exists x)(\forall y)\sim Rxy$
   c) $(\exists x)Dx,$ $(\forall x)(Dx \supset (\forall y)(\forall z)Ryz),$ $(\exists x)(\exists y)\sim Rxy$
   d) $(\exists x)(\exists y)(Rxx$ & $\sim Ryy$ & $Rxy),$ $(\forall x)(\forall y)(Rxy \supset Ryx),$
       $(\forall x)(\forall y)\forall z)[(Rxy$ & $Ryz) \supset Rxz)]$

6–6. a) List the pairs of sentences which are shown to be logically equivalent by the examples in this chapter and any of the derivations in exercises 6–1 and 6–8.

b) Write derivations which show the following three arguments to be valid. (You will see in the next part of this exercise that there is a point to your doing these trivial derivations.)

$(\forall x)Rxa$	$(\forall x)Rxx$	$(\forall x)Px$
$(\exists x)Rxa$	$(\exists x)Rxx$	$(\exists x)Px$

c) Note that the three derivations you provided in your answer to (b) are essentially the same. From the point of view of these derivations, 'Rxa' and 'Rxx' are both open sentences which we could have just as well have written as $\mathbf{P(u)}$, an arbitrary (perhaps very complex) open sentence with $\mathbf{u}$ as its only free variable. In many of the problems in 5–5 and 5–7, I threw in names and repeated variables which played no real role in the problem, just as in the first two derivations in (b) above. (I did so to keep you on your toes in applying the new rules.) Find the problems which, when recast in the manner illustrated in (b) above, do the work of proving the following logical equivalences. Here, $\mathbf{P(u)}$ and $\mathbf{Q(u)}$ are arbitrary open sentences with $\mathbf{u}$ as their only free variable. $\mathbf{A}$ is an arbitrary closed sentence.

(∀u)(P(u) & Q(u))	is logically equivalent to	(∀u)P(u) & (∀u)Q(u)
(∃u)(P(u) ∨ Q(u))	is logically equivalent to	(∃u)P(u) ∨ (∃u)Q(u)
A ⊃ (∀u)P(u)	is logically equivalent to	(∀u)(A ⊃ P(u))
A ⊃ (∃u)P(u)	is logically equivalent to	(∃u)(A ⊃ P(u))
(∀u)P(u) ⊃ A	is logically equivalent to	(∃u)(P(u) ⊃ A)
(∃u)P(u) ⊃ A	is logically equivalent to	(∀u)(P(u) ⊃ A)

d) Prove, by providing a counterexample, that the following two pairs of sentences are not logically equivalent. (A counterexample is an interpretation in which one of the two sentences is true and the other is false.)

(∀x)(Px ∨ Qx)	is not logically equivalent to	(∀x)Px ∨ (∀x)Qx
(∃x)(Px & Qx)	is not logically equivalent to	(∃x)Px & (∃x)Qx

e) Complete the work done in 6–1(c) and (d) to show that the following pairs of sentences are logically equivalent. (**R** is an arbitrary open sentence with **u** and **v** as its only two free variables.)

(∀u)(∀v)R(u, v)	is logically equivalent to	(∀v)(∀u)R(u, v)
(∃u)(∃v)R(u, v)	is logically equivalent to	(∃v)(∃u)R(u, v)

6–7. Here are some harder arguments to prove valid by providing derivations. In some cases it is easier to find solutions by using the derived rules for negated quantifiers. But in every case you should look for elegant solutions which do not use these rules.

a) (∀x)[(∃y)(Lxy ∨ Lyx) ⊃ Lxx]
   (∃x)(∃y)Lxy
   _____
   (∃x)Lxx

(Everyone who loves or is loved by someone loves themself. Someone loves someone. Therefore, someone loves themself.)

b) (∀x)(Hx ⊃ Ax)
   _____
   (∀x)[(∃y)(Hy & Txy) ⊃ (∃y)(Ay & Txy)]

(Horses are animals. Therefore horses' tails are animals' tails.)

c) (∀x)(∀y)[(∃z)Lyz ⊃ Lxy]
   (∃x)(∃y)Lxy
   _____
   (∀x)(∀y)Lxy

(Everyone loves a lover. Someone loves someone. Therefore, everyone loves everyone.)

d) (∀x)(∀y)[(∃z)(Rzy & ~Rxz) ⊃ Lxy]
   ~(∃x)Lxx
   _____
   (∀x)(∀y)(~Ryx ⊃ ~Rxy)

e) (∀x){(∃y)Lxy ⊃ (∃y)[(∀z)Lyz & Lxy]}
    (∃x)(∃y)Lxy
    ─────────────────────────────────
    (∃x)(∀y)Lxy

(Everyone who loves someone loves someone who loves everyone. Someone loves someone. Therefore, someone loves everyone.)

f) (∀x)[Px ⊃ (∀y)(Hy ⊃ Rxy)]
    (∃x)(Px & (∃y)~Rxy)
    ───────────────────────────
    ~(∀x)Hx

g) (∀x)[(Ex ⊃ (∀y)(Hy ⊃ Wxy)]
    (∃x)[Hx & (∀y)(Dy ⊃ Wxy)]
    (∀x)(∀y)(∀z)[(Wxy & Wyz) ⊃ Wxz]
    ──────────────────────────────────
    (∀x)[Ex ⊃ (∀y)(Dy ⊃ Wxy)]

(Any elephant weighs more than a horse. Some horse weighs more than any donkey. If a first thing weighs more than a second, and the second weighs more than a third, the first weighs more than the third. Therefore, any elephant weighs more than any donkey.)

h) (∀x)(∃y)(Py ⊃ Qx)
    ──────────────────
    (∃y)(∀x)(Py ⊃ Qx)

Note that in general a sentence of the form (∀x)(∃y)**X** does not imply a sentence of the form (∃y)(∀x)**X** (See problem 6−1(e)). However, in this case, the special form of the conditional makes the argument valid.

i) (∃x)Px ⊃ (∃x)Qx
    ──────────────────
    (∀x)(∃y)(Px ⊃ Qy)

j) (∃x)Px ⊃ (∀x)Qx
    ──────────────────
    (∀x)(∀y)(Px ⊃ Qy)

k) (∀x){Bx ⊃ [(∃y)Lxy ⊃ (∃y)Lyx]}
    (∀x)[(∃y)Lyx ⊃ Lxx]
    ~(∃x)Lxx
    ────────────────────────────────
    (∀x)(Bx ⊃ (∀y)~Lxy)

(All blond lovers are loved. All those who are loved love themselves. No one loves themself. Therefore, all blonds love no one.)

l) (∀x){Fx ⊃ [Hx & (~Cx & ~Kx)]}
    (∀x)[(Hx & ~(∃y)Nxy) ⊃ Dx]
    ─────────────────────────────
    (∀x)(Fx ⊃ (∃y)Nxy)

m) $(\forall y)(Cy \supset Dy)$
$(\forall x)(\exists y)[(Hx \& Cx) \& (Gy \& Ryx)]$
$(\exists x)Dx \supset (\forall y)(\forall z)(Ryz \supset Dy)$

$(\exists x)(Gx \& Cx)$

n) $(\forall x)(\forall y)[(Rdy \& Rxd) \supset Rxy]$
$(\forall x)(Bx \supset Rdx)$
$(\exists x)(Bx \& Rxd)$

$(\exists x)[Bx \& (\forall y)(By \supset Rxy)]$

CHAPTER REVIEW EXERCISES

Write short explanations in your notebook for each of the following.

a)   Contradiction Rule
b)   Quantifier Negation Rules
c)   Logical Truth of Predicate Logic
d)   Test for a Logical Truth
e)   Contradiction of Predicate Logic
f)   Test for a Contradiction
g)   Consistent Set of Sentences
h)   Inconsistent Set of Sentences
i)   Test for a Finite Set of Inconsistent Sentences
j)   Logical Equivalence of Predicate Logic Sentences
k)   Test for Logical Equivalence

Truth Trees for Predicate Logic: $\overline{7}$

Fundamentals

7–1. THE RULE FOR UNIVERSAL QUANTIFICATION

You have already learned the truth tree method for sentence logic. And now that you have a basic understanding of predicate logic sentences, you are ready to extend the truth tree method to predicate logic.

Let's go back to the basics of testing arguments for validity: To say that an argument is valid is to say that in every possible case in which the premises are true, the conclusion is true also. We reexpress this by saying that an argument is valid if and only if it has no counterexamples, that is, no possible cases in which the premises are true and the conclusion false. When we were doing sentence logic, our possible cases were the lines of a truth table, and in any one problem there were only finitely many lines. In principle, we could always check all the truth table lines to see if any of them were counterexamples. Often the truth tree method shortened our work. But the trees were really just a labor-saving device. We could always go back and check through all the truth table lines.

Predicate logic changes everything. In predicate logic our cases are interpretations, and there are always infinitely many of these. Thus we could never check through them all to be sure that there are no counterexamples. Now truth trees become much more than a convenience. They provide the only systematic means we have for searching for counterexamples.

Everything we learned about truth trees in sentence logic carries over to predicate logic. Someone gives us an argument and asks us whether it is valid. We proceed by searching for a counterexample. We begin by listing the premises and the denial of the conclusion as the beginning of a tree. Just as before, if we can make these true we will have a case in which the premises are true and the conclusion false, which is a counterexample and which shows the argument to be invalid. If we can establish that the method does not turn up a counterexample, we conclude that there is none and that the argument is valid.

We have boiled our job down to the task of systematically looking for a case which will make true the initial sentence on a tree. In sentence logic we did this by applying the rules for the connectives '&', 'v', '~', '⊃', and '≡'. These rules broke down longer sentences into shorter ones in all the minimally sufficient possible ways which would make the longer sentences true by making the shorter ones true. Since, in sentence logic, this process terminates in sentence letters and negated sentence letters, we got branches which (if they do not close) make everything true by making the sentence letters and negated sentence letters along them true. In this way you should think of each branch as a systematic way of developing a line of a truth table which will make all the sentences along the branch true.

The tree method for predicate logic works in exactly the same way, with just one change: Each branch is no longer a way of developing a line of a truth table which will make all the sentences along the branch true. Instead, a branch is a way of developing an **interpretation** which will make all the sentences along the branch true. All you have to do is to stop thinking in terms of building a line of a truth table (an assignment of truth values to sentence letters). Instead, start thinking in terms of building an interpretation.

Let's see this strategy in action. Consider the example that got us started on predicate logic, way back in chapter 1:

Everybody loves Eve.	(∀x)Lxe
Adam loves Eve.	Lae

We begin our search for an interpretation in which the premise is true and the conclusion is false by listing the premise and the denial of the conclusion as the initial lines of a tree:

```
1   (∀x)Lxe    P
2   ~Lae       ~C
```

We already know quite a bit about any interpretation of these two sentences which makes them both true. The interpretation will have to have something called 'a' and something called 'e', and '~Lae' will have to be true in the interpretation. '~Lae' is already a negated atomic sentence. We cannot make it true by making some shorter sentence true.

But we can make '(∀x)Lxe' true by making some shorter sentences true. Intuitively, '(∀x)Lxe' says that everybody loves Eve. In our interpretation we have a (Adam) and e (Eve). In this interpretation, in this little novel or story of the way the world might be, we can make it true that everybody loves Eve by making it true that Adam loves Eve and making it true that Eve loves Eve. So we extend the branch representing our interpretation with the sentences 'Lae' and 'Lee':

a, e	1	(∀x)Lxe	P
	2	~Lae	~C
	3	Lae	1, ∀
	4	Lee	1, ∀
		×	

And the branch closes! The branch includes both '~Lae' and 'Lae', where the first is the negation of the second. They cannot both be true in an interpretation. We had to include '~Lae' to get an interpretation which makes the conclusion of the argument false. We had to include 'Lae' to get an interpretation which makes '(∀x)Lxe' true. But no interpretation can make the same sentence both true and false. So there is no interpretation which makes lines 1 and 2 true—there is no counterexample to the argument. And so the argument is valid.

Let's talk more generally about how I got lines 3 and 4 out of line 1. Already, when we have just lines 1 and 2, we know that our branch will represent an interpretation with something called 'a' and something called 'e'. We know this because our interpretation must be an interpretation of all the sentences already appearing, and these sentences include the names 'a' and 'e'. Our immediate objective is to make '(∀x)Lxe' true in this interpretation. But we know that a universally quantified sentence is true in an interpretation just in case all its substitution instances are true in the interpretation. So to make '(∀x)Lxe' true in the interpretation we must make 'Lae' and 'Lee' true in the interpretation. This is because 'Lae' and 'Lee' are the substitution instances of '(∀x)Lxe' formed with the interpretation's names, 'a' and 'e'.

Notice that I did something more complicated than simply checking line 1 after working on it and putting the annotation '1,∀' after lines 3 and 4. The rule for the universal quantifier differs in this respect from all the other rules. The other rules, when applied to a "target" sentence, tell us to write something at the bottom of every open branch on which the target sentence appears. When this is done, we have guaranteed that we have made the target sentence true in all possible minimally sufficient ways. We thus will never have to worry about the target sentence again. To note the fact that we are done with the sentence, we check it.

But the rule for the universal quantifier is not like this. First, in applying the rule to a universally quantified sentence, we have to search the branch on which the target sentence appears for names. Then, at the bottom of every open branch on which the target sentence appears, we must instantiate the target sentence with each name which occurs along that branch. To help keep track of which names have already been used to instantiate the target sentence, we list them as we use them.

You might think that when we have thus accounted for all the names on the branch we are done with the target sentence and can check it. But you will see that **new names** can arise after first working on a universally quantified target sentence. In such a case we must come **back** and work on the universally quantified sentence again. Because we must recognize the possibility of having to return to a universally quantified sentence, we never check the sentence as a whole. Instead, we list the names which we have thus far used in the sentence, because once a universally quantified sentence has been instantiated with a given name, we never have to instantiate it with the same name again.

Here is a summary statement of our rule:

> *Rule $\forall$:* If a universally quantified sentence $(\forall u)(\ldots u \ldots)$ appears as the entire sentence at a point on a tree, do the following to each open branch on which $(\forall u)(\ldots u \ldots)$ appears. First, collect all the names $s_1, s_2, s_3, \ldots$ that appear along the branch. (If no name appears on the branch, introduce a name so that you have at least one name.) Then write the substitution instances $(\ldots s_1 \ldots), (\ldots s_2 \ldots), (\ldots s_3 \ldots), \ldots$ at the bottom of the branch, and write the names $s_1, s_2, s_3, \ldots$ to the left of $(\forall u)(\ldots u \ldots)$. **Do not** put a check by $(\forall u)(\ldots u \ldots)$.

Several facets of this rule bear further comment. First, in working on a universally quantified sentence on a given branch, you only need to instantiate it with the names along that branch. If the same universally quantified sentence occurs along a second branch, that second branch calls for use of the names that occur along that second branch. This is because each branch is going to represent its own interpretation. Also, when instructed to write a substitution instance, $(\ldots s \ldots)$, at the bottom of an open branch, you do not need to write it a second time if it already appears.

Next, the rule instructs you to write all of the substitution instances, $(\ldots s_1 \ldots), (\ldots s_2 \ldots), (\ldots s_3 \ldots), \ldots$ at the bottom of every open path. But if the path closes before you are done, of course you can stop. Once a path closes, it cannot represent a counterexample, and further additions will make no difference. Thus, in the last example, I could have correctly marked the path as closed after line 3, omitting line 4. You can make good use of this fact to shorten your work by choosing to write down first the substitution instances which will get a branch to close. But don't forget that if the branch does **not** close, you must list **all** the substitution instances.

Finally, listing the names used to the left of (∀u)(. . . **u** . . .) is a practical reminder of which names you have already used to instantiate (∀u)(. . . **u** . . .). But this reminder is not foolproof because it does not contain the information about which branch the substitution instance appears on. In practice, this isn't a difficulty because in almost every problem your substitution instance will appear on all branches. Indeed, when a universally quantified sentence appears on a branch it never hurts to introduce a substitution instance formed with a name which had not otherwise appeared on that branch.

Let me illustrate how the rule applies when no name appears on a path. At the same time, I will show you how we will write down counterexamples:

$$\begin{array}{cc}
A \\
\hline
\sim(\forall x)Bx
\end{array}
\qquad
\begin{array}{llll}
1 & A & P \\
\sqrt{2} & \sim\sim(\forall x)Bx & \sim C \\
a\,3 & (\forall x)Bx & 2,\, \sim\sim \\
4 & Ba & 3,\, \forall
\end{array}$$

Invalid. Counterexample: D = {a}; Ba & A

'A' is an atomic sentence letter which we make true in the counterexample. 'A' is **not** a name. So when we get to line 3 and need to instantiate '(∀x)Bx' with all the names in the interpretation we are building, we find that we don't have any names. What do we do? Every interpretation must have at least one thing in it. So when applying the rule ∀ to a universally quantified sentence on a branch which has no names, we have to introduce a name to use. This is the **only** circumstance in which the ∀ rule tells us to introduce a new name. Any name will do. In this example I used 'a'.

Notice how I indicated the counterexample to the argument provided by the open branch. The counterexample is an interpretation which makes everything along the branch true. You read the counterexample off the open branch by listing the names which occur on the branch and the atomic and negated atomic sentences which occur along the branch. The rules have been designed so that these shortest sentences make true the longer sentences from which they came, which in turn make true the still longer sentences from which they came, and so on, until finally everything along the open branch is true.

EXERCISES

7–1. Use the truth tree method to test the following arguments for validity. In each problem, state whether or not the argument is valid; if invalid, give a counterexample.

a) (∀x)(Kx & Jx)   b) (∀x)(Fx ⊃ Gx)   c) (∀x)(Cx ⊃ Ix)
─────────────   ~Ga   ─────────────
    Ka   ─────────────   Ch v Ih
                          Fa

d) A ⊃ (∀x)Mx   e) (∀x)(Bx ⊃ Cx)   f) (∀x)(Ne ≡ Px)
    A   (∀x)Bx   ─────────────
─────────────   ─────────────   Pg
    Mg & Mi   Ca & Cb

g) (∀x)(Kx v Ax)   h) (∀x)(Dx v Gx)   i) (∀x)(Sx ≡ Tx)
    ~Kj   (∀x)(Dx ⊃ Jx)   ─────────────
─────────────   (∀x)(Gx ⊃ Jx)   Sb v ~Ta
    Ad   ─────────────
                              Ja

j) ~Tfg v (∀x)Px
    Ph ⊃ (∀x)Qx
─────────────
    Tfg ⊃ Qh

7–2. THE RULE FOR EXISTENTIAL QUANTIFICATION

Consider the argument

Somebody is blond.	(∃x)Bx
Adam is blond.	Ba

As we noted in chapter 2, this argument is obviously invalid. If somebody
is blond, it does not follow that Adam is blond. The blond might well be
somebody else. We will have to keep the clear invalidity of this argument
in mind while formulating the rule for existentially quantified sentences
to make sure we get the rule right.

Begin by listing the premise and the negation of the conclusion:

1   (∃x)Bx   P
2   ~Ba   ~C

As in the last example, we already know that we have an interpretation
started, this time with one object named 'a'. We also know that '~Ba' will
have to be true in this interpretation. Can we extend the interpretation so
as also to make '(∃x)Bx' true?

We have to be very careful here. We may be tempted to think along the
following lines: An existentially quantified sentence is true in an interpretation just in case at least one of its substitution instances is true in the

interpretation. We have one name, 'a', in the interpretation, so we could make '(∃x)Bx' true by making its substitution instance, 'Ba', true. But if we do that, we add 'Ba' to a branch which already has '~Ba' on it, so that the branch would close. This would tell us that there are no counterexamples, indicating that the inference is valid. But we **know** the inference is invalid. Something has gone wrong.

As I pointed out in introducing the example, the key to the problem is that the blond might well be someone other than Adam. How do we reflect this fact in our rules? Remember that in extending a branch downward we are **building** an interpretation. In so doing, we are always free to add new objects to the interpretation's domain, which we do by bringing in **new names** in sentences on the tree. Since there is a possibility that the blond might be somebody else, we indicate this by instantiating our existentially quantified sentence with a **new name**. That is, we make '(∃x)Bx' true by writing 'Bb' at the bottom of the branch, with 'b' a **new name**. We bring the **new name**, 'b', into the interpretation to make sure that there is no conflict with things that are true of the objects which were in the interpretation beforehand.

The completed tree looks like this:

√1   (∃x)Bx   P
2   ~Ba   ~C
3   Bb   1, ∃, **New name**

Invalid. Counterexample: D = {a,b}; ~Ba & Bb

The open branch represents a counterexample. The counterexample is an interpretation with domain D = {a,b}, formed with the names which appear on the open branch. The open branch tells us what is true about a and b in this interpretation, namely, that ~Ba & Bb.

You may be a little annoyed that I keep stressing '**new name**'. I do this because the **new name** requirement is a very important aspect of the rule for existentially quantified sentences—an aspect which students have a very hard time remembering. When I don't make such a big fuss about it, at least 50 percent of a class forgets to use a new name on the next test. By making this fuss I can sometimes get the percentage down to 25 percent.

Here is the reason for the new name requirement. Suppose we are working on a sentence of the form (∃u)(. . . **u** . . .) such as '(∃x)Bx' in our example. And suppose we try to make it true along each open branch on which it appears by writing a substitution instance, (. . . **t** . . .), at the bottom of each of these branches. Now imagine, as happened in our example, that ~(. . . **t** . . .)—or something which logically implies ~(. . . **t** . . .)—already appears along one of these branches. In the example we already had '~Ba'. This would lead to the branch closing when in fact we can make a consistent interpretation out of the branch.

We can always do this by instantiating (∃**u**)(. . . **u** . . .) with a **new name**, say, **s**, a name which does not appear anywhere along the branch. We use this new name in the instantiation (. . . **s** . . .). Then (. . . **s** . . .) can't conflict with a sentence already on the branch, and we are guaranteed not to have the kind of trouble we have been considering.

Not infrequently you get the right answer to a problem even if you don't use a **new name** when instantiating an existentially quantified sentence. But this is just luck, or perhaps insight into the particular problem, but insight which cannot be guaranteed to work with every problem. We want the rules to be guaranteed to find a counterexample if there is one. The only way to guarantee this is to write the rule for existentially quantified sentences with the **new name** requirement. This guarantees that we will not get into the kind of difficulty which we illustrated with our example:

> *Rule ∃*: If an existentially quantified sentence (∃**u**)(. . . **u** . . .) appears as the entire sentence at some point on a tree, do the following to each open branch on which (∃**u**)(. . . **u** . . .) appears: First pick a **new name, s,** that is, a name which does not appear anywhere on the branch. Then write the one substitution instance (. . . **s** . . .) at the bottom of the branch. Put a check by (∃**u**)(. . . **u** . . .).

Why do we always need a new name for an existentially quantified sentence but no new name for a universally quantified sentence (unless there happens to be no names)? In making a universally quantified sentence true, we must make it true for all things (all substitution instances) in the interpretation we are building. To make it true for more things, to add to the interpretation, does no harm. But it also does no good. If a conflict is going to come up with what is already true in the interpretation, we cannot avoid the conflict by bringing in new objects. This is because the universally quantified sentence has to be true for **all** the objects in the interpretation anyway.

We have an entirely different situation with existentially quantified sentences. They don't have to be true for all things in the interpretation. So they present the possibility of avoiding conflict with what is already true in the interpretation by extending the interpretation, by making each existentially quantified sentence true of something new. Finally, since the rules have the job of finding a consistent interpretation if there is one, the rule for existentially quantified sentences must incorporate this conflict-avoiding device.

EXERCISES

7-2. Test the following arguments for validity. State whether each argument is valid or invalid; when invalid, give the counterexamples shown by the open paths.

a)   A ⊃ (∃x)Gx   b)   (∃x)Dx   c)   (∃x)(Px & Qx)
           A   (∃x)~Dx   ───────────────
      ─────────────   ───────────   Pa v Qb
           Gb   A

d)   (∃x)Px   e)   A v B
           (∃x)Qx   A ⊃ (∃x)Nx
      ─────────────   B ⊃ (∃x)Nx
         Pm ≡ Qm   ───────────────
                                   Ng

7–3. APPLYING THE RULES

Now let's apply our rules to some more involved examples. Let's try the argument

(∀x)Lxe v (∀x)~Lxa
~Lae
───────────────────
~(∃x)Lxa

I am going to write out the completed tree so that you can follow it as I explain each step. Don't try to understand the tree before I explain it. Skip over it, and start reading the explanation, referring back to the tree in following the explanation of each step.

```
√1              (∀x)Lxe v (∀x)~Lxa              P
 2                    ~Lae                      P
√3                  ~~(∃x)Lxa                   ~C
√4                   (∃x)Lxa                    3, ~~

                   ╱‾‾‾‾‾‾‾╲
 5   a, e, c (∀x)Lxe   a, e, c (∀x)~Lxa      1, v
 6         Lca              Lca              4, ∃ New Name
 7         Lae             ~Laa             5, ∀
 8         Lee             ~Lea             5, ∀
 9         Lce             ~Lca             5, ∀
            ×                ×
                  Valid
```

We begin by listing the premises and the negation of the conclusion. Our first move is to apply the rule for double negation to line 3, giving line 4. Next we work on line 1. Notice that even though '(∀x)' is the first symbol to appear on line 1, the sentence is **not** a universally quantified sentence. Ask yourself (As in chapters 8 and 9 in volume I): What is the last thing I do in building this sentence up from its parts? You take '(∀x)Lxe' and '(∀x)~Lxa' and form a disjunction out of them. So the main connective is a disjunction, and to make this sentence true in the interpretation we are building, we must apply the rule for disjunction, just as we used it in sentence logic. This gives line 5.

In lines 1 through 4 our tree has one path. Line 5 splits this path into two branches. Each branch has its own universally quantified sentence which we must make true along the branch. Each branch also has '(∃x)Lxa', which is common to both branches and so must be made true along both branches. What should we do first?

When we work on '(∃x)Lxa' we will have to introduce a new name. It is usually better to get out all the new names which we will have to introduce **before** working on universally quantified sentences. To see why, look at what would have happened if I had worked on line 5 before line 4. Looking at the right branch I would have instantiated '(∀x)~Lxa' with 'a' and 'e'. Then I would have returned to work on line 4, which would have introduced the new name 'c'. But now with a new name 'c' on the branch I must go back and instantiate (∀x)~Lxa' with 'c'. To make this sentence true, I must make it true for **all** instances. If a new name comes up in midstream, I must be sure to include its instance. Your work on a tree is more clearly organized if you don't have to return in this way to work on a universally quantified sentence a second time.

We will see in the next chapter that in some problems we cannot avoid returning to work on a universally quantified sentence a second time. (It is because sometimes we cannot avoid this situation that we must never check a universally quantified sentence.) But in the present problem we keep things much better organized by following this practical guide:

> Practical Guide: Whenever possible, work on existentially quantified sentences before universally quantified sentences.

Now we can complete the problem. I work on line 4 before line 5. Line 4 is an existentially quantified sentence. The rule ∃ tells me to pick a **new name**, to use this new name in forming a substitution instance for the existentially quantified sentence, and to write this instance at the bottom of every open path on which the existentially quantified sentence appears. Accordingly, I pick 'c' as my new name and write the instance 'Lca' on each branch as line 6. Having done this, I check line 4, since I have now ensured that it will be made true along each open path on which it appears.

Finally, I can work on line 5. On the left branch I must write substitution instances for '(∀x)Lxe' for all the names that appear along that branch. So below '(∀x)Lxe' I write 'Lae', 'Lee', and 'Lce', and I write the names 'a', 'e', and 'c' to the left of the target sentence '(∀x)Lxe' to note the fact that this sentence has been instantiated with these three names. The branch closes because 'Lae' of line 7 conflicts with '~Lae' on line 2. On the right branch I have '(∀x)~Lxa'. At the bottom of the branch I write its substitution instances for all names on the branch, giving '~Laa', '~Lea', and '~Lca'. Again, I write the names used to the left of the target sentence. '~Lca' is the negation of 'Lca' on line 6. So the right branch closes also, and the argument is valid.

One more comment about this example: The new name requirement did not actually avoid any trouble in this particular case. If I had used either of the old names 'a' or 'e', I would in this case have gotten the right answer. Moreover, the tree would have been shorter. You may be thinking: What a bother this new name requirement is! Why should I waste my time with it in a case like this? But you must follow the new name requirement scrupulously if you want to be sure that the tree method works. When problems get more complicated, it is, for all practical purposes, impossible to tell whether you can safely get away without using it. The only way to be sure of always getting the right answer is to use the new name requirement every time you instantiate an existentially quantified sentence.

Now let's try an example which results by slightly changing the first premises of the last case:

(∀x)(Lxe v ~Lxa)
~Lae
———————————
~(∃x)Lxa

Instead of starting with a disjunction of two universally quantified sentences, we start with a universal quantification of a disjunction:

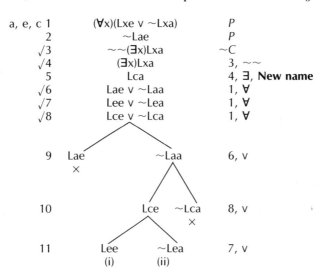

Lines 1, 2, and 3 list the premises and the negation of the conclusion. Line 4 gives the result of applying ~~ to line 3. Looking at line 1, we ask, What was the very last step performed in writing this sentence? The answer: applying a universal quantifier. So it is a universally quantified sentence. But line 4 is an existentially quantified sentence. Our practical guide tells us to work on the existentially before the universally quantified sentence. Accordingly, I pick a **new name**, 'c', and use it to instantiate '(∃x)Lxa', giving me line 5. Now I can return to line 1 and apply the rule ∀. At this point, the names on the branch are 'a', 'e', and 'c'. So I get the three instances of 1 written on lines 6, 7, and 8, and I record the names used to the left of line 1. Lines 9, 10, and 11 apply the ∨ rules to lines 6, 7, and 8. Notice that I chose to work on line 8 before line 7. I am free to do this, and I chose to do it, because I noticed that the disjunction of line 8 would close on one branch, while the disjunction of line 7 would not close on any branches.

We have applied the rules as far as they can be applied. No sentence can be made true by making shorter sentences true. We are left with two open branches, each of which represents a counterexample to the original argument. Let's write these counterexamples down.

The branch labeled (i) at the bottom has the names 'e', 'c', and 'a'. (In principle, the order in which you list information on a branch makes no difference. But it's easiest to read off the information from the bottom of the branch up.) So I indicate the domain of branch (i)'s interpretation by writing D = {e,c,a}. What is true of e, c, and a in this interpretation? The branch tells us that e bears L to itself, that c bears L to e, that a does not bear L to itself, that c bears L to a and that a does not bear L to e. In short, the interpretation is

D = {e,c,a}; Lee & Lce & ~Laa & Lca & ~Lae

To read an interpretation of an open branch, you need only make a list of the branch's names and the atomic and negated atomic sentences which appear along the branch. We use the format I have just indicated to make clear that the names are names of the objects of the domain, and the atomic and negated atomic sentences describe what is true of these objects. Check your understanding by reading the counterexample off the branch labeled (ii). You should get

D = {e,a,c}; ~Lea & Lce & ~Laa & Lca & ~Lae

Notice that neither of these counterexamples as read off the branches constitutes complete interpretations. The branches fail to specify some of the atomic facts that can be expressed with 'L', 'a', 'c', and 'e'. For example, neither branch tells us whether 'Lcc' is true or false. We have seen the same situation in sentence logic when sometimes we had a relevant sentence letter and an open branch on which neither the sentence letter nor its negation appeared as the entire sentence at a point along the branch. Here, as in sentence logic, this happens when a branch succeeds in making everything along it true before completing a selection of truth values for all relevant atomic sentences. In effect, the branch represents a whole group of interpretations, one for each way of completing the specification of truth values for atomic sentences which the branch does not mention. But for our purposes it will be sufficient to read off the interpretation as the branch presents it and call it our counterexample even though it may not yet be a complete interpretation.

EXERCISES

7–3. Test the following arguments for validity. State whether each argument is valid or invalid, when invalid, give the counterexamples shown by the open paths.

a) (∃x)(Px ⊃ Qx)   b) (∃x)Cx   c) (∃x)Jx v (∃x)Kx
　　―――――――――   ――――――   (∀x)~Jx
　　~(∀x)(Px & ~Qx)   ~(∃x)~Cx   ――――――――
　　　　　　　　　　　　　　　　　　　　　　　~(∀x)~Kx

d) (∀x)(Px ⊃ Qx)   e)   (∀x)(Gx v Hx)
　　(∃x)Px   ―――――――――――――
　　――――――――   ~(∃x)~Gx v ~(Ex)~Hx
　　~(∀x)~Qx

f) (∃x)Px & (∃x)~Px   g) ~(∀x)Px ⊃ (∃x)Qx
　　――――――――――――   ――――――――――――――
　　~(∀x)Px & ~(∀x)~Px   (∃x)~Qx ⊃ ~(∀x)~Px

h) Jq ⊃ (∃x)Kx   i) (∃x)Hx & (∃x)Gx   j)   (∃x)~Fx
　　(∀x)(Kx ⊃ Lx)   ―――――――――――   ~(∀x)Fx ⊃ (∀x)~Px
　　――――――――   ~(∀x)~(Hx & Gx)   ~(∀x)Fx ⊃ (∀x)~Qx
　　Jq ⊃ ~(∀x)~Lx   ―――――――――――――
　　　　　　　　　　　　　　　　　　　　　　　~(∀x)(Px v Qx)

7–4. NEGATED QUANTIFIED SENTENCES

To complete the rules for quantification, we still need the rules for the negation of quantified sentences. As always, we illustrate with a simple example:

Lae	*1*	Lae	P
$\overline{(\exists x)Lxe}$	2	$\sim(\exists x)Lxe$	$\sim C$

What will make line 2 true? All we need do is to make use of the equivalence rule for a negated existential quantifier, which we proved in section 3–4. (Remember: "Not one is" comes to the same thing as "All are not." If you have forgotten that material, reread the first few paragraphs of section 3–4—you will very quickly remember how it works.) '$\sim(\exists x)Lxe$' is true in an interpretation if and only if '$(\forall x)\sim Lxe$' is true in the interpretation. So we can make '$\sim(\exists x)Lxe$' true by making '$(\forall x)\sim Lxe$' true. This strategy obviously will work for any negated existentially quantified sentence. So we reformulate the $\sim\exists$ rule for logical equivalence as a rule for working on a negated existentially quantified sentence on a tree:

> *Rule* $\sim\exists$: If a sentence of the form $\sim(\exists u)(. . . u . . .)$ appears as the full sentence at any point on a tree, write $(\forall u)\sim(. . . u . . .)$ at the bottom of every open branch on which $\sim(\exists u)(. . . u . . .)$ appears. Put a check by $\sim(\exists u)(. . . u . . .)$.

With this rule, we complete our problem as follows:

1	Lae	P
$\sqrt{2}$	$\sim(\exists x)Lxe$	$\sim C$
a, e, 3	$(\forall x)\sim Lxe$	2, $\sim\exists$
4	$\sim Lae$	3, $\forall$
5	$\sim Lee$	3, $\forall$
	$\times$	
	Valid	

Note that I did **not** use a new name when I worked on line 2. The new name rule does not enter anywhere in this problem because the problem has no existentially quantified sentence as the full sentence at some point on the tree. Consequently, the rule $\exists$ never applies to any sentence in this problem. Line 2 is the **negation** of an existentially quantified sentence, and we deal with such a sentence with our new rule, $\sim\exists$. Line 2 gives line 3 to which the rule $\forall$ applies.

The story for the negation of a universally quantified sentence goes the same way as for a negation of an existentially quantified sentence. Just as "not one is" comes to the same thing as "all are not," "not all are" comes to the same thing as "some are not." In other words, we appeal to the rule $\sim\forall$ for logical equivalence in exactly the same way as we appealed to the rule $\sim\exists$ for logical equivalence. Reformulating for application to a negated universally quantified sentence on a tree, we have

> *Rule* $\sim\forall$: If a sentence of the form $\sim(\forall u)(. . . u . . .)$ appears as the full sentence at any point on a tree, write $(\exists u)\sim(. . . u . . .)$ at the bottom of

every open branch on which ~(∀u)(. . . **u** . . .) appears. Put a check by ~(∀u)(. . . **u** . . .).

Once again, this rule works because ~(∀u)(. . . **u** . . .) is equivalent to (∃u)~(. . . **u** . . .), as we noted in section 3–4 and as you proved in exercise 3–5.

Here is an example to illustrate the ~∀ rule:

$$\frac{(\exists x)Lxe}{(\forall x)Lxe}$$

√1	(∃x)Lxe	*P*
√2	~(∀x)Lxe	~C
√3	(∃x)~Lxe	2, ~∀
4	Lce	1, ∃, **New name**
5	~Lde	3, ∃, **New name**

Invalid. Counterexample: D = {d,e,c}; ~Lde & Lce

In this example, note that failure to follow the **new name** rule at step 5 would have incorrectly closed the branch. Also note that we do **not** instantiate line 2 with any of the names. Line 2 is **not** a universally quantified sentence. Rather, it is the **negation** of a universally quantified sentence which we treat with the new rule ~∀.

Now you have all the rules for quantifiers. It's time to practice them.

EXERCISES

Before you go to work, let me remind you of the three most common mistakes students make when working on trees. First of all, you must be sure you are applying the right rule to the sentence you are working on. The key is to determine the sentence's main connective. You then apply the rule for that connective (or for the first and second connectives in case of negated sentences). You should be especially careful with sentences which begin with a quantifier. Some are quantified sentences, some are not; it depends on the parentheses. '(∀x)(Px ⊃ A)' is a universally quantified sentence, so the rule ∀ applies to it. It is a universally quantified sentence because the initial universal quantifier applies to the whole following sentence as indicated by the parentheses. By way of contrast, '(∀x)(Lxa ⊃ Ba) & Lba' is not a universally quantified sentence. It is a conjunction, and the rule & is the rule to apply to it.

The second mistake to watch for especially carefully is failure to instantiate a universally quantified sentence with all the names that appear on the sentence's branch. When a universally quantified sentence appears on a branch, you are not finally done with the sentence until either the branch closes or you have instantiated it with all the names that appear on the branch.

Finally, please don't forget the **new name** requirement when you work on an existentially quantified sentence. When instantiating an existentially quantified sentence, you use only one name, but that name must not yet appear anywhere on the branch.

7–4. Use the truth tree method to test the following arguments for validity. In each problem, state whether or not the argument is valid; if invalid give a counterexample.

a1)	(∀x)Px & (∀x)Qx	a2)	(∀x)(Px & Qx)
	(∀x)(Px & Qx)		(∀x)Px & (∀x)Qx
b1)	(∃x)Px ∨ (∃x)Qx	b2)	(∃x)(Px ∨ Qx)
	(∃x)(Px ∨ Qx)		(∃x)Px ∨ (∃x)Qx
c1)	(∀x)Px ∨ (∀x)Qx	c2)	(∀x)(Px ∨ Qx)
	(∀x)(Px ∨ Qx)		(∀x)Px ∨ (∀x)Qx
d1)	(∃x)Px & (∃x)Qx	d2)	(∃x)(Px & Qx)
	(∃x)(Px & Qx)		(∃x)Px &(∃x)Qx
e1)	A ⊃ (∀x)Px	e2)	(∀x)(A ⊃ Px)
	(∀x)(A ⊃ Px)		A ⊃ (∀x)Px
f1)	A ⊃ (∃x)Px	f2)	(∃x)(A ⊃ Px)
	(∃x)(A ⊃ Px)		A ⊃ (∃x)Px
g1)	(∀x)Px ⊃ A	g2)	(∃x)(Px ⊃ A)
	(∃x)(Px ⊃ A)		(∀x)Px ⊃ A
h1)	(∃x)Px ⊃ A	h2)	(∀x)(Px ⊃ A)
	(∀x)(Px ⊃ A)		(∃x)Px ⊃ A
i1)	(∀x)Px	i2)	(∃x)Px
	(∃x)Px		(∀x)Px
j1)	(∀x)Px ⊃ A	j2)	(∀x)(Px ⊃ A)
	(∀x)(Px ⊃ A)		(∀x)Px ⊃ A
k1)	(∃x)(Px ⊃ A)	k2)	(∃x)Px ⊃ A
	(∃x)Px ⊃ A		(∃x)(Px ⊃ A)

l) $(\forall x)(Px \supset Qx)$
    $(\exists x)Px$
    _____

    $(\exists x)Qx$

m) $(\exists x)(Lxa \equiv Lex)$
    $(\forall x)Lxa$
    _____

    $(\exists x)Lex$

CHAPTER SUMMARY EXERCISES

Here are the new ideas from this chapter. Make sure you understand them, and record your summaries in your notebook.

a) Rule $\forall$ d) Rule $\sim\forall$
b) Rule $\exists$ e) Rule $\sim\exists$
c) New Name Requirement   f) Reading an Interpretation Off an Open Branch

More on Truth Trees for Predicate Logic $\underline{\overline{8}}$

8–1. CONTRADICTIONS, LOGICAL TRUTH, LOGICAL EQUIVALENCE, AND CONSISTENCY

In this section we are going to see how to apply the truth tree method to test predicate logic sentences for some familiar properties. This will be little more than a review of what you learned for sentence logic. The ideas are all the same. All we have to do is to switch to talking about interpretations where before we talked about lines of a truth table.

Let's start with logical contradiction. In sentence logic we say that a sentence is a contradiction if and only if it is false in all possible cases, where by "possible cases" we mean assignments of truth values to sentence letters—in other words, lines of the sentence's truth table. Recharacterizing the idea of a possible case as an interpretation, we have

> A closed predicate logic sentence is a *Contradiction* if and only if it is false in all of its interpretations.

The truth tree test for being a contradiction also carries over directly from sentence logic. The truth tree method is guaranteed to find an interpretation in which the initial sentence or sentences on the tree are true, if there is such an interpretation. Consequently

> To test a sentence, **X,** for being a contradiction make **X** the first line of a truth tree. If there is an interpretation which makes **X** true, the tree method

123

will find such an interpretation, which will provide a counterexample to **X** being a contradiction. If all branches close, there is no interpretation in which **X** is true. In this case, **X** is false in all of its interpretations; that is, **X** is a contradiction.

Here is a very simple example. We test '(∃x)(Bx & ~Bx)' to see whether it is a contradiction:

```
√1   (∃x)(Bx & ~Bx)    S (The sentence being tested)
√2     (Ba & ~Ba)      1, ∃, New name
 3        Ba           2, &
 4        ~Ba          2, &
           ×
```

The sentence is a contradiction.

The idea of a logical truth carries over from sentence logic in exactly the same way. In sentence logic a sentence is a logical truth if it is true for all possible cases, understood as all truth value assignments. Now, taking possible cases to be interpretations, we say

> A closed predicate logic sentence is a *Logical Truth* if and only if it is true in all of its interpretations.

To determine whether a sentence is a logical truth, we must, just as we do in sentence logic, look for a counterexample—that is, a case in which the sentence is false. Consequently

> To test a predicate logic sentence, **X,** for being a logical truth, make ~**X** the first line of a tree. If there is an interpretation which makes ~**X** true, the tree method will find such an interpretation. In such an interpretation, **X** is false, so that such an interpretation provides a counterexample to **X** being a logical truth. If all branches close, there is no interpretation in which ~**X** is true, and so no interpretation in which **X** is false. In this event, **X** is true in all of its interpretations; that is, **X** is a logical truth.

Again, let's illustrate with a simple example: Test '(∃x)Bx ∨ (∃x)~Bx' to see if it is a logical truth:

```
√1   ~[(∃x)Bx ∨ (∃x)~Bx]    ~S (The negation of the sentence being tested)
√2        ~(∃x)Bx           1, ~∨
√3       ~(∃x)~Bx           1, ~∨
a4        (∀x)~Bx           2, ~∃
a5       (∀x)~~Bx           3, ~∃
 6          ~Ba             4, ∀
 7          ~~Ba            5, ∀
             ×
```

The sentence is a logical truth.

The tree shows that there are no interpretations in which line 1 is true. Consequently, there are no interpretations in which the original sentence (the one which we negated to get line 1) is false. So this original sentence is a logical truth.

Notice that I had to introduce a name when I worked on line 4. Line 4 is a universally quantified sentence, and having no name at that point I had to introduce one to start my try at an interpretation. Line 5 is another universally quantified sentence, and when I worked on it, I already had the name 'a'. So I instantiated line 5 with 'a'. At no place on this tree did the **new name** requirement of the rule ∃ apply. This is because at no place on the tree is the entire sentence an existentially quantified sentence. In particular, the sentences of lines 2 and 3 are **negated** existentially quantified sentences, not existentially quantified sentences, so the rule ∃ and the new name requirement do not apply to them.

It's time to talk about logical equivalence. We already discussed this subject in section 3–4, which you may want to review at this point. For completeness, let's restate the definition:

> Two closed predicate logic sentences are *Logically Equivalent* if and only if in each of their interpretations the two sentences are either both true or both false.

Do you remember how we tested for logical equivalence of sentence logic sentences? Once again, everything works the same way in predicate logic. Two closed predicate logic sentences have the same truth value in one of their interpretations if and only if their biconditional is true in the interpretation. So the two sentences will agree in truth value in all of their interpretations if and only if their biconditional is true in all of their interpretations—that is, if and only if their biconditional is a logical truth. So to test for logical equivalence we just test for the logical truth of the biconditional:

> To determine whether the closed predicate logic sentences, **X** and **Y,** are logically equivalent, test their biconditional, **X≡Y,** for logical truth. That is, make ~(**X≡Y**) the first line of a tree. If all branches close, ~(**X≡Y**) is a logical truth, so that **X** and **Y** are logically equivalent. If there is an open branch, **X** and **Y** are not logically equivalent. An open branch will be an interpretation in which one of the two sentences is true and the other false, so that such an open branch provides a counterexample to **X** and **Y** being logically equivalent.

Here is another way in which you can test two sentences, **X** and **Y,** for logical equivalence. Consider the argument "**X**. Therefore **Y**." with **X** as premise and **Y** as conclusion. If this argument is invalid, there is a counterexample, an interpretation in which **X** is true and **Y** is false. Thus if "**X**. Therefore **Y**." is invalid, **X** and **Y** are not logically equivalent, and a counterexample to the argument is also a counterexample which shows **X** and **Y** not to be logically equivalent. The same goes for the argument "**Y**. Therefore **X**.", this time taking the second sentence, **Y**, as premise and the first sentence, **X**, as conclusion. If this argument is invalid there is a counterexample, that is, an interpretation in which **Y** is true and X is false, and hence again a counterexample to **X** and **Y** being logically equivalent.

Now, what happens if both the arguments "**X**. Therefore **Y**." and "**Y**. Therefore **X**." are valid? In this event every interpretation in which **X** is true is an interpretation in which **Y** is true (the validity of "**X**. Therefore **Y**."), and every interpretation in which **Y** is true is an interpretation in which **X** is true (the validity of "**Y**. Therefore **X**."). But that is just another way of saying that in each interpretation **X** and **Y** have the same truth value. If whenever **X** is true **Y** is true and whenever **Y** is true **X** is true, we can't have a situation (an interpretation) in which one is true and the other is false. Thus, if "**X**. Therefore **Y**." and "**Y**. Therefore **X**." are both valid, **X** and **Y** are logically equivalent:

> To determine whether the closed predicate logic sentences, **X** and **Y**, are logically equivalent, test the two arguments "**X**. Therefore **Y**." and "**Y**. Therefore **X**." for validity. If either argument is invalid, **X** and **Y** are not logically equivalent. A counterexample to either argument is a counterexample to the logical equivalence of **X** and **Y**. If both arguments are valid, **X** and **Y** are logically equivalent.

In fact, the two tests for logical equivalence really come to the same thing. To see this, suppose we start out to determine whether **X** and **Y** are logically equivalent by using the first test. We begin a tree with ~(**X**≡**Y**) and apply the rule ~≡:

$\checkmark$1   ~(**X**≡**Y**)   ~S

2   **X**   ~**X**   1, ~≡
3   ~**Y**   **Y**   1, ~≡

Now notice that the left-hand branch, with **X** followed by ~**Y**, is just the way we start a tree which tests the validity of the argument "**X**. Therefore **Y**.". And, except for the order of ~**X** and **Y**, the right-hand branch looks just like the tree which we would use to test the validity of the argument "**Y**. Therefore **X**.". So far as the right-hand branch goes, this order makes no difference. Because we are free to work on the lines in any order, what follows on the right-hand branch is going to look the same whether we start it with ~**X** followed by **Y** or **Y** follow by ~**X**.

In sum, lines 2 and 3 in our tree are just the beginning of trees which test the validity of "**X**. Therefore **Y**." and "**Y**. Therefore **X**.". Thus the completed tree will contain the trees which test the arguments "**X**. Therefore **Y**." and "**Y**. Therefore **X**.". And, conversely, if we do the two trees which test the arguments "**X**. Therefore **Y**." and "**Y**. Therefore **X**." we will have done all the work which appears in the tree we started above, the tree which tests **X≡Y** for logical truth. So the two ways of determining whether **X** and **Y** are logically equivalent really involve the same work.

If you did all of exercise 7–4 you have already tested 11 pairs of sentences for logical equivalence! In each of these pairs you tested two arguments, of the form "**X**. Therefore **Y**." and "**Y**. Therefore **X**.". Using our new test for logical equivalence, you can use your work to determine in each of these problems whether or not the pair of sentences is logically equivalent.

Truth trees also apply to test sets of sentences for consistency. Recall from section 9–2 in volume I that a set of sentence logic sentences is consistent if and only if there is at least one case which makes all of the sentences in the set true. Interpreting cases as interpretations, we have

> A *Model* of a set of one or more predicate logic sentences is an interpretation in which all of the sentences in the set are true.

> A set of one or more predicate logic sentences is consistent just in case it has at least one model, that is, an interpretation in which all of the sentences in the set are true.

> To test a finite set of predicate logic sentences for consistency, make the sentence or sentences in the set the initial sentences of a tree. If the tree closes, there is no interpretation which makes all of the sentences true together (no model) and the set is inconsistent. An open branch gives a model and shows the set to be consistent.

Every truth tree test of an argument is also a test of the consistency of the argument's premises with the negation of the argument's conclusion. An argument is valid if and only if its premises are inconsistent with the negation of the argument's conclusion. In other words, an argument is invalid if and only if its premises are consistent with the negation of its conclusion. Thus one can view the truth tree test for argument validity as a special application of the truth tree test for consistency of sets of sentences. (If you have any trouble understanding this paragraph, review exercise 9–7 in volume I. Everything in that exercise applies to predicate logic in exactly the same way as it does to sentence logic.)

EXERCISES

8–1. Test the following sentences to determine which are logical truths, which are contradictions, and which are neither. Show your work and state your conclusion about the sentence. Whenever you find a counterexample to a sentence being a logical truth or a contradiction, give the counterexample and state explicitly what it is a counterexample to.

a) $(\forall x)Dx \lor (\exists x)\sim Dx$ b)$(\forall x)Kx \ \& \ (\exists x)\sim Kx$
c) $(\forall x)Nx \lor (\forall x)\sim Nx$ d)$(\forall x)Jx \ \& \ (\forall x)\sim Jx$
e) $(\exists x)Bx \lor (\exists x)\sim Bx$ f)$(\exists x)Px \ \& \ (\exists x)\sim Px$
g) $[(\forall x)Gx \lor (\forall x)Hx] \ \& \ \sim(\forall x)(Gx \lor Hx)$
h) $(\forall x)(Kx \lor Jx) \supset [(\exists x)\sim Kx \supset (\exists x)Jx]$
i) $[(\forall x)Mx \supset (\forall x)\sim Nx] \ \& \ (\exists x)(\sim Mx \ \& \ Nx)$
j) $[(\exists x)Hx \supset (\forall x)(Ox \supset Nx)] \supset [(\exists x)(Hx \ \& \ Ox) \supset (\forall x)Nx]$
k) $(\exists x)[\sim Sx \ \& \ (Gx \lor Kx)] \lor [(\forall x)Gx \supset (\forall x)(Sx \lor Kx)]$
l) $[(\forall x)Fx \lor (\forall x)Gx] \equiv [(\exists x)\sim Fx \ \& \ \sim(\forall x)Gx]$

8–2. Use the truth tree method to test the following sets of sentences for consistency. In each case, state your conclusion about the set of sentences, and if the set of sentences is consistent, give a model.

a) $(\exists x)Px,$ $(\exists x)\sim Px$
b) $(\forall x)Px,$ $(\forall x)\sim Px$
c) $(\forall x)Px,$ $(\exists x)\sim Px$
d) $(\forall x)\sim Fx,$ $(\forall x)Sx,$ $(\exists x)[(\sim Fx \supset Sx) \supset Fx]$
e) $(\exists x)Gx \ \& \ (\exists x)Qx,$ $\sim(\exists x)(Gx \ \& \ Qx)$
f) $(\forall x)(Gx \lor Qx),$ $\sim[(\forall x)Gx \lor (\forall x)Qx]$
g) $(\exists x)(Jx \lor Dx),$ $(\forall x)(Jx \supset \sim Hx),$ $(\forall x)(Dx \supset Hx),$
   $(\forall x)[Jx \equiv (Dx \lor Hx)]$

8–3. Explain the connections among consistency, logical truth, and logical contradiction.

8–4. By examining your results from exercise 7–4(a) through (k), determine which pairs of sentences are logically equivalent and which are not. This is more than an exercise in mechanically applying the test for logical equivalence. For each pair of sentences, see if you can understand intuitively why the pair is or is not logically equivalent. See if you can spot any regularities.

8-2. TRUTH TREES WITH MULTIPLE QUANTIFIERS

In the last chapter I tried to keep the basics in the limelight by avoiding the complication of multiple quantifiers. Multiple quantifiers involve no new rules. But they do illustrate some circumstances which you have not yet seen.

Suppose I asked you to determine whether '$(\exists x)[Lxa \supset (\forall y)Lya]$' is a logical truth. To determine this, we must look for a counterexample to its being a logical truth, that is, an interpretation in which it is false. So we make the negation of the sentence we are testing the first line of a tree. Here are the first six lines:

√1	~(∃x)[Lxa ⊃ (∀y)Lya]	~S
a 2	(∀x)~[Lxa ⊃ (∀y)Lya]	1, ~∃
√3	~[Laa ⊃ (∀y)Lya]	2, ∀
4	Laa	3, ~⊃
√5	~(∀y)Lya	3, ~⊃
6	(∃y)~Lya	5, ~∀

We begin with the negation of the sentence to be tested. Line 2 applies the rule for a negated quantifier, and line 3 instantiates the resulting universally quantified sentence with the one name on the branch. Lines 4, 5, and 6 are straightforward, first applying the rule ~⊃ to line 3 and then the rule ~∀ to line 5.

But now the rules we have been using all along are going to force on us something we have not seen before. Applying the rule ∃ to line 6 forces us to introduce a new name, say, 'b', giving '~Lba' as line 7. This has repercussions for line 2. When we worked on line 2 we instantiated it for all the names we had on that branch **at that time.** But when we worked on line 6 we got a new name, 'b'. For the universally quantified line 2 to be true in the interpretation we are building, it must be true for all the names in the interpretation, and we now have a name which we did not have when we worked on line 2 the first time. So we must **return** to line 2 and instantiate it again with the new name, 'b'. This gives line 8. Here, with the final two easy steps, is the way the whole tree looks:

√1	~(∃x)[Lxa ⊃ (∀y)Lya]	~S
b, a 2	(∀x)~[Lxa ⊃ (∀y)Lya]	1, ~∃
√3	~[Laa ⊃ (∀y)Lya]	2, ∀
4	Laa	3, ~⊃
√5	~(∀y)Lya	3, ~⊃
√6	(∃y)~Lya	5, ~∀
7	~Lba	6, ∃, **New name**
a 8	~[Lba ⊃ (∀y)Lya]	2, ∀
9	Lba	8, ~⊃
√10	~(∀y)Lya	8, ~⊃
	×	

The sentence is a logical truth.

We do not need to work on line 10 because line 7 is the negation of line 9, and the branch thus closes. Indeed, I could have omitted line 10.

There was no way for us to avoid going back and working on line 2 a second time. There was no way in which we could have worked on the existentially quantified sentence of line 6 before working on line 2 the first time. The sentence of line 6 came from **inside** line 2. Thus we could get line 6 only by instantiating line 2 first. You should always be on the watch for this circumstance. In multiple quantified sentences it is always possible that an existentially quantified sentence will turn up from inside some larger sentence. The existential quantifier will then produce a new name which will force us to go back and instantiate all our universally quantified sentences with the new name. This is why we never check a universally quantified sentence.

Here is another example. We will test the following argument for validity:

Everyone loves someone.	$(\forall x)(\exists y)Lxy$
Anyone who loves someone loves themself.	$(\forall x)[(\exists y)Lxy \supset Lxx]$
Everyone loves themselves.	$(\forall x)Lxx$

```
a  1   (∀x)(∃y)Lxy              P
a  2   (∀x)[(∃y)Lxy ⊃ Lxx]      P
√  3   ~(∀x)Lxx                 ~C
√  4   (∃x)~Lxx                 3, ~∀
√  5   ~Laa                     4, ∃
√  6   (∃y)Lay                  1, ∀
√  7   Lab                      6, ∃, New name
√  8   (∃y)Lay ⊃ Laa            2, ∀
             /\
√  9   ~(∃y)Lay    Laa          8, ⊃
b 10   (∀y)~Lay     ×           9, ~∃
  11   ~Lab                     10, ∀
         ×
       Valid
```

Getting this tree to come out as short as I did requires some care in choosing at each stage what to do next. For example, I got line 8 by instantiating the universally quantified line 2 with just the name 'a'. The rule ∀ requires me to instantiate a universally quantified sentence with all the names on the branch. But it does not tell me when I have to do this. I am free to do my instantiating of a universally quantified sentence in any order I like, and if I can get all branches to close before I have used all available names, so much the better. In the same way, the rule ∀ requires that I return to instantiate lines 1 and 2 with the new name 'b', which arose on line 7. But the rule doesn't tell me when I have to do that. With a combination of luck and skill in deciding what to do first, I can get all branches to close before returning to line 1 or line 2 to instantiate with 'b'. In this circumstance I can get away without using 'b' in these sentences.

However, in any problem, if I instantiate with fewer than all the names and I have failed to close all the branches, then I **must** return and put the names not yet used into all universally quantified sentences which appear on open branches.

8–3. THREE SHORTCUTS

In general, it is very dangerous to do two or more steps at the same time, omitting explicitly to write down one or more steps which the rules require. When you fail to write down all the steps, it becomes too easy to make mistakes and too hard to find mistakes once you do make them. Also, omitting steps makes it extremely hard for anyone to correct your papers. However, there are three step-skipping shortcuts which are sufficiently clear-cut that, once you are proficient, you may safely use. You should begin to use these shortcuts only if and when your instructor says it is alright to do so.

Suppose you encounter the sentence ~(∀x)(∀y)Lxy on a tree. The rules as I have given them require you to proceed as follows:

$\checkmark$1   ~(∀x)(∀y)Lxy
$\checkmark$2   (∃x)~(∀y)Lxy   1, ~∀
$\checkmark$3   ~(∀y)Lay   2, ∃
$\checkmark$4   (∃y)~Lay   3, ~∀
   5   ~Lab   4, ∃, **New name**

Now look at line 2. You may be tempted to apply the rule ~∀ **inside** the sentence of line 2. In most cases, applying a rule inside a sentence is disastrous. For example, if you should try to instantiate '(∀x)Bx' inside ' ~[(∀x)Bx ∨ A]', you will make hash of your answer. But in the special case of the rule for negated quantifiers, one can justify such internal application of the rule.

In the example we have started, an internal application of the rule ~∀ gives the following first three lines of the tree:

$\checkmark$1   ~(∀x)(∀y)Lxy
$\checkmark$2   (∃x)~(∀y)Lxy   1, ~∀
   3   (∃x)(∃y)~Lxy   2, ~∀

In fact, we can sensibly skip line 2 and simply "push" the negation sign through both quantifiers, changing them both. Our tree now looks like this:

$\checkmark$1   ~(∀x)(∀y)Lxy
   2   (∃x)(∃y)~Lxy   1, ~∀, ~∀

We can do the same with two consecutive existential quantifiers or a mixture of quantifiers:

√1   ~(∃x)(∃y)Lxy
  2   (∀x)(∀y)~Lxy   1, ~∃, ~∃

√1   ~(∃x)(∀y)Lxy
√2   (∀x)(∃y)~Lxy   1, ~∃, ~∀

√1   ~(∀x)(∃y)Lxy
  2   (∃x)(∀y)~Lxy   1, ~∀, ~∃

Indeed, if a sentence is the negation of a triply quantified sentence, you could push the negation sign through all three quantifiers, changing each quantifier as you go.

Why is this shortcut justified? To give the reason in a very sketchy way, the subsentences to which we apply the negated quantifier rule are logically equivalent to the sentences which result from applying the rule. In short, we are appealing to the substitution of logical equivalents. To make all this rigorous actually takes a little bit of work (for the reasons explained in exercise 3–6), and I will leave such niceties to your instructor or to your work on logic in a future class.

Here is another shortcut: Suppose you have a multiple universally quantified sentence, such as '(∀x)(∀y)Lxy', on a tree that already has several names, say, 'a' and 'b'. Following the rules explicitly and instantiating with all the names is going to take a lot of writing:

a, b, 1   (∀x)(∀y)Lxy
a, b, 2   (∀y)Lay   1, ∀
      3   Laa   2, ∀
      4   Lab   2, ∀
a, b, 5   (∀y)Lby   1, ∀
      6   Lba   5, ∀
      7   Lbb   5, ∀

In general, it is not a good idea to skip steps, because if we need to look for mistakes it is often hard to reconstruct what steps we skipped. But we won't get into trouble if we skip steps 2 and 5 in the above tree:

1   (∀x)(∀y)Lxy   (a, a), (a, b), (b, a), (a, b)
2   Laa   1, ∀, ∀
3   Lab   1, ∀, ∀
4   Lba   1, ∀, ∀
5   Lbb   1, ∀, ∀

(In noting on line 1 what names I have used in instantiating the doubly universally quantified sentence '(∀x)(∀y)Lxy', I have written down the **pairs** of names I have used, being careful to distinguish the order in which they occurred, and I wrote them to the right of the line simply because I did not have room on the left.)

In fact, if you think you can get all branches to close by writing down just some of the lines 2 to 5, write down only what you think you will need. But if in doing so you do not get all branches to close, **you must be sure** to come back and write down the instances you did not include on all open branches on which line 1 occurs.

What about using the same shortcut for a doubly existentially quantified sentence? That is, is it all right to proceed as in this mini-tree?

1	(∃x)(∃y)Lxy	
2	Lab	1, ∃, ∃, **New names**

This is acceptable **if** you are very sure that the names you use to instantiate both existential quantifiers are both **new names,** that is, names that have not yet appeared anywhere on the branch.

Our last shortcut does not really save much work, but everyone is tempted by it, and it is perfectly legitimate: You may drop double negations anywhere they occur, as main connectives or within sentences. This step is fully justified by the law of substitution of logical equivalents from sentence logic.

A final reminder: You may use these shortcuts only if and when your instructor judges that your proficiency is sufficient to allow you to use them safely. Also, **do not** try to omit other steps. Other shortcuts are too likely to lead you into errors.

8–4. INFINITE TREES

So far, truth trees have provided a mechanical means for testing arguments for validity and sentences for consistency, logical truth, logical contradiction, or logical equivalence. But if logic were a purely mechanical procedure it could not have enough interest to absorb the attention of hundreds of logicians, mathematicians, and philosophers. However, in one way, the truth tree method is not purely mechanical.

Let's test the sentence '(∀x)(∃y)Lxy' for consistency. That is, let's look for an interpretation which makes it true:

d, c, b, a, 1	(∀x)(∃y)Lxy	S
√2	(∃y)Lay	1, ∀
3	Lab	2, ∃, **New name**
√4	(∃y)Lby	1, ∀
5	Lbc	4, ∃, **New name**
√6	(∃x)Lcy	1, ∀
7	Lcd	6, ∃, **New name**
.	.	
.	.	
.	.	

The tree starts with the universally quantified sentence '(∀x)(∃y)Lxy'. At this point the tree has no names, so I pick a name, 'a', and use it to instantiate 1, giving 2. Line 2 is an existentially quantified sentence, so I must instantiate it with a new name, 'b', giving line 3. But having the new name, 'b', I must go back and make 1 true for 'b'. This produces 4, again an existentially quantified sentence, which calls up the new name, 'c'. Now I must go back once more to 1 and instantiate it with 'c', producing the existentially quantified 6 and the new name, 'd', in 7. I am going to have to return to 1 with 'd'. By this time you can see the handwriting on the wall. This procedure is never going to end! The tree is just going to keep on growing. What does this mean? What has gone wrong?

Your immediate reaction may be that the troublesome new name requirement has clearly gummed up the works. The tree keeps on growing without end only because we keep needing to use a new name each time the existentially quantified sentence comes up. It's the new name from the existentially quantified sentence which has to be used to instantiate the universally quantified sentence which produces a new existentially quantified sentence which . . . and so on.

On the other hand, we know that without the new name requirement, the method will not always do its job. So what should we make of this situation?

First, let us understand what this infinite tree represents. It represents an interpretation with infinitely many names. The tree goes on forever, and corresponding to it we have a domain, D = {a,b,c,d, . . .}, and a specification that Lab & Lbc & Lcd & . . . . In other words, each object bears the relation L to the next.

Perhaps you have noticed that we can simplify the interpretation by supposing that there really is only one object to which all of the infinitely many names refer. This gives an interpretation in which there is only one thing, a, such that 'Laa' is true. In this interpretation it is true that for each thing (there is only one, namely a) there is something (namely a itself) such that Laa.

This is the last straw! you may well be saying to yourself. The new name requirement horribly complicates things, in this case by unnecessarily making the tree infinite. In this case the requirement prevents the method from finding the simplest interpretation imaginable which makes the original sentence true!

In fact we could rewrite the rules so that they would find this simple interpretation in the present case. But then the new rules would have some analogue of the new name requirement, an analogue which would provide a similar difficulty in some other problem. Let us say a bit more specifically what the difficulty comes to. In the infinite tree we have seen, it is very easy to tell that the tree will go on forever. And it is easy to figure out what infinite interpretation the infinite tree will provide. But in more complicated problems it will not be so easy. The rub is that there can be no mechanical way which will apply to all cases to tell us, in some limited number of steps, whether or not the tree will eventually close. There will always be cases in which, even after thousands of pages, we will still not know whether the tree will close in just a few more steps or whether it will go on forever.

One can show that this problem, or some analogue of it, will come up no matter how we write the rules of logic. Indeed, this is one of the many exciting things about logic. The rules can be mechanically applied. But logic will always leave room for insight and ingenuity. For in difficult problems the mechanical rules may never tell you whether the tree will eventually close. In these cases you can find out only by being clever.

Unfortunately, we must stop at this point. But I hope that all of you have been able to get a glimpse of one of the ways in which logic can be exciting. If you continue your study of logic beyond this course, you will come to understand why and how the problem of infinite trees is really a very general fact about all formulations of predicate logic, and you will understand the essential limitations of predicate logic in a much more thorough way.

EXERCISES

8–5. Test the following sentences to determine which are logical truths, which are contradictions, and which are neither. Show your work and state your conclusion about the sentence. Whenever you find a counterexample to a sentence being a logical truth or a contradiction, give the counterexample and state explicitly what it is a counterexample to.

  a) $(\forall x)[(\forall y)Py \supset Px]$
  b) $(\forall x)[(\exists y)By \supset Bx]$
  c) $(\forall x)[(\exists y)Cy \ \& \sim Cx]$
  d) $(\exists x)(\exists y)(Lxy \ \& \sim Lyx)$
  e) $(\exists y)[(\forall x)Rxy \supset (\forall x)Ryx]$
  f) $(\forall x)[(\forall y)Txy \ \& \ (\exists x)\sim Tyx]$
  g) $(\exists x)(\forall y)(Fx \supset Fy)$
  h) $(\forall x)(\exists y)(Rxy \ \& \sim Ryx)$

8-6. Use the truth tree method to test the following sets of sentences for consistency. In each case, state your conclusion about the sets of sentences, and if the set of sentences is consistent, give a model.

  a) $(\exists x)(\exists y)Lxy$, $(\exists x)(\exists y)\sim Lxy$
  b) $(\forall x)(\forall y)Lxy$, $(\forall x)(\forall y)\sim Lyx$
  c) $(\forall x)(\exists y)Kxy$, $(\exists x)(\forall y)\sim Kxy$

d) (∀x)Ax, ~(∃x)Bx, (∀x){(∃y)(Ax & ~By) ⊃ [(∃y)Ay ⊃ (∀y)~By]}
e) (∀x)(∃y)Mxy, (∃y)(∀x)~Mxy
f) (∃x)(∃y)(Rxx & ~Ryy & Rxy),   (∀x)(∀y)(Rxy ⊃ Ryx),
    (∀x)(∀y)∀z)[(Rxy & Ryz) ⊃ Rxz]

8–7. Use the truth tree method to determine which of the following
are logically equivalent. Give counterexamples as appropriate.

a) (∀x)(∀y)(Px & Qy)   and   (∀x)Px & (∀x)Qx
b) (∃x)(∃y)(Px & Qy)   and   (∃x)Px & (∃x)Qx
c) (∀x)(∀y)(Px ∨ Qy)   and   (∀x)Px ∨ (∀x)Qx
d) (∃x)(∃y)(Px ∨ Qy)   and   (∃x)Px ∨ (∃x)Qx
e) (∀x)(∀y)(Px ⊃ Qy)   and   (∃x)Px ⊃ (∀x)Qx
f) (∃x)(∃y)(Px ⊃ Qy)   and   (∀x)Px ⊃ (∃x)Qx
g) (∃x)(∀y)(Px ⊃ Qy)   and   (∀x)Px ⊃ (∀x)Qx
h) (∀x)(∃y)(Px ⊃ Qy)   and   (∃x)Px ⊃ (∃x)Qx
i) (∀x)(∃y)Lxy   and   (∃y)(∀x)Lxy
j) (∀y)[(∃x)Bx & Hy]   and   (∃x)Bx & (∀y)Hy

8–8. Are the following arguments valid? If not, give a counterexample.

a) (∃x)(∃y)[(∀z)Lzx ⊃ Lxy]   b) (∀x)(∃y)Lxy
    ―――――――――――――――   (∀x)[(∃y)Lxy ⊃ Lxx]
    (∃x)(∃y)Lxy   ―――――――――――――――
                                   (∀x)Lxx

c) (∀x)(∃y)Lyx   d) (∀x)(∀y)(∀z)[(Jxy & Jyz) ⊃ Jxz]
    (∀x)(∀y)(Lxy ⊃ Txy)   (∀x)(∀y)(Jxy ⊃ Jyx)
    ――――――――――――――   ――――――――――――――――――――
    (∀x)(∃y)Tyx   (∀x)Jxx

e) (∀x)(∃y)Lxy   f)   (∀x)(Cx ⊃ Ax)
    ――――――――――   ――――――――――――――――――――――――――――
    (∃y)(∀x)Lxy   (∀x)[(∃y)(Cy & Txy) ⊃ (∃y)(Ay & Txy)]

                     (All cats are animals. Therefore all
                     tails of cats are tails of animals.)

CHAPTER SUMMARY EXERCISES

Here are items from this chapter for you to review and record in
summary:

a) Contradiction
b) Truth Tree Test for Contradictions
c) Logical Truth

Identity, Functions, and Definite Descriptions

9

9–1. IDENTITY

Clark Kent and Superman would seem to be entirely different people. Yet it turns out they are one and the same. We say that they are *Identical*. Since identity plays a special role in logic, we give it a permanent relation symbol. We express 'a is identical to b' with 'a = b', and the negation with either '~(a = b)' or 'a ≠ b'.

'=' is not a connective, which forms longer sentences from shorter sentences. '=' is a new logical symbol which we use to form atomic sentences out of names and variables. But as we did with the connectives, we can explain exactly how to understand '=' by giving truth conditions for closed sentences in interpretations. Just follow the intuitive meaning of identity: To say that **s** = **t** is to say that the thing named by **s** is identical to the thing named by **t**; that is, that the names **s** and **t** refer to the same object. (Logicians say that **s** and **t** have the same referent, or that they are *Co-Referential*.) To summarize

> '=' flanked by a name or a variable on either side is an atomic sentence. If **s** and **t** are names, **t** = **s** is true in an interpretation if **s** and **t** name the same thing. **s** = **t** is false if **s** and **t** name different things. The negation of an identity sentence can be written either as ~(**s** = **t**) or as **s** ≠ **t.**

Identity is easy to understand, and it is extraordinarily useful in expressing things we could not say before. For example, '(∃x)' means that there is one **or more** x such that. . . . Let's try to say that there is exactly one x such that . . . , for which we will introduce the traditional expression '(∃x!)' (read "E shriek"). We could, of course, introduce '(∃x!)' as a new connective, saying, for example, that '(∃x!)Bx' is true in an interpretation just in case exactly one thing in the interpretation is B. But, with the help of identity, we can get the same effect with the tools at hand, giving a rewriting rule for '(∃x!)' much as we did for subscripted quantifiers in chapter 4.

To say that there is exactly one person (or thing) who is blond is to say, first of all, that someone is blond. But it is further to say that nothing else is blond, which we can reexpress by saying that if anything is blond, it must **be** (that is, be identical to) that first blond thing. In symbols, this is '(∃x)[Bx & (∀y)(By ⊃ y = x)]'.

Before giving a general statement, I want to introduce a small, new expository device. Previously I have used the expression '(. . . **u** . . .)' to stand for an arbitrary sentence with **u** the only free variable. From now on I am going to use expressions such as **P(u)** and **Q(u)** for the same thing:

> Boldface capital letters followed by a variable in parentheses, such as **P(u)** and **Q(u)**, stand for arbitrary sentences in which **u,** and only **u,** may be free. Similarly, **R(u,v)** stands for an arbitrary sentence in which at most **u** and **v** are free.

In practice **P(u)**, **Q(u)**, and **R(u,v)** stand for open sentences with the indicated variable or variables the only free variable. However, for work in Part II of this Volume, I have written the definition to accommodate degenerate cases in which **u,** or **u** and **v**, don't actually occur or don't occur free. If you are not a stickler for detail, don't worry about this complication: Just think of **P(u)**, **Q(u)**, and **R(u,v)** as arbitrary open sentences. But if you want to know why I need, to be strictly correct, to cover degenerate cases, you can get an idea from exercise 13–3.

With this notation we can give the E! rewrite rule:

> *Rule for rewriting* ∃!:   For any open formula **P(u)** with **u** a free variable, (∃u!)**P(u)** is shorthand for (∃u)[**P(u)** & (v)(**P(v)** ⊃ v = u)], where **v** is free for **u** in **P(u)**, that is, where **v** is free at all the places where **u** is free in **P(u)**.

Once you understand how we have used '=' to express the idea that exactly one of something exists, you will be able to see how to use '=' to express many related ideas. Think through the following exemplars until you see why the predicate logic sentences expresses what the English expresses:

> There are at least two x such that Fx:
> (∃x)(∃y)[x ≠ y & Fx & Fy].

There are exactly two x such that Fx:
$(\exists x)(\exists y)\{x \neq y \ \& \ Fx \ \& \ Fy \ \& \ (\forall z)[Fz \supset (z = x \lor z = y)]\}$.

There are at most two x such that Fx:
$(\forall x)(\forall y)(\forall z)[(Fx \ \& \ Fy \ \& \ Fz) \supset (x = y \lor x = z \lor y = z)]$.

We can also use '=' to say some things more accurately which previously we could not say quite correctly in predicate logic. For example, when we say that everyone loves Adam, we usually intend to say that everyone **other** than Adam loves Adam, leaving it open whether Adam loves himself. But '$(\forall x)$' means absolutely everyone (and thing), and thus won't exempt Adam. Now we can use '=' explicitly to exempt Adam:

Everyone loves Adam (meaning, everyone except possibly Adam himself):
$(\forall x)(x \neq a \supset Lxa)$.

In a similar way we can solve a problem with transcribing 'Adam is the tallest one in the class'. The problem is that no one is taller than themself, so we can't just use '$(\forall x)$', which means absolutely everyone. We have to say explicitly that Adam is taller than all class members **except Adam**.

Adam is the tallest one in the class:
$(\forall x)[(Cx \ \& \ x \neq a) \supset Tax]$.

To become familiar with what work '=' can do for us in transcribing, make sure you understand the following further examples:

Everyone except Adam loves Eve:
$(\forall x)(x \neq a \supset Lxe) \ \& \ {\sim}Lae$.

Only Adam loves Eve:
$(\forall x)(Lxe \equiv x = a)$, or $Lae \ \& \ (\forall x)(Lxe \supset x = a)$.

Cid is Eve's only son:
$(\forall x)(Sxe \equiv x = c)$, or $Sce \ \& \ (\forall x)(Sxe \supset x = c)$.

EXERCISES

9–1. Using Cx: x is a clown, transcribe the following:

a) There is at least one clown.
b) There is no more than one clown.
c) There are at least three clowns.
d) There are exactly three clowns.
e) There are at most three clowns.

9–2. Use the following transcription guide:

a:	Adam	Sxy:	x is smarter than y
e:	Eve	Qxy:	x is a parent of y
Px:	x is a person	Oxy:	x owns y
Rx:	x is in the classroom	Mxy:	x is a mother of y
Cx:	x is a Cat		
Fx:	x is furry		

Transcribe the following:

a) Three people love Adam. (Three or more)
b) Three people love Adam. (Exactly three)
c) Eve is the only person in the classroom.
d) Everyone except Adam is in the classroom.
e) Only Eve is smarter than Adam.
f) Anyone in the classroom is smarter than Adam.
g) Eve is the smartest person in the classroom.
h) Everyone except Adam is smarter than Eve.
i) Adam's only cat is furry.
j) Everyone has exactly one maternal grandparent.
k) No one has more than two parents.

9–2. INFERENCE RULES FOR IDENTITY

You now know what '=' means, and you have practiced using '=' to say various things. You still need to learn how to use '=' in proofs. In this section I will give the rules for '=' both for derivations and for trees. If you have studied only one of these methods of proof, just ignore the rules for the one you didn't study.

As always, we must guide ourselves with the requirement that our rules be truth preserving, that is, that when applied to sentences true in an interpretation they should take us to new sentences also true in that interpretation. And the rules need to be strong enough to cover all valid arguments.

To understand the rules for both derivations and trees, you need to appreciate two general facts about identity. The first is that everything is self-identical. In any interpretation which uses the name 'a', 'a = a' will be true. Thus we can freely use statements of self-identity. In particular, self-identity should always come out as a logical truth.

The second fact about identity which our rules need to reflect is just this: If a = b, then anything true about a is true about b, and conversely.

I'm going to digress to discuss a worry about how general this second fact really is. For example, if Adam believes that Clark Kent is a weakling and if in addition Clark Kent is Superman, does it follow that Adam believes that Superman is a weakling? In at least one way of understanding these sentences the answer must be "no," since Adam may well be laboring under the false belief that Clark Kent and Superman are different people.

Adam's believing that Clark Kent is a weakling constitutes an attitude on Adam's part, not just toward a person however named, but toward a person known under a name (and possibly under a further description as well). At least this is so on one way of understanding the word 'believe'. On this way of understanding 'believe', Adam's attitude is an attitude not just about Clark Kent but about Clark Kent under the name 'Clark Kent'. Change the name and we may change what this attitude is about. What is believed about something under the name 'a' may be different from what is believed about that thing under the name 'b', whether or not in fact a = b.

This problem, known as the problem of substitutivity into belief, and other so-called "opaque" or "intensional" contexts, provides a major research topic in the philosophy of language. I mention it here only to make clear that predicate logic puts it aside. An identity statement, 'a = b', is true in an interpretation just in case 'a' and 'b' are names of the same thing in the interpretation. Other truths in an interpretation are specified by saying which objects have which properties, which objects stand in which relations to each other, and so on, irrespective of how the objects are named. In predicate logic all such facts must respect identity.

Thus, in giving an interpretation of a sentence which uses the predicate 'B', one must specify the things in the interpretation, the names of these things, and then the things of which 'B' is true and the things of which 'B' is false. It is most important that this last step is independent of which names apply to which objects. Given an object in the interpretation's domain, we say whether or not 'B' is true of that **object**, however that thing happens to be named. Of course, we may use a name in saying whether or not 'B' is true of an object—indeed, this is the way I have been writing down interpretations. But since interpretations are really characterized by saying which predicates apply to which objects, if we use names in listing such facts, we must treat names which refer to the same thing, so-called *Co-Referential Names*, in the same way. If 'a' and 'b' are names of the same thing and if we say that 'B' is true of this thing by saying that 'Ba' is true, then we must also make 'Bb' true in the interpretation.

In short, given the way we have defined truth in an interpretation, if 'a = b' is true in an interpretation, and if something is true of 'a' in the interpretation, then the same thing is true of 'b' in the interpretation. Logicians say that interpretations provide an *Extensional Semantics* for predicate logic. "Semantics" refers to facts concerning what is true, and facts concerning meaning, insofar as rules of meaning have to do with what comes out true in one or another circumstance. "Extensional" means that the *Extension* of a predicate—the collection of things of which the predicate is true—is independent of what those things are called. Parts of English (e.g., 'Adam believes Clark Kent is a weakling') are not extensional. Predicate logic deals with the special case of extensional sentences. Because predicate logic deals with the restricted and special case of extensional sentences, in predicate logic we can freely substitute one name for another when the names name the same thing.

Now let's apply these two facts to write down introduction and elimination rules for identity in derivations. Since, for any name, **s**, **s** = **s** is always true in an interpretation, at any place in a derivation which we can simply introduce the identity statement **s** = **s**:

$\boxed{\enclose{circle}{\mathbf{s=s}}}$ = I   Where **s** is any name.

If **s** does not occur in any governing premises or assumptions, it occurs arbitrarily and gets a hat. To illustrate, let's demonstrate that '$(\forall x)(x = x)$' is a logical truth:

$$
\begin{array}{l|ll}
1 & \hat{a} = \hat{a} & = I \\
2 & (\forall x)(x = x) & 2, \forall I
\end{array}
$$

The second fact, that co-referential names can be substituted for each other, results in the following two rules:

$$
\begin{array}{ll}
\left|\begin{array}{l} \mathbf{s = t} \\[4pt] \mathbf{P(s)} \end{array}\right. & \left|\begin{array}{l} \mathbf{s = t} \\[4pt] \mathbf{P(t)} \end{array}\right. \\[18pt]
\enclose{circle}{\mathbf{P(t)}} \ = E & \enclose{circle}{\mathbf{P(s)}} \ = E
\end{array}
$$

The indicated substitutions may be for any number of occurrences of the name substituted for.

To illustrate, let's show that '$(\forall x)(\forall y)[x = y \supset (Fx \supset Fy)]$' is a logical truth:

```
1    │    │ a = b                           A
2    │    │ │ Fa                            A
3    │    │ │ a = b                         1, R
4    │    │ │ Fb                            2, 3, = E
5    │    │ │ Fa ⊃ Fb                       2 – 4, ⊃I
6    │ â b̂ ⊃ (Fâ ⊃ Fb̂)                     1 – 5, ⊃I
7    │ (∀y)[â = y ⊃ (Fâ ⊃ Fy)]             6, ∀I
8    │ (∀x)(∀y)[x = y ⊃ (Fx ⊃ Fy)]         7, ∀I
```

Now we'll do the rules for trees. We could proceed much as we did with derivations and require that we write identities such as 'a = a' wherever this will make a branch close. An equivalent but slightly simpler rule instructs us to close any branch on which there appears a negated self-identity, such as 'a ≠ a'. This rule makes sense because a negated self-identity is a contradiction, and if a contradiction appears on a branch, the branch cannot represent an interpretation in which all its sentences are true. In an exercise you will show that this rule has the same effect as writing self-identities, such as 'a = a', wherever this will make a branch close.

Rule ≠ :   For any name, **s**, if **s ≠ s** appears on a branch, close the branch.

Let's illustrate by proving '(∀x)(x = x)' to be a logical truth:

```
√1    ~(∀x)(x = x)      ~S
√2    (∃x)(x ≠ x)       1, ~∀
 3     a ≠ a            2, ∃
        ×
```

The second rule for trees looks just like the corresponding rules for derivations. Substitute co-referential names:

Rule = :   For any names, **s** and **t**, if **s = t** appears on a branch, substitute **s** for **t** and **t** for **s** in any expression on the branch, and write the result at the bottom of the branch if that sentence does not already appear on the branch. Cite the line numbers of the equality and the sentence into which you have substituted. But do not check either sentence. Application of this rule to a branch is not completed until either the branch closes or until all such substitutions have been made.

Let's illustrate, again by showing '(∀x)(∀y)[x = y ⊃ (Fx ⊃ Fy)]' to be a logical truth:

$\checkmark$1   ~($\forall$x)($\forall$y)[x = y $\supset$ (Fx $\supset$ Fy)]   ~S
$\checkmark$2   ($\exists$x)($\exists$y)~[x = y $\supset$ (Fx $\supset$ Fy)]   1, ~$\forall$, ~$\forall$
$\checkmark$3   ~[a = b $\supset$ (Fa $\supset$ Fb)]   2, $\exists$, $\exists$
4   a = b   3, ~$\supset$
$\checkmark$5   ~(Fa $\supset$ Fb)   3, ~$\supset$
6   Fa   5, ~$\supset$
7   ~Fb   5, ~$\supset$
8   ~Fa   4, 7, =
    ×

Before closing this discussion of identity, I should mention that identity provides an extreme example of what is called an *Equivalence Relation*. Saying that identity is an equivalence relation is to attribute to it the following three characteristics:

Identity is *Reflexive*. Everything is identical with itself: $(\forall x)(x = x)$. In general, to say that relation **R** is reflexive is to say that $(\forall x)R(x,x)$.

Identity is *Symmetric*. If a first thing is identical with a second, the second is identical with the first: $(\forall x)(\forall y)(x = y \supset y = x)$. In general, to say that relation **R** is symmetric is to say that $(\forall x)(\forall y)(\textbf{R}(x,y) \supset \textbf{R}(y,x))$.

Identity is *Transitive*. If a first thing is identical with a second, and the second is identical with a third, then the first is identical with the third: $(\forall x)(\forall y)(\forall z)[(x = y \ \& \ y = z) \supset x = z]$. In general, to say that relation **R** is transitive is to say that $(\forall x)(\forall y)(\forall z)[(\textbf{R}(x,y) \ \& \ \textbf{R}(y,z)) \supset \textbf{R}(x,z)]$.

You can prove that identity is an equivalence relation using either derivations or trees.

Here are some other examples of equivalence relations: being a member of the same family, having (exactly) the same eye color, being teammates on a soccer team. Items which are related by an equivalence relation can be treated as the same for certain purposes, depending on the relation. For example, when it comes to color coordination, two items with exactly the same color can be treated interchangeably. Identity is the extreme case of an equivalence relation because "two" things related by identity can be treated as the same for **all** purposes.

Equivalence relations are extremely important in mathematics. For example two numbers are said to be *Equal Modulo 9* if they differ by an exact multiple of 9. Equality modulo 9 is an equivalence relation which is useful in checking your arithmetic (as you know if you have heard of the "rule of casting out 9s").

EXERCISES

9–3. Show that each of the two = E rules can be obtained from the other, with the help of the = I rule.

9–4. Show that the rule $\neq$ is equivalent to requiring one to write, on each branch, self-identities for each name that occurs on the branch. Do the following three exercises using derivations, trees, or both:

9–5. Show that the following are logical truths:

a) $(\exists x)(x = a)$
b) $(\forall x)(\forall y)[\sim(Fx \supset Fy) \supset x \neq y]$
c) $(\forall x)[Px \equiv (\exists y)(x = y \ \& \ Py)]$
d) $Pa \equiv (\forall x)(x = a \supset Pa)$
e) $(\exists x)(\exists y)(Fx \ \& \sim Fy) \supset (\exists x)(\exists y)(x \neq y)$

9–6. Show that $(\exists x)(\forall y)(Fy \equiv y = x)$ and $(\exists x!)Fx$ are logically equivalent.

9–7. Prove that $=$ is an equivalence relation.

9–8. Show the validity of the following arguments:

a) $\dfrac{(\forall x)(x = a \supset Fx)}{Fa}$ b) $\dfrac{Fa}{(\forall x)(x = a \supset Fx)}$ c) $\dfrac{(\exists x)(Fx \ \& \ x = a)}{Fa}$

d) $\dfrac{\begin{array}{l}(\forall x)(x = a \supset Fx)\\(\forall x)(Fx \supset Fb)\end{array}}{Fb}$ e) $\dfrac{\begin{array}{c}Pa\\(\exists y)(y = a \ \& \ y = b)\end{array}}{Pb}$ f) $\dfrac{a = b}{Fa \equiv Fb}$

g) $\dfrac{a = b}{(\forall x)(a = x \equiv b = x)}$ h) $\dfrac{(\forall x)(a = x \equiv b = x)}{a = b}$ i) $\dfrac{\begin{array}{c}(\exists x)(\forall y)(Py \equiv y = x)\\Pa\\Pb\end{array}}{a = b}$

j) $\dfrac{\begin{array}{c}(\exists x)Px\\(\forall x)(x = a \ v \ x = b)\end{array}}{Pa \ v \ Pb}$ k) $\dfrac{(\exists x)(\forall y)(x = y)}{(\exists x)Px \supset (\forall x)Px}$ l) $\dfrac{\begin{array}{c}(\forall x)(\exists y)Rxy\\(\forall x)\sim Rxx\end{array}}{(\exists x)(\exists y)(x \neq y)}$

m) $\dfrac{\begin{array}{c}(\forall x)(\exists y)Rxy\\(\forall x)\sim Rxx\end{array}}{(\forall x)(\exists y)(Rxy \ \& \ x \neq y)}$ n) $\dfrac{\begin{array}{c}(\exists x)(Kx \ \& \ Jx)\\(\exists x)(Kx \ \& \sim Jx)\end{array}}{(\exists x)(\exists y)(Kx \ \& \ Ky \ \& \ x \neq y)}$

o) $\dfrac{\begin{array}{c}(\exists x!)Px\\(\exists x)(Px \ \& \ Qx)\end{array}}{(\forall x)(Px \supset Qx)}$ p) $\dfrac{\begin{array}{c}\sim(\exists!x)Fx\\(\exists x)Fx\end{array}}{(\exists x)(\exists y)(Fx \ \& \ Fy \ \& \ x \neq y)}$

9–9. I stated that being teammates on a soccer team is an equivalence relation. This is right, on the assumption that no one belongs to more than one soccer team. Why can the relation, *being teammates on a soccer team,* fail to be an equivalence relation if someone belongs to two teams? Are there any circumstances under which being team-mates on a soccer team is an equivalence relation even though one or more people belong to more than one team?

9–3. FUNCTIONS

Often formal presentations of functions leave students bewildered. But if you have done any high school algebra you have an intuitive idea of a function. So let's start with some simple examples from algebra.

For our algebraic examples, the letters 'x', 'y', and 'z' represent variables for numbers. Consider the expression 'y = 2x + 7'. This means that if you put in the value 3 for x you get the value $2 \times 3 + 7 = 13$ for y. If you put in the value 5 for x, you get the value $2 \times 5 + 7 = 17$ for y. Thus the expression 'y = 2x + 7' describes a rule or formula for calculating a value for y if you give it a value for x. The formula always gives you a definite answer. Given some definite value for x, there is exactly one value for y which the formula tells you how to calculate.

Mathematicians often use expressions like '$f(x)$' for functions. Thus, instead of using the variable y in the last example, I could have written '$f(x) = 2x + 7$' This means exactly what 'y = 2x + 7' means. When you put in a specific number for x, '$f(x)$' serves as a name for the value y, so that we have $y = f(x)$. In particular, '$f(3)$' is a name for the number which results by putting in the value 3 for x in 2x + 7. That is, '$f(3)$' is a name for the number 13, the number which results by putting in the value 3 for x in $f(x) = 2x + 7$.

This is all there is to functions in logic. Consider the name 'a'. Then '$f(a)$' acts like another name. To what does '$f(a)$' refer? That depends, of course, on what function $f(\ )$ is, which depends on how '$f(\ )$' is interpreted. In specifying an interpretation for a sentence in which the function symbol '$f(\ )$' occurs, we must give the rule which tells us, for any name **s,** what object $f(\mathbf{s})$ refers to. When we deal with interpretations in which there are objects with no names, this must be put a little more abstractly: We must say, for each object (called the *Argument* of the function), what new object (called the *Value* of the function) is picked out by the function $f(\ )$ when $f(\ )$ is applied to the first object. The function must be well defined, which means that for each object to which it might be applied, we must specify exactly **one** object which the function picks out. For each argument there must be a unique value.

So far I have talked only about one place functions. Consider the example of the mathematical formula 'z = 3x + 5y − 8', which we can also write as '$z = g(x,y)$' or as '$g(x,y) = 3x + 5y − 8$'. Here $g(\ , \ )$ has two arguments. You give the function two input numbers, for example, x = 2 and y = 4, and the function gives you a single, unique output—in this case, the number $3 \times 2 + 5 \times 4 - 8 = 18$. Again, the idea carries over to logic. If '$g(\quad , \quad)$' is a two place function symbol occurring in a sentence, in giving an interpretation for the sentence we must specify the unique object the function will pick out when you give it a **pair** of objects. If our interpretation has a name for each object the same requirement can be expressed in this way: For any two names, **s** and **t**, '$g(\mathbf{s},\mathbf{t})$' refers to a unique object, the one picked out by the function $g(\quad , \quad)$ when $g(\quad , \quad)$ is applied to the arguments **s** and **t**. We can characterize functions with three, four, or any number of argument places in the same kind of way.

To summarize

> The interpretation of a one place function specifies, for each object in the interpretation's domain, what object the function picks out as its value when the function is applied to the first object as its argument. The interpretation of a two place function similarly specifies a value for each pair of arguments. Three and more place functions are interpreted similarly.

Incidentally, the value of a function does not have to differ from the argument. Depending on the function, these may be the same or they may be different. In particular, the trivial identity function defined by $(\forall x)(f(x) = x)$ is a perfectly well-defined function.

In the last sentence I applied a function symbol to a variable instead of a name. How should you understand such an application? In an interpretation, a name such as 'a' refers to some definite object. A variable symbol such as 'x' does not. Similarly, '$f(a)$' refers to some definite object, but '$f(x)$' does not. Nonetheless, expressions such as '$f(x)$' can be very useful. The closed sentence '$(\forall x)Bf(x)$' should be understood as saying that every value of '$f(x)$' has the property named by 'B'. For example, let us understand 'Bx' as 'x is blond' and '$f(x)$' as referring to the father of x. That is, for each person, x, $f(x)$ is the father of x, so that '$f(a)$' refers to Adam's father, '$f(e)$' refers to Eve's father, and so on. Then '$(\forall x)Bf(x)$' says that everyone's father is blond.

In sum, function symbols extend the kind of sentences we can write. Previously we had names, variables, predicate symbols, and connectives. Now we introduce function symbols as an extension of the category of names and variables. This involves the new category called *Terms*:

> We extend the vocabulary of predicate logic to include *Function Symbols*, written with lowercase italicized letters followed by parentheses with places for writing in one, two, or more arguments.

> All names and variables are *Terms*. A function symbol applied to any term or terms (a one place function symbol applied to one term, a two place function symbol applied to two terms, etc.) is again a term. Only such expressions are terms.

In forming sentences, terms function exactly as do names and variables. One may be written after a one place predicate, two after a two place predicate, and so on.

Do not confuse function symbols (lowercase italicized letters followed by parentheses with room for writing in arguments) with such expressions as **P(u)** and **R(u,v)**. These latter expressions are really not part of predicate logic at all. They are part of English which I use to talk about arbitrary open predicate logic sentences.

Notice that these definitions allow us to apply functions to functions: If '$f(\ )$' is a one place function symbol, '$f(f(a))$' is a well-defined term. In practice, we leave out all but the innermost parentheses, writing '$f(f(a))$' as '$ff(a)$' What does such multiple application of a function symbol mean? Well, if $f(x) = x^2$, then $ff(x)$ is the square of the square of x. If x = 3, then $ff(3) = (3^2)^2 = 9^2 = 81$. In general, you determine the referent of— that is, the object referred to by —'$ff(a)$' as follows: Look up the referent of 'a'. Apply the function f to that object to get the referent of '$f(a)$'. Now apply f a second time to this new object. The object you get after the second application of f is the referent of '$ff(a)$'.

Function symbols can be combined to form new terms in all kinds of ways. If '$f(\ )$' is a one place function symbol and '$g(\ ,\ )$' is a two place function symbol, the following are all terms: '$f(a)$', '$f(y)$', '$g(a,x)$', '$fg(a,x)$'— that is, $f[g(a,x)]$, '$g[f(a), f(b)]$', and $g[f(x), g(a,b)]$'.

We need one more definition:

A term in which no variables occur is called a *Constant* or a *Constant Term*.

Only constant terms actually refer to some specific object in an interpretation. But closed sentences which use nonconstant terms still have truth values. In applying the truth definitions for quantifiers, we form substitution instances, substituting names for variables within function symbols as well as elsewhere. Thus, in applying the definition for the truth of a universally quantified sentence in an interpretation to '$(\forall x)Laf(x)$', we look at the substitution instances '$Laf(a)$', '$Laf(b)$', '$Laf(c)$', and so on. We then look to see if the relation L holds between a and the object $f(a)$, between a and the object $f(b)$, and so on. Only if all these instances hold is '$(\forall x)Laf(x)$' true in the interpretation.

The rules for functions simply reflect the fact that constant terms formed by applying function symbols to other constant terms have definite referents, just as names do. However, the generality of these new referring terms may be restricted. For example, the constant function f defined by $(\forall x)(f(x) = a)$ can only refer to one thing, namely, a. Thus, when it is important that nothing be assumed about a constant term we must use a name and not a function symbol applied to another constant term.

For derivations this means that we should treat constant terms all alike in applying the rules ∀E and ∃I. In applying ∃E, our isolated name must still be a name completely isolated to the subderivation to which the ∃E rule applies. (Strictly speaking, if you used an isolated function symbol applied to an isolated name, no difficulty would arise. But it's simpler just to let the isolated name requirement stand as a requirement to use an isolated name.)

In applying ∀I only names can occur arbitrarily. For example, we must never put a hat on a term such as '$f(a)$'. The hat means that the term could refer to absolutely **anything,** but often the value of a function is restricted to only part of an interpretation's domain. So we can't apply ∀I to a function symbol. However, if a name appears in no governing premise or assumption and occurs **as the argument** of a function symbol, we can apply ∀I to the name. For example, if 'a' appears in no governing premise or assumption, we could have '$Bf(â)$' as a line on a derivation, to which we could apply ∀I to get '$(x)Bf(x)$'. To summarize

> In derivations, treat all constant terms alike in applying ∀E and ∃I. Apply ∀I and ∃E only to names.

Let's try this out by showing that '$(\forall x)(\exists y)(f(x) = y)$' is a logical truth. This sentence says that for each argument a function has a value. The way we treat functions in giving interpretations guarantees that this statement is true in all interpretations. If our rules are adequate, this fact should be certified by the rules:

$$
\begin{array}{l|ll}
1 & f(\hat{a}) = f(\hat{a}) & = \mathrm{I} \\
2 & (\exists y)(f(\hat{a}) = y) & 1, \exists\mathrm{I} \\
3 & (\forall x)(\exists y)(f(x) = y) & 2, \forall\mathrm{I}
\end{array}
$$

Note that this derivation works without any premise or assumption. = I allows us to introduce the identity of line 1. Since 'a' does not occur in any governing premise or assumption, it occurs arbitrarily, although the larger term '$f(a)$' does not occur arbitrarily. 'a' could refer to absolutely anything—that is, the argument to which the function is applied could be any object at all. However, the result of applying the function f to this arbitrary object might not be just anything. In line 2 we apply ∃I to the whole term '$f(a)$', not just to the argument 'a'. This is all right because we are **existentially,** not universally, generalizing. If $f(\hat{a}) = f(\hat{a})$, then $f(\hat{a})$ is identical with **something.** Finally, in line 3, we universally generalize on the remaining arbitrarily occurring instance of 'a'.

Let's try something harder. '$(\forall x)(\exists y)[f(x) = y \ \& \ (\forall z)(f(x) = z \supset z = y)]$' says that for each argument the function f has a value and furthermore this value is unique. Again, the way we treat functions in giving interpretations guarantees that this statement is true in all interpretations. So our rules had better enable us to show that this sentence is a logical truth:

1	$f(\hat{a}) = f(\hat{a})$ $= I$	
2	$f(a) = b$ A	
3	$f(a) = f(a)$ $= I$	
4	$b = f(a)$ 2, 3, $= E$	
5	$f(\hat{a}) = \hat{b} \supset \hat{b} = f(\hat{a})$	2– 4, $\supset I$
6	$(\forall z)(f(\hat{a}) = z \supset z = f(\hat{a}))$	5, $\forall I$
7	$f(\hat{a}) = f(\hat{a}) \ \& \ (\forall z)(f(\hat{a}) = z \supset z = f(\hat{a}))$	1, 6, &I
8	$(\exists y)(f(\hat{a}) = y \ \& \ (\forall z)(f(\hat{a}) = z \supset z = y)]$	7, $\exists I$
9	$(\forall x)(\exists y)[f(x) = y \ \& \ (\forall z)(f(x) = z \supset z = y)]$	8, $\forall I$

One more example will illustrate $\exists E$ and $\forall E$ as applied to terms using function symbols. Note carefully how in applying $\forall E$ the constant term to use in this problem is not a name, but '$f(a)$', a function symbol applied to a name:

1	$(\exists x)(\forall y)[f(x) = g(y)]$ P	
2	a $(\forall y)[f(a) = g(y)]$ A	
3	$f(a) = gf(a)$ 2, $\forall E$	
4	$(\exists x)[f(x) = gf(x)]$ 3, $\exists I$	
5	$(\exists x)[f(x) = gf(x)]$ 1, 2– 4, $\exists E$	

Similar thinking goes into the rules for trees. All constant terms act as names when it comes to the rule $\forall$. But for the rule $\exists$ we want a name that could refer to anything in the interpretation—that was the reason for requiring that the name be new to the branch. So for $\exists$ we need a new name, which must be a name, not a function symbol, applied to another constant term:

> In trees, instantiate all universally quantified sentences with all constant terms that occur along the branch, unless the branch closes. Instantiate each existentially quantified sentence with a **new name**.

Let us illustrate the new rules with the same sentence as before, '$(\forall x)(\exists y)[f(x) = y \ \& \ (\forall z)(f(x) = z \supset z = y)]$'. As I mentioned, this sentence says that f has a unique value for each argument. Since the way we treat functions in giving interpretations ensures that this sentence is true in all interpretations, our rules had better make this sentence come out to be a logical truth:

$\sqrt{}$1 $\sim(\forall x)(\exists y)\{f(x)=y \;\&\; (\forall z)[f(x)=z \supset z=y]\}$ $\sim S$
$\sqrt{}$2 $(\exists x)(\forall y)\sim\{f(x)=y \;\&\; (\forall z)[f(x)=z \supset z=y]\}$ 1, $\sim\exists$, $\sim\forall$
$f(a)$ 3 $(\forall y)\sim\{f(a)=y \;\&\; (\forall z)[f(a)=z \supset z=y]\}$ 2, $\exists$
$\sqrt{}$4 $\sim\{f(a)=f(a) \;\&\; (\forall z)[f(a)=z \supset z=f(a)]\}$ 3, $\forall$

$\sqrt{}$5 $f(a)\neq f(a)$ $\sim(\forall z)[f(a)=z \supset z=f(a)]$ $\sim\&$
$\sqrt{}$6 $\times$ $(\exists z)\sim[f(a)=z \supset z=f(a)]$ 5, $\sim\forall$
$\sqrt{}$7 $\sim[f(a)=b \supset b=f(a)]$ 6, $\exists$
8            $f(a)=b$ 7, $\sim\supset$
9            $b\neq f(a)$ 7, $\sim\supset$
10            $f(a)\neq f(a)$ 8, 9, =
                $\times$

Notice that to get everything to close I used the term '$f(a)$' in substituting into line 3. Also, note that the right branch does not close at line 9. Line 9 is not, strictly speaking, the negation of line 8 since, strictly speaking, '$f(a)=b$' and '$b=f(a)$' are different sentences.

The occurrence of functions in trees has an unpleasant feature. Suppose that a universally quantified sentence such as '$(\forall x)Pf(x)$' appears on a tree. This will be instantiated, at least once, say, with 'a', giving '$Pf(a)$'. But now we have a new constant, '$f(a)$', which we must put into '$(\forall x)Pf(x)$', giving '$Pff(a)$'. This in turn gives us a further constant, '$ff(a)$'—and clearly we are off on an infinite chase. In general, open trees with function symbols are infinite when, as in '$(\forall x)Pf(x)$', a function symbol occurs as a nonconstant term inside the scope of a universal quantifier.

EXERCISES

9–10. Provide derivations and/or trees to establish that the following are logical truths:

a) $(\forall x)(\forall y)(\forall z)[(f(z)=x \;\&\; f(z)=y) \supset x=y]$
b) $(\exists x)[Ff(x) \vee \sim Ff(x)]$

9–11. Provide derivations and/or trees to establish the validity of the following arguments:

a) $\dfrac{(\forall x)Fx}{(\forall x)Fg(x)}$ b) $\dfrac{(\forall x)(\forall y)(x=y)}{(\forall x)(f(x)=x)}$ c) $\dfrac{(\forall x)(f(x)\neq x)}{(\exists x)(\exists y)(x\neq y)}$

d) $\dfrac{(\exists x)(f(x)\neq x)}{(\exists x)(\exists y)(fx\neq y)}$ e) $\dfrac{(\exists x)(\forall y)(f(y)=x)}{(\forall x)(\forall y)[f(x)=f(y)]}$

f) $\dfrac{(\forall x)(\forall y)[g(x,y)=g(y,x)]}{(\forall x)(\forall y)[Fg(x,y) \supset Fg(y,x)]}$ g) $\dfrac{}{(\forall x)(ff(x)=x)}$ $\dfrac{}{(\forall x)(\forall y)[f(x)=f(y) \supset x=y]}$

h) $\dfrac{(\exists x)(\forall y)(\forall z)(g(y,z)=x)}{(\forall x)(\forall y)(\forall z)(\forall w)[g(x,y)=g(z,w)]}$ i) $\dfrac{(\forall z)(\exists x)(\exists y)[z=g(x,y)]}{(\forall x)(\forall y)Fg(x,y) \supset (\forall x)Fx}$

j) $\dfrac{(\exists x)(\exists y)[Ff(x) \ \& \ {\sim}Ff(y)]}{(\exists x)(\exists y)[f(x) \neq f(y)]}$

k) $\dfrac{(\forall x)(\forall y)[x \neq y \supset g(x,y) \neq g(y,x)]}{(\forall x)(\forall y)\{x \neq y \supset g[g(x,y),g(y,x)] \neq g[g(y,x),g(x,y)]\}}$

l) $\dfrac{(\forall x)(\forall y)\{x \neq y \supset [Fg(x,y) \equiv {\sim}Fg(y,x)]\}}{(\forall x)(\forall y)[(x \neq y \supset g(x,y) \neq g(y,x)]}$

9–4. DEFINITE DESCRIPTIONS

Let's transcribe

    (1)   The one who loves Eve is blond.

We need a predicate logic sentence which is true when (1) is true and false when it is false. If there is exactly one person who loves Eve and this person is blond, (1) is true. If this person is not blond, (1) clearly is false. But what should we say about (1) if no one loves Eve, or more than one do?

If no one, or more than one love Eve, we surely can't count (1) as true. If we insist that every sentence is true or false, and since (1) can't be true if none or more than one love Eve, we will have to count (1) as false under these conditions. Thinking about (1) in this way results in transcribing it as

    (1a) $(\exists x!)(Lxe \ \& \ Bx).$

which is true if exactly one person loves Eve and is blond, and is false if such a person exists and is not blond **or** if there are none or more than one who love Eve.

From a perspective wider than predicate logic with identity we do not have to take this stand. We could, instead, suggest that there being exactly one person who loves Eve provides a precondition for, or a *Presupposition* of, the claim that the one who loves Eve is blond. This means that the condition that there is exactly one person who loves Eve must hold for (1) to be either true or false. If the presupposition holds—if there is exactly one person who loves Eve—then (1) is true if this unique person is blond and false if he or she is not blond. If the presupposition fails—if there is none or more than one who love Eve—then we say that (1) is neither true nor false. One can design more complex systems of logic in which to formalize this idea, but predicate logic with identity does not have these resources. Hence, (1a) is the best transcription we can provide.

Grammatically, 'the one who loves Eve' functions as a term. It is supposed to refer to something, and we use the expression in a sentence by attributing some property or relation to the thing purportedly referred to. We can mirror this idea in predicate logic by introducing a new kind of expression, (The **u**)**P**(**u**), which, when there is a unique **u** which is **P**, refers to that object. We would then like to use (The **u**)**P**(**u**) like a name or other constant term in combination with predicates. Thus we would transcribe (1) as

(1b)   B(The x)Lxe.

Read this as the predicate 'B' applied to the "term" '(The x)Lxe'. 'The one who loves Eve' and '(The x)Lxe' are called *Definite Descriptions*, respectively in English and in logic. Traditionally, the definite description forming operator, (The **u**), is written with an upside-down Greek letter iota, 'ι', like this: (ι**u**)**P**(**u**).

Here are some examples of definite descriptions transcribed into predicate logic:

   a)   The present king of France: (The x)Kx.
   b)   The blond son of Eve: (The x)(Bx & Sxe).
   c)   The one who loves all who love themselves: (The x)($\forall$y)(Lyy $\supset$ Lxy).

But we can't treat (The x)**P**(x) like an ordinary term, because sometimes such "terms" don't refer. Consequently, we need a rewriting rule, just as we did for subscripted predicates and '($\exists$x!)', to show that expressions like (1b) should be rewritten as (1a):

> Rule for rewriting *Definite Descriptions Using '(The **u**)'*:   **Q**[(The **u**)**P**(**u**)] is shorthand for ($\exists$**u**!)[**P**(**u**) & **Q**(**u**)], where **P**(**u**) and **Q**(**u**) are open formulas with **u** the only free variable.

This treatment of definite descriptions works very smoothly, given the limitations of predicate logic. It does, however, introduce an oddity about the negations of sentences which use a definite description. How should we understand

(2)   The one who loves Eve is not blond.

Anyone who holds a presupposition account will have no trouble with (2): They will say that if the presupposition holds, so that there is just one person who loves Eve, then (2) is true if the person is not blond and false if he or she is blond. If the presupposition fails, then (2), just as (1), is neither true nor false.

But what should we say in predicate logic about the transcription of
(2)? We can see (2) as the negation of (1) in two very different ways. We
can see (2) as the definite description '(The x)Lxe applied to the negated
predicate '~B' in which case we have

(2a) ~B(The x)Lxe, rewritten as ($\exists$x!)(Lxe & ~Bx).

When we think of (1) and (2) this way, we say that the definite description
has *Primary Occurrence* or *Wide Scope*.
Or we can see (2) as the negation of the whole transcribed sentence:

(2b) ~[B(The x)Lxe], rewritten as ~($\exists$x!)(Lxe & Bx).

Thinking of (1) and (2) in this second way, we say that the definite description has *Secondary Occurrence* or *Narrow Scope*. When transcribing an
English sentence with a definite description into logic, you will always
have to make a choice between treating the definite description as having
primary or secondary occurrence.

EXERCISES

Transcription Guide

a:	Adam	Dx: x is dark-eyed
e:	Eve	Fxy: x is a father of y
c:	Cain	Sxy: x is a son of y
Bx:	x is blond	Cxy: x is more clever than y
		Lxy: x loves y

9–12. Transcribe the following. Expressions of the form (The **u**) and
($\exists$**u**!) should not appear in your final answers.

  a) The son of Eve is blond.
  b) The son of Eve is more clever than Adam.
  c) Adam is the father of Cain.
  d) Adam loves the son of Eve.
  e) Adam loves his son.
  f) Cain loves the blond.
  g) The paternal grandfather of Adam is dark-eyed.
  h) The son of Eve is the son of Adam.
  i) The blond is more clever than the dark-eyed one.
  j) The most clever son of Adam is the father of Eve.
  k) The son of the father of Eve is more clever than the father of the
      son of Adam.

9–13. Transcribe the negations of the sentences of exercise 9–12, once with the definite description having primary occurrence and once with secondary occurrence, indicating which transcription is which. Comment on how you think the notions of primary and secondary occurrence should work when a sentence has two definite descriptions.

CHAPTER SUMMARY EXERCISES

This chapter has introduced the following terms and ideas. Summarize them briefly.

a) Identity
b) Referent
c) Co-Referential
d) ($\exists \mathbf{u}!$)
e) Self-Identity
f) Extensional
g) Extensional Semantics
h) Rule $=$I for Derivations
i) Rule $=$E for Derivations
j) Rule $=$ for Trees
k) Rules $\neq$ for Trees
l) Reflexive Relation
m) Symmetric Relation
n) Transitive Relation
o) Equivalence Relation
p) Function
q) One Place Function
r) Two and Three Place Functions
s) Arguments of a Function
t) Function Symbols
u) Term
v) Constant, or Constant Term
w) Rules for Function Symbols in Derivations
x) Rules for Function Symbols in Trees
y) Presupposition
z) Definite Description
aa) Rewrite Rule for Definite Descriptions
bb) Primary Occurrence (Wide Scope) of a Definite Description
cc) Secondary Occurrence (Narrow Scope) of a Definite Description

Metatheory

The Basic Concepts

10

10-1. OBJECT LANGUAGE AND METALANGUAGE

In metatheory, we analyze and prove facts **about** logic, as opposed to **using** logic. To proceed clearly, we must bear in mind that the language in which we do logic is distinct from the language in which we study logic—that is, that the language of sentence and predicate logic is distinct from English. The distinction has been implicit throughout the text. It is time to make this distinction explicit and give it a name.

Since the language of sentence and predicate logic is the language we study and talk about, we call it an *Object language.*

> An *Object Language* is a language we study and talk abut. Our object language is the language of sentence and predicate logic.

Our object language has an infinite stock of sentence letters, names, one place predicates, two place predicates, and in general, n-place predicates. (In section 15–5 we also add function symbols.)

We contrast our object language with the language, called a *Metalanguage*, which we use to talk about our object language. Our metalanguage is English, to which we add a few convenient items. Most of these you have already seen. For example, think about how we have been using boldface capital 'X' and 'Y' to range over sentences in the object language. In so doing, we are really using 'X' and 'Y' as a simple extension of English, as a new linguistic device which we use in talking about the lan-

157

guage of sentence and predicate logic. We have used 's', 't', 'u', 'v', 'P(u)', and 'R(u,v)' similarly. Since these are variables used in the metalanguage to range over object language sentences, names, variables, and open sentences, we call them *Metavariables*.

I will now add three more kinds of metavariables to be used as part of English in talking about our object language. I will use boldface script capitals '$\mathcal{X}$', '$\mathcal{Y}$', and '$\mathcal{Z}$' to talk generally about **sets** of object language sentences. A set of sentences is just a collection of one, two, or more sentences where the order of the sentences does not matter. I will also include among sets of sentences infinite sets, with infinitely many sentences in them, and the somewhat funny case of the *Empty Set*, that is, the degenerate case in which the set contains nothing.

Next, I will use '$\mathbf{I}$', '$\mathbf{J}$', . . . as metavariables ranging over interpretations. When, as in chapter 15, we will be concerned with predicate logic sentences, interpretations will be described by a generalization of the idea I introduced in chapter 2. For chapters 11 to 14, in which we will be concerned only with sentence logic, interpretations will just be assignments of truth values to atomic sentence letters, that is, specifications of conditions which determine truth values for sentence logic sentences. I will use '$\mathbf{I}$' and '$\mathbf{J}$' as part of English to talk generally about interpretations, as when I say that two sentences, **X** and **Y,** are logically equivalent if and only if, for each **I** which is an interpretation of both **X** and **Y,** either **X** and **Y** are both true in **I** or **X** and **Y** are both false in **I**.

As a last metavariable I will use '$\mathbf{T}$' to range over truth trees.

I will also add to English the special symbol '$\therefore$' as an abbreviation of the word 'Therefore'. $\mathcal{Z}\backslash\mathbf{X}$ stands for the argument which has sentences in the set $\mathcal{Z}$ as its premises and **X** as its conclusion. This is exactly what I have previously written as "$\mathcal{Z}$. Therefore **X**." I did not previously introduce '$\therefore$' as an abbreviation for 'therefore' because I wanted to be sure that you did not mistakenly think that '$\therefore$' was part of the object language. But now that we have made the object language/metalanguage distinction explicit, I can introduce '$\therefore$' as an abbreviation for 'therefore' and ask you to be careful to understand that '$\therefore$' is an abbreviation in English, not a connective of the object language we are studying. To summarize

A *Metalanguage* is a language, distinct from the object language, which we use to talk about the object language. Our metalanguage is English, augmented with metavariables as follows: '**X**', '**Y**', '**Z**', . . . range over object language sentences; '$\mathcal{X}$', '$\mathcal{Y}$', '$\mathcal{Z}$', . . . range over sets of object language sen-

---

*Only after typesetting made large-scale changes in type a practical impossibility, I learned that the compositor's capital boldface italic was almost indistinguishable from the roman boldface type. However, I have used $\mathcal{Z}$ everywhere as my metavariable for sets of sentences, with only two minor exceptions (where I use $\mathcal{W}$); and $\mathbf{Z}$ never occurs as a metavariable for sentences. By remembering that $\mathcal{Z}$ ranges over sets of sentences, I hope that the reader will be able to make the needed contrast. I regret not having provided a truly distinctive typeface.

tences*; 's', 't', . . . range over names in the object language; '**u**', '**v**', . . . range over variables of the object language; '**P(u)**' and '**R(u, v)**' . . . range over sentences of the object language in which **u** (or **u** and **v**) may be free; '**I**', '**J**', . . . range over interpretations; and '**T**' ranges over trees. We also use '∴' as an abbreviation for 'therefore' in the metalanguage, so that '**Z∴X**' stands for the argument with premises taken from the sentences in the set **Z** and conclusion the sentence **X**.

To understand better the interplay between object and metalanguage, you also need to understand the distinction between *Use* and *Mention*. Let's talk for a moment about Adam: In so doing I mention (that is, I refer to) this **person**. I might say about Adam that he is blond. Now, let us talk, not about the person, Adam, but about this person's **name**, 'Adam'. For example, I might say that 'Adam' is spelled with four letters. Note how I accomplished this. To talk about the name, I take the name and enclose it in single quotation marks. If I use the name without quotes, I use the name to mention (that is, to talk about) the person. If I use the name enclosed in quotes, I use the quoted name—really a name of the name—to mention (talk about) the name.

Throughout this text I have tried hard (but not always successfully!) to observe the distinction between use and mention. Thus, when in the text I have talked about an object language sentence, such as 'A&B', I have been careful always to enclose it in quotes. When such a sentence is displayed as an example, like this

 A&B

I omit the quotes. This is because of the convention, universal in logic and philosophy, that offsetting a formal expression functions just like quoting it, so that you know that we are talking about what has been displayed rather than using what is displayed to make a statement or reference.

In contrast, when I use a metavariable I do not put quotes around it. Thus I might say that if the sentence **X** is a conjunction, then **X** contains the symbol '&'. Notice that there are no quotes around the boldface letter. This is because I was **using** it to make a general statement, not mentioning the letter. In contrast, I do use quotes when I **mention** (that is, talk about) the boldface letter, as in the following statement: In the previous example I used the symbol '**X**' as an example of how metavariables can be used.

Now let's look at a problematic case. Suppose I say that any sentence of the form **X&Y** is true just in case **X** and **Y** are both true. I have, writing in the metalanguage, used '**X**' and '**Y**' to make a general statement. But in so doing I used the expression '**X&Y**', which contains the object language symbol '&'. Furthermore, in some sense I made a statement **about** the symbol '&'. I didn't assert a conjunction. Instead, I talked about all sentences which have '&' as their main connective.

Here's the problem. I was tacitly talking **about** the symbol '&'. But I didn't quote it. I really should have used quotes around '&'. But it's not clear how I could do that without putting quotes around 'X' and 'Y', which I was using and not mentioning!

Philosophers have invented some fancy notation to make more precise what is going on in such cases. But introducing this further notation would be to pass the point of diminishing returns for our present needs. Instead, I am simply going to ask you to understand that such "mixed" cases of use and mention, formed with metalanguage boldface variables and object language connectives, are a device which I use to talk generally about all sentences of the indicated form.

I must mention one further twist in our conventions. Our object language provides a very precise and compact way of expressing truth functional facts. It would be a shame not to be able to use this compact notation in our metalanguage and to have to write everything out in imprecise, long-winded English. So we will occasionally allow ourselves the luxury of using expressions of the object language to make statements as part of the metalanguage. You can think of the metalanguage, English, as incorporating or being extended by a copy of the object language.

You can always tell when I talk about, or mention, logical notation as part of the object language, for in these cases I will always quote or display the expressions. When I use, as opposed to mention, logical notation as part of the metalanguage, the notation will not be quoted. Furthermore, when I use, as opposed to mention, logical notation as part of the metalanguage, I will use the notation with metalanguage variables. You can spot these metalanguage variables as belonging to the metalanguage because I always write them in boldface. Strictly speaking, my notation does not distinguish between use of logical notation in the metalanguage

---

EXERCISES

10–1. For each of the underlined expressions, say whether the expression is being used as part of the metalanguage, mentioned as part of the metalanguage, used as part of the object language, or mentioned as part of the object language.

 a) If there is a proof of a sentence <u>**X**</u>, then there is a proof of the sentence **X**v**Y**.
 b) The sentence '<u>(∀x)(Bx ∨ ~Bx)</u>' is a logical truth.
 c) Any sentence of the form <u>(∀**u**)[**P**(**u**) ∨ ~**P**(**u**)]</u> is a logical truth.
 d) '<u>**Y**</u>' is a metavariable.

and the mixed use-mention cases which I described two paragraphs back. But in practice this imprecision causes no confusion.

10–2. SYNTAX AND SEMANTICS

Much of metatheory deals with connections between syntax and semantics, another distinction which I have tacitly observed throughout the text. A fact of *Syntax* is a fact which concerns symbols or sentences insofar as the fact can be determined from the **form** of the symbols or sentences, from the way they are written. The point is that facts of syntax do not depend on what the symbols mean.

A fact of *Semantics,* on the other hand, concerns the referents, interpretation, or (insofar as we understand this notion) the meaning of symbols and sentences. In particular, semantics has to do with the referents of expressions, the truth of sentences, and the relations between various cases of these.

Here are some examples: Syntactic facts include the fact that 'A&B' is a well-formed sentence of sentence logic, that 'AB&' is not a well-formed sentence, and that 'A&B' is a conjunction. Syntactic facts include more general facts which can be determined from form alone, such as the fact that the derivation rule &E and the truth tree rule & apply to any sentence of the form **X&Y** and that any sentence of the form **XvY** is derivable from (that is, there is a proof from) a sentence of the form ~**X** ⊃ **Y**.

One thing to keep in mind is that whether or not a given string of sentences counts as a formal proof (a derivation or a tree) is a syntactic fact. All the rules of proof have been carefully stated so that they appeal only to facts about how sentences are written, not about how they are interpreted. Whether or not a string of sentences qualifies as a proof depends only on the form, not on the content of the sentences. To see this clearly, consider that you could program a computer to check and construct proofs. The computer need not know **anything** about how the sentences are interpreted. For example, the computer need not know that you are supposed to think of '&' as meaning 'and'. It need only be programmed so that if a sentence of the form **X&Y** appears on a derivation or tree, then below this sentence it can write both the sentences **X** and **Y**.

Examples of semantic facts include the fact that any interpretation which makes 'A⊃B' true makes '~B⊃~A' true, that '(∀x)(Px ∨ ~Px)' is true in all interpretations, and that '(∀x)Px' is true in some interpretations and false in others. Semantic facts include more general facts such as the fact that any existentially quantified sentence is true in an interpretation if one of its substitution instances is true in the interpretation.

To summarize the distinction between syntactic and semantic facts

Facts of *Syntax* are facts having to do with the form of expressions. Syntactic facts contrast with facts of *Semantics* which have to do with the truth, reference, and the meaning of expressions.

EXERCISES

10–2. Which of the following facts are syntactic facts and which semantic facts?

    a)   Any interpretation which makes '$(\forall x)(Ax \ \& \ Bx)$' true makes '$(\forall x)Ax$' true

    b)   The expression '$A\&B\lor C$' is not a well-formed sentence, though it would be if parentheses were put around the '$A\&B$'.

    c)   A sentence of the form $\sim\sim \mathbf{X}$ can be derived from a sentence of the form $\mathbf{X}$.

    d)   In some interpretations 'a' and 'b' have the same referent. In some interpretations they do not.

    e)   If $\mathbf{X}$ and $\mathbf{Y}$ are well-formed sentences, then so is their conjunction.

    f)   If the argument $\mathbf{X}\backslash\mathbf{Y}$ is valid, then so is the argument $\sim\mathbf{Y}\backslash\sim\mathbf{X}$.

    g)   A model of a set of sentences (that is, an interpretation in which each sentence in the set is true) is a model for any subset of the set (that is, any smaller set of sentences all the sentences of which are contained in the original set).

    h)   If there is a proof of the sentence $\mathbf{X}$ from the sentences in the set $\mathbf{Z}$, then there is a proof of $\mathbf{X}$ from any superset of $\mathbf{Z}$, that is, any set which contains all the sentences of $\mathbf{Z}$ as well as one or more additional sentences.

10–3. SOUNDNESS AND COMPLETENESS

Students often have difficulty appreciating the difference between the question of whether an argument, $\mathbf{Z}\backslash\mathbf{X}$, is valid (a semantic question) and the question of whether there is a proof from $\mathbf{Z}$ to $\mathbf{X}$ (a syntactic question). And no wonder! The syntactic rules of proof have been carefully crafted so that there is a proof from $\mathbf{Z}$ to $\mathbf{X}$ if and only if the argument, $\mathbf{Z}\backslash\mathbf{X}$, is valid. Of course, we have done this so that we can use proofs to ascertain validity. But this must not obscure the fact that *Derivability*—that is, the existence of a proof—is one thing and validity is another. That these two very different concepts go together is something we must demonstrate. Indeed, this fundamental result about logic is what the rest of this book is about.

To help in talking about these ideas, we will use two new abbreviations in the metalanguage. (The following definitions also use the abbreviation 'iff', which is just shorthand for the metalanguage expression 'if and only if'.)

> D1: $Z \vdash X$ iff **X** is *Derivable* from **Z**, that is, iff there is a formal proof of **X** using only sentences in **Z**.
>
> D2: $Z \vDash X$ iff the argument $Z \backslash X$ is valid, that is, iff every interpretation which makes all of the sentences in **Z** true also makes **X** true.

The symbol '$\vdash$' is called the *Single Turnstyle*. $Z \vdash X$ asserts that a **syntactic** relation holds between the sentences in the set of sentences, **Z**, and the sentence, **X**, that the latter is derivable from the former. The symbol '$\vDash$' is called the *Double Turnstyle*. $Z \vDash X$ asserts that a **semantic** relation holds between the set of sentences, **Z**, and the sentence, **X**, that any interpretation which makes all of the sentences in **Z** true will also make **X** true.

Here's a mnemonic to help remember which turnstyle is which. '$\vDash$' has *m*ore bars and so has to do with *m*eaning. '$\vdash$' has *l*ess bars and so has to do with the form of *l*anguage.

Using the turnstyle notation, we can express the close relation between derivability and validity in two convenient parts:

> D3: A system of formal proof is *Sound* iff for all **Z**, **X**, if $Z \vdash X$, then $Z \vDash X$.

To say that a system of formal proof is sound is to say that whenever you have a proof from **Z** to **X**, then any interpretation which makes all of the sentences in **Z** true also makes **X** true.

> D4: A system of formal proof is *Complete* iff for all **Z**, **X**, if $Z \vDash X$, then $Z \vdash X$.

To say that a system of formal proof is complete is to say that in every case of an argument, $Z \backslash X$, which is valid (that is, any interpretation which makes every sentence in **Z** true also makes **X** true), there exists a proof from **Z** to **X**. Completeness means that there is a proof in every case in which there ought to be a proof.

Once more, derivability and validity are distinct concepts. But derivability has been set up so that it can be used as a surefire test of validity. To give a crude analogy, derivability is like the litmus test for acids. If you put a piece of litmus paper in a liquid and the paper turns red, you know that the liquid is an acid. If the litmus paper does not turn red, the liquid is not an acid. Derivability is a kind of litmus test for validity. Proving that the test works, proving soundness and completeness, is the fundamental metatheoretical result in logic.

This litmus test analogy is a good way to emphasize the fact that derivability and validity are distinct but related ideas. However, I must be sure that the analogy does not mislead you in the following respect. Derivability is a surefire test for validity in the sense that if there is a proof, then the corresponding argument is valid, and if an argument is valid, then there exists a proof which establishes that validity. But there may not be any surefire way to establish whether or not such a proof exists! We might look for a proof from **Z** to **X** until the cows come home and still not know for sure whether or not a proof exists.

In predicate logic there is no mechanical means to determine whether or not a proof from **Z** to **X** exists, no means guaranteed to give a definite yes or no answer in some finite number of steps. This fact about predicate logic is known as *Undecidability*, and constitutes a second fundamental metatheoretical result. (Sentence logic is decidable.) If you learned the tree method, I can give you a hint of what is involved by reminding you of the problem of infinite trees. The same fact will turn up for derivations when we get to chapter 15. However, further study of undecidability goes beyond what you will study in this text.

EXERCISES

10–3. Some one might propose a set of rules of inference different from our natural deduction or truth tree rules. Explain what is involved in such a new set of rules being *Unsound* (not sound) or *Incomplete* (not complete).

In fact, logicians have proposed many, many sets of inferential rules. Some such sets are sound and complete, some are not. Whenever someone proposes a new set of inference rules it is important to determine whether or not the rules are sound and complete.

Exercises 10–4 to 10–6 concern the idea of *Rule Soundness*. To say that an individual rule of inference is sound is to say that if the rule is applied to a sentence or sentences which is (are) true in a case, then the sentence which the rule licenses you to draw is also true in that case. We can state the rules of inference for derivations using the turnstyle notation, and we can also use this notation to assert the soundness of these rules. For example, the rule &I is expressed by saying that if $Z \vdash X$ and $Z \vdash Y$, then $Z \vdash X \& Y$. We can state, in one way, that the rule &I is sound by stating that if $Z \vDash X$ and $Z \vDash Y$, then $Z \vDash X \& Y$.

10–4. Show that the rule &I is sound.

10–5. State the other primitive rules for derivations using the turnstyle notation and show that they are sound.

10–6. Consider the following new rules for derivations. Determine which are sound and which are not. In each case, give an informal demonstration of your conclusion about the rules.

a) If $Z \vdash X \supset Y$ and $Z \vdash Y$, then $Z \vdash X$.
b) If $Z \vdash X \equiv Y$ and $Z \vdash \sim X$, then $\vdash \sim Y$.
c) If $Z \vdash [(\forall u)P(u) \lor (\forall u)Q(u)]$, then $Z \vdash (\forall u)[P(u) \lor Q(u)]$.
d) If $Z \vdash (\exists u)P(u)$, then $Z \vdash P(s)$.
e) If $Z \vdash [(\exists u)P(u) \& (\exists u)Q(u)]$, then $Z \vdash (\exists u)[P(u) \& Q(u)]$.

10–7. Refresh your memory of the truth table method of establishing validity in sentence logic (see exercise 4–2 in chapter 4 of volume I). Then show that this method provides a decision procedure for sentence logic. That is, show that, given a sentence logic argument, the truth table method is guaranteed in a finite number of steps to give you a yes or no answer to the question of whether or not the argument is valid.

10–4. SOME FURTHER NOTATION AND DEFINITIONS

Some further notation and definitions will prove very useful in the following chapters, and will also give you a chance to practice the concepts of the last three sections.

First, here's an obvious and trivial extension of the turnstyle notation, a fussy logician's point which you might not even notice. For example, if I write '$Z \vdash X$', I have used Z as a metavariable over **sets** of sentences. What if I want to look at the special case in which Z contains just one sentence? Then I may just use 'Z', a metavariable over individual sentences, writing '$Z \vdash X$'. Or, if I want more explicitly to list the sentences that come before the turnstyle, I may do just that, explicitly giving the list, for example, writing $W,Z \vdash X$. I may use the same latitude in notation with the double turnstyle.

A little less trivially, I have glossed over an important point about using the single turnstyle. '$Z \vdash X$' means that there is a proof of X from the sentences in the set Z. But by proof, do I mean a derivation or a closed tree? It is important to keep separate these very distinct kinds of formal proof. Strictly speaking, I should use one kind of turnstyle, say, '$\vdash_d$' to mean derivations. Thus '$Z \vdash_d X$' means that there is a derivation which uses premises in Z and has X as its last line. And I should use a second kind of turnstyle, say, '$\vdash_t$', to mean trees. Thus '$Z \vdash_t X$' means that there is a closed tree of which the initial sentences are $\sim X$ and sentences taken from Z. Other systems of formal proof (and there are **many** others) must be distinguished from these with further subscripts on the single turnstyle. When there is any danger of confusion about what kind of proof is in question, we must use a disambiguating subscript on the turnstyle. Usually, context will make it quite plain which kind of proof is in question, In which case we may omit the subscript.

EXERCISE

10–8. Do we need corresponding subscripts on the double turnstyle? Explain why or why not.

Here is one more refinement. How should we understand the turnstyle notation when the set Z has infinitely many sentences? In the case of '$Z \vDash X$' this should be clear enough. This asserts that every interpretation which makes **all** of the infinitely many sentences in **Z** true also makes **X** true. But what do we mean by '$Z \vdash X$'? A formal proof can use only finitely many sentences. So by '$Z \vdash X$' we mean that there is a proof of **X** each premise of which is a sentence in the set **Z**. This formulation leaves it open whether all of the sentences in **Z** get used as premises. If **Z** is infinite, only finitely many sentences can be used in a proof from **Z**. If **Z** is finite, all or only some of the sentences in **Z** may get used. Reread definition D1 and be sure that you understand 'formal proof of **X using only sentences in Z**', as just explained, to mean a proof which uses any number of, but not necessarily all, the sentences in **Z** as premises. We even allow the case of using no premises at all. Any proof of a sentence, **X**, from no premises makes $Z \vdash X$ true for any set of sentences, **Z**.

EXERCISES

10–9. '$Z \subset W$' means that every sentence in **Z** is a sentence in **W**. We say that **Z** is a *Subset of W*. Show that if $Z \vdash X$ and $Z \subset W$, then $W \vdash X$.
10–10. Show that if $Z \vDash X$ and $Z \subset W$, then $W \vDash X$.
10–11. If **Z** is the empty set, we write $\vdash X$ for $Z \vdash X$ and $\vDash X$ for $Z \vDash X$. Explain what $\vdash X$ and $\vDash X$ mean.

If you have studied truth trees, you have already encountered (in section 9–2, volume I, and section 8–1, this volume) the idea of a *Model* of a set of sentences. It's not complicated: An interpretation, **I**, is a model of a set of sentences, **Z**, iff every sentence in **Z** is true in **I**. That is, a model, **I**, of a set of sentences, **Z**, makes all the sentences in **Z** true. For example, consider the truth value assignment, **I** which makes 'A' true, 'B' false, and 'C' true. **I** is a model for the set of sentences $\{(A \lor B),(\sim B \supset C)\}$, but is not a model for the set of sentences $\{(A \& \sim B),C,(B \equiv C)\}$. Be sure you understand why this is so. To check, work out the truth values of each sentence in the two sets in the truth value assignment, **I**, and apply the definition of model just given.

In the following chapter we will use the notion of a model so often that it's worth introducing an abbreviation:

> D5: '**Mod**' is a predicate in the metalanguage (an abbreviation in English), defined as **Mod(I,Z)** iff all the sentences in the set **Z** are true in the interpretation, **I**. If **Mod(I,Z)**, **I** is said to be a *Model* for the sentences in **Z**. **I** is also said to *Satisfy* the sentences in **Z**.

As with the turnstyle notation, we can use metavariables for sentences, such as '**Z**', where the metavariable, '**Z**', for sets of sentences occurs in the definition of '**Mod**'.

We will also lean heavily on the notations of consistency and inconsistency, already introduced in exercise 7–8 and section 9–2 (in volume I) and in sections 6–3 and 8–1 (in this volume). To get ready for this work, and to practice this chapter's ideas, here is a pair of equivalent definitions for each of these concepts. (The slash through the double turnstyle in D6′ means just what a slash through an equal sign means—the double turnstyle relation does **not** hold.)

> D6: The set **Z** of sentences is *Consistent* iff (∃**I**)**Mod(I,Z)**.

> D6′: The set **Z** of sentences is *Consistent* iff **Z**⊭A&~A.

> D7: The set Z of sentences is *Inconsistent* iff (∀**I**)~**Mod(I,Z)**, that is, iff **Z** is not consistent, that is, iff there is no model for all the sentences in **Z**.

> D7′: The set Z of sentences is *Inconsistent* iff **Z**⊨A&~A.

EXERCISES

10–12. Show that D6 and D6′ are equivalent.

10–13. Show that D7 and D7′ are equivalent.

10–14. Explain why the notions of consistency and inconsistency are semantic and not syntactic notions. Modify definitions D6′ and D7′ to provide corresponding syntactic notions, and label your new definitions D6″ and D7″. You will then have a pair of notions, *Semantic Consistency* and *Syntactic Consistency*, and a second pair, *Semantic Inconsistency* and *Syntactic Inconsistency*. You must always carefully distinguish between these semantic and syntactic ideas. Whenever I speak about consistency and inconsistency without specifying whether it is the semantic or syntactic notion, I will always mean the semantic notion.

10–15. What do you think the relation is between semantic and syntactic consistency, and between semantic and syntactic inconsistency? What would you guess is the connection between this question and the ideas of soundness and completeness? Write a paragraph informally explaining these connections as best you can.

CHAPTER CONCEPTS

Here are the important concepts which I have introduced and discussed in this chapter. Review them carefully to be sure you understand them.

a) Object Language
b) Metalanguage
c) Metavariable
d) Use
e) Mention
f) Syntactic Fact
g) Semantic Fact
h) Derivability
i) ⊢
j) ⊨
k) Soundness
l) Completeness
m) Set of sentences
n) Subset
o) Model
p) Consistency
q) Inconsistency

Mathematical Induction

<u>**11**</u>

The point of metatheory is to establish facts about logic, as distinguished from using logic. Sentence and predicate logic themselves become the object of investigation. Of course, in studying logic, we must use logic itself. We do this by expressing and using the needed logical principles in our metalangauge. It turns out, however, that to prove all the things we want to show about logic, we need **more** than just the principles of logic. At least we need more if by 'logic' we mean the principles of sentence and predicate logic which we have studied. We will need an additional principle of reasoning in mathematics called *Mathematical Induction*.

You can get the basic idea of mathematical induction by an analogy. Suppose we have an infinite number of dominos, a first, a second, a third, and so on, all set up in a line. Furthermore, suppose that each domino has been set up close enough to the next so that if the prior domino falls over, it will knock over its successor. In other words, we know that, for all n, if the nth domino falls then the n + 1 domino will fall also. Now you know what will happen if you push over the first domino: They will all fall.

To put the idea more generally, suppose that we have an unlimited or infinite number of cases, a first case, a second, a third, and so on. Suppose that we can show that the first case has a certain property. Furthermore, suppose that we can show, for all n, that if the nth case has the property,

169

then the n + 1 case has the property also. Mathematical induction then licenses us to conclude that all cases have the property.

If you now have the intuitive idea of induction, you are well enough prepared to read the informal sections in chapters 12 and 13. But to master the details of the proofs in what follows you will need to understand induction in more detail.

11–2. THE PRINCIPLE OF WEAK INDUCTION

Let's look at a more specific example. You may have wondered how many lines there are in a truth table with n atomic sentence letters. The answer is 2^n. But how do we prove that this answer is correct, that for all n, an n-letter truth table has 2^n lines?

If n = 1, that is, if there is just one sentence letter in a truth table, then the number of lines is $2 = 2^1$. So the generalization holds for the first case. This is called the *Basis Step* of the induction. We then need to do what is called the *Inductive Step*. We assume that the generalization holds for n. This assumption is called the *Inductive Hypothesis*. Then, using the inductive hypothesis, we show that the generalization holds for n + 1.

So let's assume (inductive hypothesis) that in an n-letter truth table there are 2^n lines. How many lines are there in a truth table obtained by adding one more letter? Suppose our new letter is 'A'. 'A' can be either true or false. The first two lines of the n + 1 letter truth table will be the first line of the n-letter table plus the specification that 'A' is true, followed by the first line of the n-letter table plus the specification that 'A' is false. The next two lines of the new table will be the second line of the old table, similarly extended with the two possible truth values of 'A'. In general, each line of the old table will give rise to two lines of the new table. So the new table has twice the lines of the old table, or $2^n \times 2 = 2^{n+1}$. This is what we needed to show in the inductive step of the argument.

We have shown that there are 2^n lines of an n-letter truth table when n = 1 (basis step). We have shown that if an n-letter table has 2^n lines, then an n + 1 letter table has 2^{n+1} lines. Our generalization is true for n = 1, and if it is true for any arbitrarily chosen n, then it is true for n + 1. The princple of mathematical induction then tells us we may conclude that it is true for all n.

We will express this principle generally with the idea of an *Inductive Property*. An inductive property is, strictly speaking, a property of integers. In an inductive argument we show that the integer 1 has the inductive property, and that for each integer n, if n has the inductive property, then the integer n + 1 has the inductive property. Induction then licenses us to conclude that all integers, n, have the inductive property. In the last example, *All n letter truth tables have exactly 2^n lines,* a proposition about the integer n, was our inductive property. To speak generally, I will use '**P**(n)' to talk about whatever inductive property might be in question:

Principle of Weak Induction

a) Let **P**(n) be some property which can be claimed to hold for (is defined for) the integers, n = 1, 2, 3, . . . (the *Inductive Property*).

b) Suppose we have proved **P**(1) (*Basis Step*).

c) Suppose we have proved, for any n, that if **P**(n), then **P**(n + 1) (*Inductive Step*, with the assumption of **P**(n), the *Inductive Hypothesis*).

d) Then you may conclude that **P**(n) holds for all n from 1 on.

e) If in the basis step we have proved **P**(i), we may conclude that **P**(n) holds for n = i, i + 1, i + 2,. . . . .

(e) simply says that our induction can really start from any integer, as long as the inductive property is defined from that integer onward. Often it is convenient to start from 0 instead of from 1, showing that **P**(n) holds for n = 0, 1, 2,. . . . .

Most of the inductions we will do involve facts about sentences. To get you started, here is a simple example. The conclusion is so obvious that, ordinarily, we would not stop explicitly to prove it. But it provides a nice illustration and, incidentally, illustrates the fact that many of the generalizations which seem obvious to us really depend on mathematical induction.

Let's prove that if the only kind of connective which occurs in a sentence logic sentence is '~', then there is a truth value assignment under which the sentence is true and another in which it is false. (For short, we'll say that the sentence "can be either true or false.") Our inductive property will be: *All sentences with n occurrences of '~' and no other connectives can be either true or false.* A standard way of expressing an important element here is to say that we will be *doing the induction on the number of connectives,* a strategy for which you will have frequent use.

We restrict attention to sentences, **X,** in which no connectives other than '~' occur. Suppose (basis case, with n = 0) that **X** has no occurrences of '~'. Then **X** is an atomic sentence letter which can be assigned either t or f. Suppose (inductive hypothesis for the inductive step) that all sentences with exactly n occurrences of '~' can be either true or false. Let **Y** be an arbitrary sentences with n + 1 occurrences of '~'. Then **Y** has the form ~**X,** where **X** has exactly n occurrences of '~'. By the inductive hypothesis, **X** can be either true or false. In these two cases, ~**X,** that is, **Y,** is, respectively, false and true. Since **Y** can be any sentence with n + 1 occurrences of '~', we have shown that the inductive property holds for n + 1, completing the inductive argument.

EXERCISES

11–1. By a *Restricted Conjunctive Sentence*, I mean one which is either an atomic sentence or is a conjunction of an atomic sentence with another restricted conjunctive sentence. Thus the sentences 'A' and '[C&(A&B)]&D' are restricted conjunctive sentences. The sentence 'A &[(C&D)&(H&G)]' is not, because the component, '(C&D)&(H&G)', fails to be a conjunction one of the components of which is an atomic sentence letter.

Here is a rigorous definition of this kind of sentence:

    a)   Any atomic sentence letter is a restricted conjunctive sentence.
    b)   Any atomic sentence letter conjoined with another restricted conjunctive sentence is again a restricted conjunctive sentence.
    c)   Only such sentences are restricted conjunctive sentences.

Such a definition is called an *Inductive Definition.*

Use weak induction to prove that a restricted conjunctive sentence is true iff all the atomic sentence letters appearing in it are true.

11–2. Prove that the formula

$$1 + 2 + 3 + \ldots + n = n(n + 1)/2$$

is correct for all n.

11–3. STRONG INDUCTION

Let's drop the restriction in exercise 11–1 and try to use induction to show that any sentence in which '&' is the only connective is true iff all its atomic sentence letters are true. We restrict attention to any sentence logic sentence, **X**, in which '&' is the only connective, and we do an induction on the number, n, of occurrences of '&'. If n = 0, **X** is atomic, and is true iff all its atomic sentence letters (namely, itself) are true. Next, let's assume, as inductive hypothesis, that any sentence, **X**, in which there are exactly n occurrences of '&' is true iff all its atomic sentence letters are true. You should try to use the inductive hypothesis to prove that the same is true of an arbitrary sentence, **Y**, with n + 1 occurrences of '&'.

If you think you succeeded, you must have made a mistake! There is a problem here. Consider, for example, the sentence '(A&B)&(C&D)'. It has three occurrences of '&'. We would like to prove that it has the inductive property, relying on the inductive hypothesis that all sentences with two occurrences of '&' have the inductive property. But we can't do that by appealing to the fact that the components, '(A&B)' and '(C&D)', have the inductive property. The inductive hypothesis allows us to appeal only to components which have two occurrences of '&' in them, but the components '(A&B)' and '(C&D)' have only one occurrence of '&' in them.

The problem is frustrating, because in doing an induction, by the time we get to case n, we have proved that the inductive property also holds for **all** previous cases. So we should be able to appeal to the fact that the inductive property holds, not just for n, but for all previous cases as well. In fact, with a little cleverness one can apply weak induction to get around this problem. But, more simply, we can appeal to another formulation of mathematical induction:

> *Weak Induction, Strong Formulation:*   Exactly like weak induction, except in the inductive step assume as inductive hypothesis that $P(i)$ holds for all $i \leq n$, and prove that $P(n + 1)$.

EXERCISE

11-3. Using the strong formulation of weak induction, prove that any sentence logic sentence in which '&' is the only connective is true iff all its atomic sentence letters are true.

You could have done the last problem with yet another form of induction:

> *Strong Induction:*   Suppose that an inductive property, $P(n)$, is defined for $n = 1, 2, 3, \ldots$. Suppose that for arbitrary n we use, as our inductive hypothesis, that $P(n)$ holds for all $i < n$; and from that hypothesis we prove that $P(n)$. Then we may conclude that $P(n)$ holds for all n from $n = 1$ on.

If $P(n)$ is defined from $n = 0$ on, or if we start from some other value of n, the conclusion holds for that value of n onward.

Strong induction looks like the strong formulation of weak induction, except that we do the inductive step for all $i < n$ instead of all $i \leq n$. You are probably surprised to see no explicit statement of a basis step in the statement of strong induction. This is because the basis step is actually covered by the inductive step. If we are doing the induction from $n = 1$ onward, how do we establish $P(i)$ for all $i < 1$? There aren't any cases of $i < 1$! When $n = 1$, the inductive hypothesis holds vacuously. In other words, when $n = 1$, the inductive hypothesis gives us no facts to which to appeal. So the only way in which to establish the inductive step when $n = 1$ is just to prove that $P(1)$. Consequently, the inductive step really covers the case of the basis step. Similar comments apply if we do the induction from n = 0 onward, or if we start from some other integer.

You may be wondering about the connections among the three forms of induction. Weak induction and weak induction in its strong formulation are equivalent. The latter is simply much easier to use in problems such as the last one. Many textbooks use the name 'strong induction' for what I have called 'weak induction, strong formulation'. This is a mistake. Strong induction is the principle I have called by that name. It is truly a stronger principle than weak induction, though we will not use its greater strength in any of our work. As long as we restrict attention to induction on the finite integers, strong and weak induction are equivalent. Strong induction shows its greater strength only in applications to something called "transfinite set theory," which studies the properties of mathematical objects which are (in some sense) greater than all the finite integers.

Since, for our work, all three principles are equivalent, the only difference comes in ease of use. For most applications, the second or third formulation will apply most easily, with no real difference between them. So I will refer to both of them, loosely, as "strong induction." You simply need to specify, when doing the inductive step, whether your inductive hypothesis assumes $P(i)$ for all $i < n$, on the basis of which you prove $P(n)$, or whether you assume $P(i)$ for all $i \leq n$, on the basis of which you prove $P(n + 1)$. In either case, you will, in practice, have to give a separate proof for the basis step.

I should mention one more pattern of argument, one that is equivalent to strong induction:

> *Least Number Principle:* To prove that $P(n)$, for all integers n, assume that there is some least value of n, say m, for which $P(m)$ fails and derive a contradiction.

The least number principle applies the reductio argument strategy. We want to show that, for all n, $P(n)$. Suppose that this is not so. Then there is some collection of values of n for which $P(n)$ fails. Let m be the least such value. Then we know that for all $i < m$, $P(i)$ holds. We then proceed to use this fact to show that, after all, $P(m)$ must hold, providing the contradiction. You can see that this form of argument really does the same work as strong induction: We produce a general argument, which works for any value of m, which shows that if for all $i < m$ $P(i)$ holds, then $P(m)$ must hold also.

You will notice in exercises 11–7 to 11–9 that you are proving things which in the beginning of Volume I we simply took for granted. Again, this illustrates how some things we take for granted really turn on mathematical induction.

EXERCISES

11-4. Prove that any sentence logic sentence in which 'v' is the only connective is true iff at least one of its atomic sentence letters is true.

11-5. Consider any sentence logic sentence, **X**, in which '&' and 'v' are the only connectives. Prove that for any such sentence, there is an interpretation which makes it true and an interpretation which makes it false. Explain how this shows that '&' and 'v', singly and together, are not expressively complete for truth functions, as this idea is explained in section 3-4, (volume I).

11-6. Consider any sentence logic sentence, **X**, in which '~' does not appear (so that '&', 'v', '⊃', and '≡' are the only connectives). Prove that for any such sentence there is an interpretation which makes **X** true. Explain how this shows that '&', 'v', '⊃', and '≡' are, singly and together, not expressively complete for truth functions.

11-7. Prove for all sentence logic sentences, **X**, and all interpretations, **I**, that either **I** makes **X** true or **I** makes **X** false, but not both.

11-8. Prove for all sentence logic sentences, **X**, that if two truth value assignments, **I** and **I'**, agree on all the atomic sentence letters in **X**, then **I** and **I'** assign **X** the same truth value.

11-9. Prove the law of substitution of logical equivalents for sentence logic.

CHAPTER CONCEPTS

In reviewing this chapter, be sure you understand clearly the following ideas:

    a) Weak Induction
    b) Inductive Property
    c) Basis Step
    d) Inductive Hypothesis
    e) Inductive Step
    f) Induction on the Number of Connectives
    g) Strong Formulation of Weak Induction
    h) Strong Induction
    i) Least Number Principle

Soundness and Completeness for Sentence Logic Trees

12

12–1. PRELIMINARIES

This chapter will explain the soundness and completeness of sentence logic for the tree method. Section 12–2 gives an informal statement which you will be able to follow without having studied more than the first short section of chapter 11, on mathematical induction. Section 12–3 gives full details.

Before getting started, I want to make a general point which will be useful in discussing both trees and derivations. I am going to make a statement which uses a new bit of notation. '∪' indicates set union. That is, $Z \cup W$ is the set consisting of all the members of the set Z together with the members of the set W. Also, if X is a sentence, $\{X\}$ is the set which has X as its only member. Now, to say that the $Z\backslash X$ is valid, that is, that $Z \vDash X$, is to say that every interpretation which makes all the sentences in Z true also makes X true. Keep in mind that X is true in an interpretation iff $\sim X$ is false in that interpretation. Consequently

L1: $Z \vDash X$ iff $Z \cup \{\sim X\}$ is inconsistent.

(The 'L' in 'L1' stands for 'lemma'. A lemma is a statement which may not be of great interest in itself but which we prove because it will be useful in proving our main results.)

L1 shows that validity of an argument comes to the same thing as the inconsistency of a certain set of sentences, namely, the premises and negation of the conclusion of the argument. You will soon see that L1's equivalent formulation of validity provides a particularly convenient way to study soundness and completeness.

EXERCISE

12–1. Prove L1.

12–2. SOUNDNESS AND COMPLETENESS OF THE TREE METHOD: INFORMAL STATEMENT

Soundness and completeness tell us that there is an exact correspondence between a semantic concept—validity—and a corresponding syntactic concept—proofs. Let's be explicit about what counts as a proof in the tree method: Given some premises and a conclusion, a tree method proof is a closed tree (a tree with all its branches closed) which has the premises and negation of the conclusion as its initial sentences. Closed trees are the syntactic objects which need to correspond to the semantic concept of validity. So proving soundness and completeness for the tree method means proving that we have the right sort of correspondence between validity and closed trees.

To become clear on what correspondence we need, let's go back to the way I introduced the tree method. I said that, given an argument, $Z\backslash X$, the argument is valid just in case it has no counterexamples, that is, no interpretations in which the premises, Z, are all true and the conclusion, X, is false. I then went on to develop truth trees as a method of looking for counterexamples, a way which is guaranteed to find a counterexample if there is one. If the whole tree closes, there are no counterexamples, and we know the argument is valid. But a closed tree is what counts as a proof. So if there is a proof, the argument is valid. If you look back at definition D3 in chapter 10, you will see that this is what we call soundness.

On the other hand, if there is an open branch (and so no proof), there is a counterexample, and thus the argument is invalid. A little thinking indicates that the last statement is just completeness: "If no proof, then invalid" comes to the same as "If valid, then there is a proof," which is completeness, as defined by D4 in chapter 10. I have used the law of contraposition: $X \supset Y$ is logically equivalent to $\sim Y \supset \sim X$.

The first time through, this argument is bound to seem very slick. It is also incomplete: I have yet to prove that the truth tree method is guaranteed to find a counterexample if there is one.

To sort all of this out more carefully, we need to examine the connection between a counterexample and lemma L1. A counterexample to the argument Z\X is just an interpretation which shows the set of sentences, Z∪{~X} to be consistent. (Remember that such an interpretation is called a model of the set of sentences.) Now, look at lemma L1, and you will start to see that all this talk about counterexamples is just another way of saying what lemma L1 says.

EXERCISE

12–2. Show that lemma L1 is equivalent to the statement that an argument is valid iff it has no counterexamples.

Lemma L1 tells us that we can forget about validity and talk about consistency and inconsistency instead. Indeed, conceptually, the tree method is really a method for determining whether the initial sentences on a tree form a consistent set. It is a method which is guaranteed to find a model for a tree's initial sentences if there is one, thereby showing the set of sentences to be consistent. Conversely, if a set is inconsistent, it has no model, and a tree starting with the sentences in the set is bound to close.

The real work we have to do is to show that the tree method is guaranteed to find a model for a set of sentences if the set has a model. We'll worry later about connecting this up with validity—lemma L1 assures us that we will be able to do so. For now, we will connect the semantic concept of a model with the syntactic concept of an open branch. Remember that an open branch always represents an interpretation in which all sentences on the branch are true. Hence, if there is an open branch, there is an interpretation in which all the sentences on the branch, including the tree's initial sentences, are true.

Here is how we proceed: We will show that a finite set of sentences is consistent if and only if we always get an open branch on a finished tree which starts from the sentences in the set. Equivalently, a set is inconsistent if and only if we always get a closed tree if we start from the sentences in the set. This gives us the connection between a syntactic concept—open and closed trees—and a semantic concept—consistency and inconsistency. Lemma L1 tells us we will be able to connect the latter with validity and invalidity.

To keep track of how we will carry out this program, let's talk about it in terms of an example, say, the tree which results from using as initial sentences the sentences in the set {~(DvB), (A&B)v(C⊃D)}:

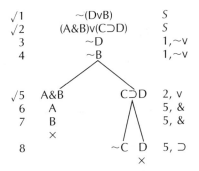

√1		~(DvB)	S
√2		(A&B)v(C⊃D)	S
3		~D	1,~v
4		~B	1,~v

√5   A&B   C⊃D   2, v
6   A   5, &
7   B   5, &
     ×
8   ~C   D   5, ⊃
                ×

We must first show that tree method is what I will call *Downwardly Adequate*. This means that the tree method applied to a consistent set of sentences always results in at least one open branch. Why is the tree method downwardly adequate? Remember that the rules are written so that when a rule is applied to a sentence, the rule instructs you to write, on separate branches, all the minimally sufficient ways of making the original sentence true. In effect, this means that, for any assignment of truth values to sentence letters which makes the original sentence true, all the sentences of at least one of the resulting stacks of sentences will be true also for the same assignment of truth values.

This fact is easiest to grasp by example. In applying the rule v to line 2, we produce two branches, on line 5. Suppose that we have an assignment that makes line 2 true. This can only be because it makes at least one of the two disjuncts true. But then, on this assignment, at least one of the sentences on the two branches of line 5 will be true for the same assignment.

Or consider application of the rule ~v to line 1, and suppose that we have a truth value assignment which makes line 1 true. A negated disjunction can be true only if both disjuncts are false. Consequently, an assignment which makes line 1 true will make lines 3 and 4 true.

As I introduced the rules, I made sure that they are all, as in these two examples, what I will call *Downwardly Correct*. In outline, the downward correctness of the rules works to show that the tree method is downwardly adequate as follows: Suppose that the initial sentences on a tree are consistent, so that there is an interpretation, **I**, which assigns truth values to sentence letters making all the initial sentences true. Now apply a rule to one of the sentences. The downward correctness of the rules means that applying the rule will result in at least one branch on which all the new sentences are true in **I**. Of course, all the former sentences along this branch were true in **I**. So at this stage we have at least one branch along which all sentences are true in **I**. Now we just do the same thing over again: Apply one of the rules to a sentence on this branch. We get at least one extension of the branch on which all sentences are true in **I**.

This process will eventually come to an end because each application of a rule produces shorter sentences. At the end we have at least one branch on which all the sentences are true in **I**. But this branch must be open. Since all the sentences along the branch are true in **I**, no sentence and its negation can both appear on the branch! In sum, if the original sentences are consistent, there will be an open branch.

We are half done. We must still show that the tree method is *Upwardly Adequate,* that is, that if there is an open branch, then the set of initial sentences is consistent. So now let us suppose that we have a tree with an open branch. Since an open branch never has both a sentence and its negation, I can consistently assign the truth value t to all atomic sentences on the branch and the truth value f to all those atomic sentences whose negations occur on the branch. Call this assignment **I**. I will also make the longer sentences on the branch true.

Look, for instance, at the open branch in the last example. Reading up from the bottom, this branch specifies the assignment 'C', 'B', and 'D' all false. Call this assignment **I**. If 'C' is false, that is, if '~C' is true in **I**, then 'C⊃D' is true in **I**. In turn, 'C⊃D' being true in **I** will make line 2, '(A&B)v(C⊃D)' true in **I**. Likewise, lines 3 and 4, '~D' and '~B', true in **I** will make line 1, '~(DvB)', true in **I**.

All the rules have the property just used, called *Upward Correctness:* If **I** makes true the sentence or sentences which a rule produced from a previous sentence, **I** makes that previous sentence true also. Upward correctness will apply to any open branch in any tree just as it did in the example. Choose an interpretation, **I**, as the one which makes all the atomic sentences on the open branch true and all the negated atomic sentences false. Apply upward correctness again and again. You can see that, finally, all the sentences along the open branch are true in **I**. So the open branch provides an interpretation, **I**, which makes all the sentences along the branch true, including the initial sentences. So if there is an open branch there is a model for the initial sentences, which is to say that the initial sentences form a consistent set, which is just what we mean by upward adequacy.

Let's pull the threads together. The tree method is downwardly adequate. That is, if the initial sentences are consistent, then there is an open branch. By contraposition, if there is no open branch, that is, if there is a proof, then the initial sentences form an inconsistent set. Lemma 1 tells us that then the corresponding argument is valid. This is soundness.

The tree method is also upwardly adequate. If there is an open branch, and so no proof, then the initial set of sentences is consistent. By contraposition, if the set of initial set of sentences is inconsistent, then there is a proof. Lemma 1 then connects the inconsistency with validity: If the corresponding argument is valid, there is a proof. This is completeness.

If you are starting to see how soundness and completeness work for trees, this section is doing its job. Doing the job fully requires further precision and details, presented in the next section. If in the next section you start to feel lost in a forest of definitions (as I often do) reread this section, which contains all the concepts. Reviewing the intuitively presented concepts will help you to see how the following formal details fit together.

12–3. SOUNDNESS AND COMPLETENESS FOR SENTENCE LOGIC TREES: FORMAL DETAILS

In this section I am going to make a very natural simplifying assumption: I will restrict discussion to **finite** sets of sentences **Z**. This restriction is natural because intuitively we think of arguments as only having finitely many premises anyway. Generalization to the case of infinite sets of sentences involves a complication which would only distract us from the main line of argument. Chapter 14 will take care of the generalization.

For precision and efficiency of statement, we need the following definitions:

> D8: A *Minimal Sentence* is a sentence which is either atomic or the negation of an atomic sentence.

> D9: A truth tree is *Finished* iff each branch is either closed or has all applicable rules applied to all nonminimal sentences.

> D10: 'Tr', 'Op', and 'Cl' are predicates of the metalanguage (abbreviations in English) which are defined as

> > a) **Tr(T,Z)** iff **T** is a finished tree with all the sentences in **Z** its initial sentences.
> > b) **Op(T)** iff the tree **T** is open, that is, if **T** has an open branch.
> > c) **Cl(T)** iff ~**Op(T)**, that is, if **T** is closed, that is, if all of **T**'s branches are closed.

A proof of $Z \backslash X$ is just a closed tree which starts with sentences in **Z** and the sentence ~**X**. Expressed with our abbreviations, this is

> D11: A tree, **T**, *is a proof of* **X** *from* **Z** iff **Tr(T,Z∪{~X})** and **Cl(T)**.

Next, recall that $Z \vdash X$ just means that **there exists** a proof of **X** using premises in **Z**, where here a proof just means a tree as described in D11. So applying D11 to the definition of ⊢, we have

> L2: For finite sets, **Z**, $Z \vdash X$ iff $(\exists T)[\mathbf{Tr(T,Z∪\{\sim X\})}\ \&\ \mathbf{Cl(T)}]$.

Of course, throughout this section '⊢' means ⊢$_t$, that is, derivability according to the tree method.

EXERCISE

12–3. In chapter 10 I specified that **Z**⊢**X** means that there is a proof of **X** using any number of sentences in **Z**, but not necessarily all of them. (I did this to accommodate the eventual generalization to infinite sets.) But D11 defines **T** as being a proof of **X** from **Z** in terms of **Tr(T,Z∪{~X})**, which specifies a tree, **T**, which has **all** the sentences of **Z∪{~X}** as its initial sentences.

Prove L2, taking care to deal with this apparent difficulty. Use the fact that L2 is stated with the existential quantifier, '(∃**T**)'.

Now remember how we used L1 to show that we could exchange the study of validity and invalidity for the study of the consistency and inconsistency of a certain set of sentences, namely, the premises together with negation of the conclusion. Our next step is to connect the consistency of this set with the syntactic notion of an open branch. We do this with the idea of upward and downward adequacy of the tree method. Downward adequacy says that if the set **Z** is consistent, that is, if there is a model for **Z**, then the tree starting from **Z** has an open branch. Using definitions D5 and D6, this becomes

> D12: The tree method is *Downwardly Adequate* iff for all finite, nonempty sets of sentences **Z**, if (∃I)**Mod(I,Z)**, then (∀**T**)[**Tr(T,Z)** ⊃ **Op(T)**].

Upward adequacy is the converse: If there is an open branch, the initial set is consistent:

> D13: The tree method is *Upwardly Adequate* iff for all finite, nonempty sets of sentences **Z**, if (∀**T**)[**Tr(T,Z)** ⊃ **Op(T)**], then (∃I)**Mod(I,Z)**].

A detail in D12 and D13 requires comment. If we start a tree with the sentences in **Z**, we can come up with more than one tree because we can apply the rules in different orders. So when I give a formal definition of upward and downward adequacy, I must make a choice whether to define these in terms of **all** open trees starting from **Z** or **some** open tree starting from **Z**.

In terms of the proof of upward and downward adequacy, I could do either because, in essence, the proof will show that, for a given set of initial sentences, one tree is open iff all are. I choose to define upward and downward adequacy in terms of all open trees for the following reason: When we connect adequacy with soundness and completeness, I will be taking a converse. This will introduce a negation sign, and when the negation sign gets pushed through the quantifier, 'all' turns into 'some'. At that point I will be talking about "some closed tree". That is just what we will need to get a smooth fit with derivability, which is defined in terms of "there is **some** proof", where a proof is just a closed tree. If I had defined upward and downward adequacy in terms of some instead of all open trees, it would be a mess to make the connection with soundness and completeness.

EXERCISE

12-4. Assume (as we will prove shortly) that if a tree has at least one open branch, then the initial sentences of the tree form a consistent set. Also assume downward adequacy. Prove that for all the finished trees starting from the same set of initial sentences, one is open iff all are.

The next step is to show that upward adequacy is equivalent to soundness and downward adequacy is equivalent to completeness. The connection will not sink in unless you do the work! But I will break the job down into several steps.

First we define a version of soundness and completeness for the tree method:

D3': The tree method is *Sound* iff for all finite, nonempty sets of sentences **Z**, if $(\exists T)[\mathbf{Tr}(\mathbf{T},\mathbf{Z})$ & $\mathbf{Cl}(\mathbf{T})]$, then $(\forall I){\sim}\mathbf{Mod}(\mathbf{I},\mathbf{Z})$.

D4': The tree method is *Complete* iff for all finite, nonempty sets of sentences **Z**, if $(\forall I){\sim}\mathbf{Mod}(\mathbf{I},\mathbf{Z})$, then $(\exists T)[\mathbf{Tr}(\mathbf{T},\mathbf{Z})$ & $\mathbf{Cl}(\mathbf{T})]$.

Now it is not hard to prove that downward adequacy is soundness and upward adequacy is completeness in the form of four new lemmas:

L3: The tree method is sound according to D3 iff it is sound according to D3'.

L4: The tree method is complete according to D4 iff it is complete according to D4'.

L5: The tree method is sound according to D3' iff it is downwardly adequate.

L6: The tree method is complete according to D4' iff it is upwardly adequate.

EXERCISES

12–5. Prove lemmas L3 and L4. You will need to use lemmas L1 and L2.

12–6. Prove lemmas L5 and L6. You will need to use contraposition and the laws of logical equivalence for negated quantifiers as laws applied to statements in the metalanguage.

We have reduced the problem of proving soundness and completeness to that of proving that the tree method is downwardly and upwardly adequate, which the last section indicated we would do by appealing to the downward and upward correctness of the rules. Some further terminology will enable us to state rule correctness more clearly.

When we apply a truth tree rule to a sentence, the rule instructs us to write one or two branches and on each branch one or two new sentences. For example, the ≡ rule is

We will call the sentence to which the rule is applied, **X≡Y** in the example, the *Input Sentence*. The rule instructs you to write one or two lists of sentences (each "list" containing one or two sentences). We will call each such list an *Output List*. In the example, **X,Y** is one output list and ~**X**,~**Y** is the second output list. The rule

has only one output list, namely, **X,Y**. In summary

> D14: The sentence to which a tree method rule is applied is called the *Input Sentence*. The sentence or (sentences) along one branch which the rule directs you to write is (are) called an *Output List of Sentences*.

Here is what we must require of a correct truth tree rule. Suppose that I give you an interpretation (an assignment of truth values to sentence letters) which makes true the input sentence of a rule. Then that same interpretation must make true all the sentences on at least one (but perhaps not all) output lists. This is downward correctness. And suppose I give you an interpretation which makes all the sentences on one output list true. Then that same interpretation must make the input sentence true. This is upward correctness.

> D15: A tree method rule is *Downwardly Correct* iff any interpretation which makes the input sentence true also makes true all the sentences of at least one output list.

> D16: A tree method rule is *Upwardly Correct* iff any interpretation which makes all the sentences of one output list true also makes the input sentence true.

EXERCISES

12–7. Show that all of the truth tree rules for sentence logic are downwardly and upwardly correct.

12–8. Consider the following two proposed truth tree rules:

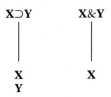

Determine which of these is downwardly correct and which is upwardly correct. In each case show correctness or failure of correctness.

We are now ready to prove

> T1: The truth tree method for sentence logic is downwardly adequate.

(The 'T' stands for 'theorem'.) Suppose we are given a finite nonempty set of sentences, **Z**, and a tree, **T**, which has the sentences of **Z** as its initial sentences. Now suppose that there is a model, **I**, of the sentences in **Z**. What we will do is to look at successively larger initial segments of one branch of **T** and show that all these initial segments of the branch are open.

Start with just the sentences in **Z**, that is, the initial sentences of **T**. This initial segment of a branch must so far be open. Why? Well, a branch closes only if it contains both a sentence and the negation of that same sentence. But **Z** can't contain a sentence and its negation. This is because there is a model, **I**, of all the sentences in **Z**. That is, **I** makes **all** the sentences in **Z** true. But no sentence and its negation can both be true in the same interpretation! If **I** makes one sentence true, it makes its negation false. So far we have an initial segment—let's call it the first segment—of a branch, all the sentences of which are true in **I**, and which consequently is (so far) open.

Next, in constructing the tree **T**, we apply a rule to one of the sentences in this first initial segment of our so far open branch. The input sentence for this rule is true in **I**. By the downward correctness of the rules, there will be at least one output list all the sentences of which are true in **I**. Pick one such output list (say, the left one if there are more than one). Look at the extension of the first segment of our branch extended by this output list. Call this extension the second initial segment. This second segment now has all its sentences true in **I**.

You can see the handwriting on the wall. We just do the same thing over and over again. At the nth stage we start with a branch all the sentences of which are true in **I**. The tree grows by application of some rule to some sentence on the nth initial segment. Downward correctness guarantees that at least one output list will have all its sentences true in **I** also. We pick the leftmost such output list as the extension of the nth initial segment to the n + 1st initial segment. Then the n + 1st initial segment has all its sentences true in **I**, and we can start all over again.

In a sentence logic tree, the sentences get shorter with each application of a rule, so this process must eventually end. When it does, we have a branch all the sentences of which are true in **I**. For exactly the same reason that the first initial segment must be open, this final branch must be open also: All its sentences are true in **I**, and no sentences and its negation can both be true in the same interpretation.

EXERCISE

12–9. Formulate the foregoing argument sketch into an explicit use of mathematical induction to prove T1. There are many correct ways to apply induction. For example, begin by supposing that you are given a finite, nonempty set of sentences, **Z**, a model **I** of **Z**, and a finished tree, **T**, with initial sentences **Z**. Break the tree up into stages: The nth stage of the tree includes all lines written down in the first through nth application of a rule. Your inductive property will be: There is a branch through the nth stage of the tree all the sentences of which are true in I. Or you can similarly organize the inductive property around the number of lines to be checked: The first line to be checked, the first and second lines to be checked, and so on. Be sure to show explicitly how the results from the induction establish downward adequacy.

I have suggested a formulation for this proof which I hope you will find to be relatively intuitive, but the logical form of the suggested proof is actually a bit convoluted. In this formulation you use both universal introduction and induction. That is, for an arbitrary, finite, nonempty set **Z**, model **I** of **Z**, and tree **T** with initial sentences in **Z**, you show how induction gives the desired result in that case. Then, since you have assumed nothing else about the **Z**, **I**, and **T**, what you have shown is true for all such **Z**, **I**, and **T**. In addition, the induction is a finite induction. In a specific case it runs only from the first through the number of stages in the tree in question.

Logicians prefer a more abstract but "pure" way of doing this kind of problem. In the inductive step you assume that in any tree with n stages (or n checked sentences) and interpretation **I** which makes all initial sentences true, there is a path all the sentences of which are true in **I**. You then use downward rule correctness to show that the same is true in any n + 1-stage tree. To do this you consider an arbitrary n + 1-stage tree and the n-stage tree (or trees) which result by deleting the first sentence to which a rule was applied in the original n + 1-stage tree. The downward rule correctness of the applied rule shows that if the inductive hypothesis holds of the subtree, it holds of the full n + 1-stage tree.

But I will leave the details to you and your instructor!

Let's turn to

T2: The truth tree method for sentence logic is upwardly adequate.

The proof works similarly to that for downwardly adequate, differing in that we use upward correctness of the rules and we look at successively longer and longer sentences on a branch instead of successively longer and longer initial segments of a branch.

Suppose we are given a tree with an open branch. Take one open branch (say, the leftmost). Because this branch is open, and so has no sentence and its negation, we can consistently assign the truth value t to all the atomic sentence letters which appear on the branch and the truth value f to all atomic sentence letters the negation of which appear on the branch. This constitutes an interpretation **I**—an assignment of truth values to sentence letters. We are going to show that all the sentences along this branch are true in **I**.

By the *Length* of a sentence let us understand the total number of connectives and sentence letters that appear in the sentence. So far, all minimal sentences along the branch are true in **I**—that is, all sentences of length 1 or 2. Now, consider any sentence along the branch (if there are any) of length 3. When a rule was applied to such a sentence, the rule produced an output list the sentences of which are each shorter than the input sentence; that is, each has fewer total connectives plus sentence letters. (You should check this.) But all such shorter sentences of the branch, that is, sentences of length 1 or 2, are already known to be true in **I**. Upward rule correctness then tells us that the sentence of length 3 is true in **I**. The same goes for any length 3 sentence on the branch. So now we know that all sentences of length 1, 2, and 3 on the branch are true in **I**.

Again, you can see how this will go: We do the same thing over and over again. At stage n we know that all sentences of the branch of length n or less are true in **I**. Consider any sentence of length n + 1. The rule applied to it produced shorter sentences, already known to be true in **I**. By upward correctness of the applied rule, the sentence of length n + 1 is then also true in **I**. The same goes for any sentence of length n + 1 on the branch, so that we now have shown that all of the branch's sentences of length n + 1 are true in **I**. Ultimately, the process shows that all the sentences in the branch are true in **I**. This includes the initial sentences, which are the initial sentences of the tree.

EXERCISE

12–10. Formulate the foregoing argument sketch into an explicit inductive argument. That is, given a tree and an open branch on the tree, show that there is an interpretation which can be shown by induction to make all sentences (and hence the initial sentences) along the branch true.

Comments exactly parallel to those on your proof of T1, about the logical "purity" of the proof, also apply here. Just as for T1, one can also do the induction on the "size" of the tree. In the inductive step, you assume that all open trees with no more than n checked sentences have the desired characteristic—that open paths represent interpretations which make all the sentences on the path true—and you then use upward rule correctness to show that all trees with n + 1 checked sentences also have this characteristic. In outline, the idea is that any tree with n + 1 checked sentences has one or more subtrees with no more than n checked sentences—namely, the tree or trees obtained by deleting the first checked sentence in the original tree. You then apply the inductive hypothesis assumed to hold for the shorter trees.

We have shown that, given some tree with an open branch, there is an interpretation, **I**, in which all of the tree's initial sentences are true. How does this show upward adequacy? Suppose we are given a finite, non-empty set of sentences, **Z**. Assume the antecedent in the statement of upward adequacy. That is, assume that any tree starting from **Z** is open. There is always at least one tree, **T**, starting from **Z**. Since all such trees are being assumed to be open, **T** is open, that is, **T** has an open branch. But in the previous paragraphs we have shown that this open branch provides an interpretation in which all initial sentences of **T**, that is, all the sentences in **Z**, are true.

We have now completed the proof of T2.

T1 and T2, with the help of lemmas L3, L4, L5, and L6, complete our proof of soundness and completeness for the tree method. As you can check in a moment, T1, L3, and L5 immediately give

> T3: The tree method for sentence logic is sound.

T2, L4, and L6 immediately give

> T4: The tree method for sentence logic is complete.

EXERCISES

12–11. This exercise makes precise the work you did informally in exercises 10–14 and 10–15. Recall that when I refer to consistency and inconsistency without qualification, I always mean semantic consistency and inconsistency. We want a notion of *Syntactic Consistency and Inconsistency*, that is, a syntactic notion which will work as a test for semantic consistency and inconsistency. These are

> D17: **Z** is *Syntactically Consistent* iff $(\forall \mathbf{T})[\mathbf{Tr(T,Z)} \supset \mathbf{Op(T)}]$.

> D18: **Z** is *Syntactically Inconsistent* iff $(\exists \mathbf{T})[\mathbf{Tr(T,Z)} \& \mathbf{Cl(T)}]$.

(Throughout this problem, be sure to assume that **Z** is finite and nonempty.)

- a) Show that a set of sentences is syntactically consistent according to D17 iff it is not syntactically inconsistent according to D18.
- b) Show that **Z** is syntactically consistent iff $\mathbf{Z} \nvdash \mathbf{A} \& {\sim}\mathbf{A}$.
- c) Show that **Z** is syntactically inconsistent iff $\mathbf{Z} \vdash \mathbf{A} \& {\sim}\mathbf{A}$.
- d) Show that **Z** is syntactically inconsistent iff for any **X**, $\mathbf{Z} \vdash \mathbf{X}$.
- e) Reexpress lemma L2 and definitions D12, D13, D3′, and D4′ in terms of semantic and syntactic consistency.

CHAPTER CONCEPTS

To check your understanding of this chapter, make sure that you understand all of the following:

a) Input Sentence of a Rule
b) Output Sentence of a Rule
c) Downward Rule Correctness
d) Upward Rule Correctness
e) Downward Adequacy
f) Upward Adequacy
g) Minimal Sentence
h) Finished Tree
i) $\mathbf{Tr(T,Z)}$
j) $\mathbf{Op(T)}$
k) $\mathbf{Cl(T)}$
l) Tree **T** is a proof of **X** from **Z**
m) Syntactic Consistency
n) Semantic Consistency

Soundness and Completeness for Sentence Logic Derivations

13

13–1. SOUNDNESS FOR DERIVATIONS: INFORMAL INTRODUCTION

Let's review what soundness comes to. Suppose I hand you a correct derivation. You want to be assured that the corresponding argument is valid. In other words, you want to be sure that an interpretation which makes all the premises true also makes the final conclusion true. Soundness guarantees that this will always be so. With symbols, what we want to prove is

T5 (Soundness for sentence logic derivations): For any set of sentences, Z, and any sentence, X, if $Z \vdash X$, then $Z \vDash X$.

with '$\vdash$' meaning derivability in the system of sentence logic derivations.

The recipe is simple, and you have already mastered the ingredients: We take the fact that the rules for derivations are truth preserving. That is, if a rule is applied to a sentence or sentences (input sentences) which are true in I, then the sentence or sentences which the rule licenses you to draw (output sentences) are likewise true in I. We can get soundness for derivations by applying mathematical induction to this truth preserving character of the rules.

Consider an arbitrary derivation and any interpretation, I, which makes all of the derivation's premises true. We get the derivation's first conclusion by applying a truth preserving rule to premises true in I. So this first conclusion will be true in **I**. Now we have all the premises and the first conclusion true in **I**. Next we apply a truth preserving rule to sentences taken from the premises and/or this first conclusion, all true in **I**. So the second conclusion will also be true in **I**. This continues, showing each conclusion down the derivation to be true in **I**, including the last.

Mathematical induction makes this pattern of argument precise, telling us that if all the initial premises are true in **I** (as we assume because we are interested only in such **I**), then all the conclusions of the derivation will likewise be true in **I**.

This sketch correctly gives you the idea of the soundness proof, but it does not yet deal with the complication arising from rules which appeal to subderivations. Let's call a rule the inputs to which are all sentences a *Sentence Rule* and a rule the inputs to which include a subderivation a *Subderivation Rule*. My foregoing sketch would be almost all we need to say if all rules were sentence rules. However, we still need to consider how subderivation rules figure in the argument.

What does it mean to say that the subderivation rule, ⊃I, is truth preserving? Suppose we are working in the outermost derivation, and have, as part of this derivation, a subderivation which starts with assumption **X** and concludes with **Y**. To say that ⊃I is truth preserving is to say that if all the premises of the outer derivation are true in **I**, then **X⊃Y** is also true in **I**. Let's show that ⊃I is truth preserving in this sense.

We have two cases to consider. First, suppose that **X** is false in **I**. Then **X⊃Y** is true in **I** simply because the antecedent of **X⊃Y** is false in **I**. Second, suppose that **X** is true in **I**. But now we can argue as we did generally for outer derivations. We have an interpretation **I** in which **X** is true. All prior conclusions of the outer derivation have already been shown to be true in **I**, so that any sentence reiterated into the subderivation will also be true in **I**. So by repeatedly applying the truth preserving character of the rules, we see that **Y**, the final conclusion of the subderivation, must be true in **I** also. Altogether, we have shown that, in this case, **Y** as well as **X** are true in **I**. But then **X⊃Y** is true in **I**, which is what we want to show.

This is roughly the way things go, but I hope you haven't bought this little argument without some suspicion. It appeals to the truth preserving character of the rules as applied in the subderivation. But these rules include ⊃I, the truth preserving character of which we were in the middle of proving! So isn't the argument circular?

The problem is that the subderivation might have a sub-subderivation to which ⊃I will be applied within the subderivation. We can't run this argument for the subderivation until we have run it for the sub-subderivation. This suggests how we might deal with our problem. We hope we can descend to the deepest level of subderivation, run the argument without appealing to ⊃I, and then work our way back out.

Things are sufficiently entangled to make it hard to see for sure if this strategy is going to work. Here is where mathematical induction becomes indispensable. In chapter 11 all my applications of induction were trivial. You may have been wondering why we bother to raise induction to the status of a **principle** and make such a fuss about it. You will see in the next section that, applied with a little ingenuity, induction will work to straighten out this otherwise very obscure part of the soundness argument.

EXERCISES

13–1. Using my discussion of the ⊃I rule as a model, explain what is meant by the rule ~I being truth preserving and argue informally that ~I is truth preserving in the sense you explain.

13–2. Explain why, in proving soundness, we only have to deal with the primitive rules. That is, show that if we have demonstrated that all derivations which use only primitive rules are sound, then any derivation which uses any derived rules will be sound also.

13–2. SOUNDNESS FOR DERIVATIONS: FORMAL DETAILS

The straightforward but messy procedure in our present case is to do a double induction. One defines the complexity of a derivation as the number of levels of subderivations which occur. The inductive property is that all derivations of complexity n are sound. One then assumes the inductive hypothesis, that all derivations with complexity less than n are sound, and proves that all derivations of complexity n are sound. In this last step one does another induction on the number of lines of the derivation. This carries out the informal thinking developed in the last section. It works, but it's a mess. A different approach takes a little work to set up but then proceeds very easily. Moreover, this second approach is particularly easy to extend to predicate logic.

This approach turns on a somewhat different way of characterizing the truth preserving character of the rules, which I call *Rule Soundness,* and which I asked you to explore in exercises 10–4, 10–5, and 10–6. One might argue about the extent to which this characterization corresponds intuitively to the idea of the rules being truth preserving. I will discuss this a little, but ultimately it doesn't matter. It is easy to show that the rules are truth preserving in the sense in question. And using the truth preserving character thus expressed, proof of soundness is almost trivial.

Here is the relevant sense of rule soundness, illustrated for the case of &I. Suppose we are working within a derivation with premises **Z**. Suppose we have already derived **X** and **Y**. Then we have **Z⊢X** and **Z⊢Y**. &I then licenses us to conclude **X&Y**. In other words, we can state the &I rule by saying

    &I Rule: If **Z⊢X** and **Z⊢Y**, then **Z⊢X&Y**.

There is a fine point here, about whether this really expresses the &I rule. The worry is that '**Z⊢X**' means **there exists** a derivation from **Z** to **X**, and '**Z⊢Y**' means that **there exists** a derivation from **Z** to **Y**. But the two derivations may well not be the same, and they could both differ extensively from some of the derivations in virtue of which '**Z⊢X&Y**' is true.

For sentence rules, this worry can be resolved. But it's really not important because, as with rule soundness, this way of stating the rules will provide us with all we need for the soundness proof. We proceed by introducing the sense in which the &I rule is sound. We do this by taking the statement of the rule and substituting '⊨' for '⊢':

    L7 (Soundness of &I): If **Z⊨X** and **Z⊨Y**, then **Z⊨X&Y**.

Why should we call this soundness of the &I rule? First, it has the same form as the rule &I. It is the semantic statement which exactly parallels the syntactic statement of the &I rule. And it tells us that if we start with any interpretation **I** which makes the premises **Z** true, and if we get as far as showing that **X** and **Y** are also true in **I**, then the conjunction **X&Y** is likewise true in **I**.

In particular, you can show that L7 directly implies that &I is truth preserving in the original sense by looking at the special case in which **Z** = {**X,Y**}. {**X,Y**}⊨**X** and {**X,Y**}⊨**Y** are trivially true. So L7 says that {**X,Y**}⊨**X&Y**, which just says that any interpretation which makes **X** true and also makes **Y** true makes the conjunction **X&Y** true.

We treat the other sentence rules in exactly the same way. This gives

    L8 (Soundness of &E: If **Z⊨X&Y**, then **Z⊨X**; and if **Z⊨X&Y**, then **Z⊨Y**.

    L9 (Soundness of ∨I): If **Z⊨X**, then **Z⊨X∨Y**; and if **Z⊨Y**, then **Z⊨X∨Y**.

    L10 (Soundness of ∨E): If **Z⊨X∨Y** and **Z⊨~X**, then **Z⊨Y**; and if **Z⊨X∨Y** and **Z⊨−Y**, then **Z⊨X**.

    L11 (Soundness of ~E): If **Z⊨~~X**, then **Z⊨X**.

    L12 (Soundness of ⊃E): If **Z⊨X⊃Y** and **Z⊨X**, then **Z⊨Y**.

    L13 (Soundness of ≡I): If **Z⊨X⊃Y** and **Z⊨Y⊃X**, then **Z⊨X≡Y**.

    L14 (Soundness of ≡E): If **Z⊨X≡Y**, then **Z⊨X⊃Y**; and if **Z⊨X≡Y**, then **Z⊨Y⊃X**.

EXERCISES

13–3. Prove lemmas L7 to L14. Note that in proving these you do not need to deal with ⊢ at all. For example, to prove L7, you need to show, using the antecedent, that $Z \vDash X\&Y$. So you assume you are given an **I** for which all sentences in **Z** are true. You then use the antecedent of L7 to show that, for this **I**, **X&Y** is also true.

13–4. In this problem you will prove that for sentence rules, such as the rules described in L7 to L14, what I have called rule soundness and the statement that a rule is truth preserving really do come to the same thing. You do this by giving a general expression to the correspondence between a syntactic and a semantic statement of a rule:

Suppose that **X, Y,** and **W** have forms such that

(i) $(\forall \mathbf{I})\{[\mathbf{Mod}(\mathbf{I},\mathbf{X}) \,\&\, \mathbf{Mod}(\mathbf{I},\mathbf{Y})] \supset \mathbf{Mod}(\mathbf{I},\mathbf{W})\}$.

That is, for all **I**, if **I** makes **X** true and makes **Y** true, then **I** makes **W** true. Of course, this won't be the case for just any **X, Y,** and **W**. But in special cases, **X, Y,** and **W** have special forms which make (i) true. For example, this is so if **X** = **U**, **Y** = **U⊃V**, and **W** = **V**. In such cases, thinking of **X** and **Y** as input sentences of a rule and **W** as the output sentence, (i) just says that the rule that allows you to derive **W** from **X** and **Y** is truth preserving in our original sense.

Now consider

(ii)   If $Z \vDash X$ and $Z \vDash Y$, then $Z \vDash W$.

This is what I have been calling soundness of the rule stated by saying that if Z⊢X and Z⊢Y, then Z⊢W. (ii) gives turnstyle expression to the statement that the rule which licenses concluding **W** from **X** and **Y** is truth preserving.

Here is your task. Show that, for all **X, Y,** and **W**, (i) holds iff and (ii) holds. This shows that for sentence rules (rules which have only sentences as inputs) the two ways of saying that a rule is truth preserving are equivalent. Although for generality, I have expressed (i) and (ii) with two input sentences, your proof will work for rules with one input sentence. You can show this trivially by letting **Y** = Av~A for rules with one input sentence.

I have not yet discussed the two subderivation rules, ⊃I and ~I. Soundness of these rules comes to

L15 (Soundness of ⊃I): If $Z \cup \{X\} \vDash Y$, then $Z \vDash X \supset Y$.

L16 (Soundness of ~I): If $Z \cup \{X\} \vDash Y$ and $Z \cup \{X\} \vDash \sim Y$, then $Z \vDash \sim X$.

In the case of ⊃I and ~I there is a more substantial question of whether, and in what sense, L15 and L16 also express the intuitive idea that these rules are truth preserving. The problem is that the turnstyle notion makes no direct connection with the idea of subderivations. Thus, if the syntactic counterpart of L15 is assumed (if $Z \cup \{X\} \vdash Y$, then $Z \vdash X \supset Y$), it is not clear whether, or in what sense, one can take this to be a statement of the ⊃I rule. (The converse is clear, as you will show in exercise 13–6.) However, this issue need not sidetrack us, since L15 and L16 will apply directly in the inductive proof, however one resolves this issue.

EXERCISES

13–5. Prove L15 and L16.

13–6. Prove that if the system of derivations includes the rule ⊃I, then if $Z \cup \{X\} \vdash Y$, then $Z \vdash X \supset Y$. Also prove that if the system of derivations includes the rule ~I, then if both $Z \cup \{X\} \vdash Y$ and $Z \cup \{X\} \vdash \sim Y$, then $Z \vdash \sim X$.

We are now ready to prove T5, soundness for derivations. Here is an outline of the proof: We will start with an arbitrary derivation and look at an arbitrary line, n. We will suppose that any interpretation which makes governing premises and assumptions true makes all prior lines true. Rule soundness will then apply to show that the sentence on line n must be true too. Strong induction will finally tell us that all lines are true when their governing premises and assumptions are true. The special case of the derivation's last line will constitute the conclusion we need for soundness.

To help make this sketch precise, we will use the following notation:

X_n is the sentence on line n of a derivation. Z_n is the set of premises and assumptions which govern line n of a derivation.

Now for the details. Suppose that for some Z and X, $Z \vdash X$. We must show that $Z \vDash X$. The assumption $Z \vdash X$ means that there is some derivation with premises a subset of Z, final conclusion X, and some final line number which we will call n*. The initial premises are the sentences, Z_{n*}, governing the last line, n*; and the final conclusion, X, is the sentence on the last line, which we are calling X_{n*}. We will show that $Z_{n*} \vDash X_{n*}$. This will establish $Z \vDash X$ because $X_{n*} = X$ and Z_{n*} is a subset of Z. (Remember exercise 10–10.)

We will establish $Z_{n*} \vDash X_{n*}$ by showing that $Z_n \vDash X_n$ for all n, $1 \leq n \leq n^*$. And in turn we will establish this by applying strong induction. We will use the

Inductive property: $Z_i \vDash X_i$.

and the

Inductive hypothesis: $Z_i \vDash X_i$ holds for all $i < n$.

So let's consider an arbitrary line, n, and assume the inductive hypothesis. What we have to do is to consider each of the ways in which line n might be justified and, applying the inductive hypothesis, show that the inductive property holds for line n.

First, X_n might be a premise or an assumption. Notice, by the way, that this covers the special case of the first line ($n = 1$), since the first line of a derivation is either a premise or, in the case of a derivation with no premises, the assumption of a subderivation. But if X_n is a premise or assumption, X_n is a member of Z_n. Therefore, $Z_n \vDash X_n$.

Next we consider all the sentence rules. I'll do one for you and let you do the rest. Suppose that X_n arises by application of &I to two previous lines, X_i and X_j, so that $X_n = X_i \& X_j$. By the inductive hypothesis

$Z_i \vDash X_i$ and $Z_j \vDash X_j$ (Inductive hypothesis)

Since we are dealing with a sentence rule, X_i, X_j, and X_n all occur in the same derivation. Consequently, $Z_i = Z_j = Z_n$. So

$Z_n \vDash X_i$ and $Z_n \vDash X_j$.

This is just the antecedent of lemma 7, which thus applies to the last line to give $Z_n \vDash X_n$.

EXERCISE

13–7. Apply lemmas L8 to L14 to carry out the inductive step for the remaining sentence rules. Your arguments will follow exactly the same pattern just illustrated for &I.

Turning to the other rules, suppose that X_n arises by reiteration from line i. That is just to say that $X_n = X_i$. We have as inductive hypothesis that $Z_i \vDash X_i$. If lines i and n are in the same derivation, $Z_n = Z_i$, so that $Z_n \vDash X_n$, as we require. If we have reiterated X_i into a subderivation, Z_n

differs from Z_i by adding the assumption of the subderivation (or the assumptions of several subderivations if we have reiterated several levels down). That is, Z_i is a subset of Z_n. But as you have shown in exercise 10–10, if $Z_i \vdash X_n$ and Z_i is a subset of Z_n, then $Z_n \vdash X_n$.

Now suppose that X_n arises by $\supset$I. Then on previous lines there is a subderivation, beginning with assumption X_i and concluding with X_j, so that $X_n = X_i \supset X_j$. By inductive hypothesis,

$Z_j \vdash X_j$ (Inductive hypothesis for line j)

The trick here is to notice that the subderivation has one more assumption than Z_n. Though not perfectly general, the following diagram will give you the idea:

Set of Premises and Assumptions

$$
\begin{array}{ll}
Z & Z_n \\
\cdot & \\
\cdot & \\
\cdot & \\
X_i & Z_i = Z_n \cup \{X_i\} \\
\cdot & \\
\cdot & \\
\cdot & \\
X_j & Z_j = Z_n \cup \{X_i\} \\
X_n \, (= X_i \supset X_j) & Z_n
\end{array}
$$

When we start the subderivation with the assumption of X_i, we **add** the assumption X_i to Z_n to get $Z_i = Z_n \cup \{X_i\}$ as the total set of premises and assumptions on line i. When we get to line n and discharge the assumption of X_i, moving back out to the outer derivation, we revert to Z_n as the set of governing premises and assumptions.

Since $Z_j = Z_n \cup \{X_i\}$, we can rewrite what the inductive hypothesis tells us about line j as

$Z_n \cup \{X_i\} \vdash X_j$.

But this is just the antecedent of lemma L15! Thus lemma L15 immediately applies to give $Z_n \vdash X_i \supset X_j$, or $Z_n \vdash X_n$, since $X_n = X_i \supset X_j$.

EXERCISE

13–8. Carry out the inductive step for the case in which X_n arises by application of $\sim$I. Your argument will appeal to lemma L16 and proceed analogously to the case for $\supset$I.

We have covered all the ways in which X_n can arise on a derivation. Strong inducton tells us that $Z_n \vDash X_n$ for all n, including n*, the last line of the derivation. Since Z_{n*} is a subset of Z and $X_{n*} = X$, this establishes $Z \vDash X$, as was to be shown.

13–3. COMPLETENESS FOR DERIVATIONS: INFORMAL INTRODUCTION

We still need to prove

> T6 (Completeness for sentence logic derivations): For any finite set of sentences, Z, and any sentence, X, if $Z \vDash X$, then $Z \vdash X$.

where '$\vdash$' is understood to mean $\vdash_d$, derivability in our natural deduction system. The proof in this section assumes that Z is finite. Chapter 14 will generalize to the case of infinite Z.

The proof of completeness for derivations is really an adaptation of the completeness proof for trees. If you have studied the tree completeness proof, you will find this and the next section relatively easy. The connection between trees and derivations on this matter is no accident. Historically, the tree method was invented in the course of developing the sort of completeness proof that I will present to you here.

Begin by reading section 12–1, if you have not already done so, since we will need lemma L1 and the notation from that section. Also, do exercises 12–1 and 12–2. (If you have not studied trees, you will need to refresh your memory on the idea of a counterexample; see section 4–1, volume I.) For quick reference, I restate L1:

> L1: $Z \vDash X$ iff $Z \cup \{\sim X\}$ is inconsistent.

The basis of our proof will be to replace completeness with another connection between semantic and syntactic notions. Let us say that

> D19: Z is *Syntactically Inconsistent* iff $Z \vdash A \& \sim A$.

Semantic inconsistency is just what I have been calling 'inconsistency', defined in chapter 10, D7, as $(\forall I) \sim \textbf{Mod}(I, Z)$. L1 says that an argument is valid iff the premises together with the negation of the conclusion form a semantically inconsistent set. Analogously

> L17: $Z \cup \{\sim X\} \vdash A \& \sim A$ iff $Z \vdash X$.

says that ~**X** together with the sentences in **Z** form a syntactically inconsistent set iff there is a proof using sentences in **Z** as premises to the
conclusion **X**. Together, L1 and L17 show that T6 is equivalent to

> T7: For any finite set of sentences, **Z**, if **Z** is semantically inconsistent, then
> **Z** is syntactically inconsistent; that is, if (∀I)~**Mod**(I,**Z**), then **Z**⊢A&~A.

EXERCISES

13–9. Prove L17.

13–10. Using L1 and L17, prove that T6 is equivalent to T7.

We have boiled our problem down to proving T7. We do this by developing a specialized, mechanical kind of derivation called a *Semantic Tableau Derivation.* Such a derivation provides a systematic way of deriving a
contradiction if the original premises form an inconsistent set.

If you haven't done trees, it is going to take you a little time and pa-
tience to see how this method works. On a first reading you may find the
next few paragraphs very hard to understand. Read them through even
if you feel quite lost. The trick is to study the two examples. If you go
back and forth several times between the examples and the text you will
find that the ideas will gradually come into focus. The next section will
add further details and precision.

A semantic tableau derivation is a correct derivation, formed with a
special recipe for applying derivation rules. Such a derivation is broken
into segments, each called a *Semantic Tableau,* marked off with double
horizontal lines. We will say that one tableau *Generates* the next tableau.
Generating and generated tableaux bear a special relation. If all of a generated tableau's sentences are true, then all the sentences of previous generating tableaux are true also. In writing a derivation, each tableau we
produce has shorter sentences than the earlier tableaux. Thus, as the derivation develops, it provides us with a sequence of tableaux, each a list of
sentences such that the sentences in the later tableaux are shorter. The
longer sentences in the earlier tableaux are guaranteed to be true if all of
the shorter sentences in the later tableaux are true.

A tableau derivation works to show that if a set, **Z**, of sentences is semantically inconsistent, then it is syntactically inconsistent. Such derivations accomplish this aim by starting with the sentences in **Z** as its premises. The derivation is then guaranteed to have 'A&~A' as its final
conclusion if **Z** is (semantically) inconsistent.

To see in outline how we get this guarantee, suppose that **Z** is an arbitrary finite set of sentences, which may or may not be inconsistent. (From
now on, by 'consistent' and 'inconsistent' I will always mean **semantic** con-

sistency and inconsistency, unless I specifically say 'syntactic consistency' or 'syntactic inconsistency'.) A tableau derivation, starting from **Z** as premises, will continue until it terminates in one of two ways. In the first way, some final tableau will have on it only atomic and/or negated atomic sentences, none of which is the negation of any other. You will see that such a list of sentences will describe an interpretation which will make true all the sentences in that and all previous tableaux. This will include the original premises, **Z**, showing this set of sentences to be consistent. Furthermore, we will prove that if the initial sentences form a consistent set, the procedure **must** end in this manner.

Consequently, if the original set of sentence forms an **inconsistent** set, the tableau procedure cannot end in the first way. It then ends in the second way. In this alternative, all subderivations end with a contradiction, 'A&~A'. As you will see, argument by cases will then apply repeatedly to make 'A&~A' the final conclusion of the outermost derivation.

Altogether we will have shown that if **Z** is (semantically) inconsistent, then **Z**⊢A&~A, that is, **Z** is syntactically inconsistent.

To see how all this works you need to study the next two examples. First, here is a tableau derivation which ends in the first way (in writing lines 3 and 4, I have omitted a step, '~B&~C', which gives 3 and 4 by &E):

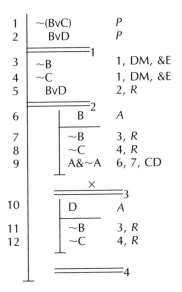

You can see that this is a correct derivation in all but two respects: I have abbreviated by omitting the step '~B&~C', which comes from 1 by DM and gives 3 and 4 by &E; and I have not discharged the assumptions of the subderivations to draw a final conclusion in the outer derivation.

Each tableau is numbered at the end of the double lines that mark its end. A tableau may generate one new tableau *(Sequential Generation):* In this example tableau 1 generated tableau 2 by applying the rules DM, &E, and R. Or a tableau may generate two new tableaus *(Branching Generation):* In the example tableau 2 generated tableaux 3 and 4 by starting two new subderivations, each using for its assumption one of the disjuncts, 'B' and 'D' of 'BvD' on line 5, and each reiterating the rest of tableau 2.

Tableau 3 ends in a contradiction. It can't describe an interpretation. We mark it with an '×' and say that it is *Closed.* Tableau 4, however is *Open.* It does not contain any sentence and the negation of the same sentence; and all its sentences are *Minimal,* that is, either atomic or negated atomic sentences. Tableau 4 describes an interpretation by assigning f to all sentence letters which appear negated on the tableau and t to all the unnegated sentence letters. In other words, the interpretation is the truth value assignment which makes true all the sentences on this terminal tableau.

Note how the interpretation described by tableau 4 makes true all the sentences on its generator, tableau 2. The truth of '~B' and '~C' carries upward simply because they are reiterated, and the truth of 'D' guarantees the truth of 'BvD' by being a disjunct of the disjunction. You should check for yourself that the truth of the sentences in tableau 2 guarantees the truth of the sentences in tableau 1.

Examine this example of a tableau derivation which ends in the second way:

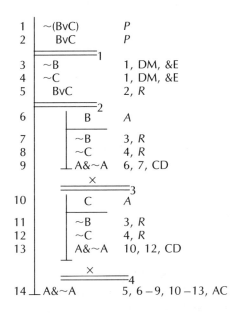

In this example, all terminal tableaux (3 and 4) close, that is, they have both a sentence and the negation of the same sentence, to which we apply the rule CD. We can then apply AC to get the final desired conclusion, 'A&~A'.

Again, here is the key point: I am going to fill in the details of the method to guarantee that a consistent initial set of sentences will produce a derivation like the first example and that an inconsistent set will give a result like the second example. More specifically, we will be able to prove that if there is an open terminal tableau, like tableau 4 in the first example, then that tableau describes an interpretation which makes true all its sentences and all the sentences on all prior tableaux. Thus, if there is an open terminal tableau, there is an interpretation which constitutes a model of all the initial sentences, showing them to form a consistent set. Conversely, if the original set is inconsistent, all terminal tableaux must close. We will than always be able to apply argument by cases, as in the second example, to yield 'A&~A' as a final conclusion. But the last two sentences just state T7, which is what we want to prove.

To help you get the pattern of the argument, here is a grand summary which shows how all our lemmas and theorems connect with each other. We want to show T6, that if $Z \nvDash X$, then $Z \vdash X$. We will assume $Z \nvDash X$, and to take advantage of lemmas L1 and L17, we then consider a semantic tableau derivation with the sentences in $Z \cup \{\sim X\}$ as the initial tableau. Then we argue

(1) $Z \nvDash X$. (Assumption)
(2)   If $Z \nvDash X$, then $Z \cup \{\sim X\}$ is inconsistent. (By L1)
(3)   If some terminal tableau is open, then $Z \cup \{\sim X\}$ is consistent. (By L18, to be proved in the next section)
(4)   If $Z \cup \{\sim X\}$ is inconsistent, then all terminal tableaux close. (Contrapositive of (3))
(5)   If all terminal tableaux close, then $Z \cup \{\sim X\} \vdash A \& \sim A$. (L20, to be proved in the next section)
(6)   If $Z \cup \{\sim X\} \vdash A \& \sim A$, then $Z \vdash X$. (By L17)

Now all we have to do is to discharge the assumption, (1), applying it to (2), (4), (5), and (6), giving

T6: If $Z \nvDash X$, then $Z \vdash X$.

In the next section we carry out this strategy more compactly by proving T7 (corresponding to (4) and (5) above), which you have already proved to be equivalent to T6.

13–4. COMPLETENESS FOR DERIVATIONS: FORMAL DETAILS

To keep attention focused on the main ideas, I'm going to restrict consideration to sentences in which '~' and 'v' are the only connectives used.

Once you understand this special case, extension to the other connectives will be very easy. As I mentioned, I will also carry out the proof only under the restriction that the initial set of sentences, **Z**, is finite. Chapter 14 will generalize the result to infinite sets, **Z**.

To help fix ideas, I'll start with a slightly more extended example. Skip over it now and refer back to it as an illustration as you read the details.

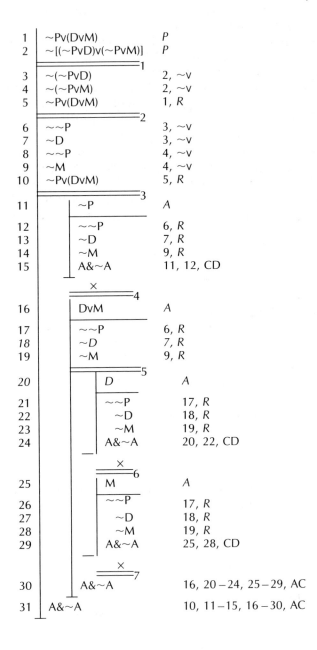

1	~Pv(DvM)	P
2	~[(~PvD)v(~PvM)]	P
═══════════════1		
3	~(~PvD)	2, ~v
4	~(~PvM)	2, ~v
5	~Pv(DvM)	1, R
═══════════════2		
6	~~P	3, ~v
7	~D	3, ~v
8	~~P	4, ~v
9	~M	4, ~v
10	~Pv(DvM)	5, R
═══════════════3		
11	~P	A
12	~~P	6, R
13	~D	7, R
14	~M	9, R
15	A&~A	11, 12, CD
×		
═══════════════4		
16	DvM	A
17	~~P	6, R
18	~D	7, R
19	~M	9, R
═══════════════5		
20	D	A
21	~~P	17, R
22	~D	18, R
23	~M	19, R
24	A&~A	20, 22, CD
×		
═══════════════6		
25	M	A
26	~~P	17, R
27	~D	18, R
28	~M	19, R
29	A&~A	25, 28, CD
×		
═══════════════7		
30	A&~A	16, 20–24, 25–29, AC
31	A&~A	10, 11–15, 16–30, AC

The method of semantic tableau derivations constitutes a way of testing a finite initial set of sentences for consistency. Here are the rules for generating such a derivation:

> **R1** *Initial Tableau:*   The method begins by listing the sentences in the set to be tested as the premises of the derivation. This initial list constitutes the initial tableau.

Lines 1 and 2 in the example are an initial tableau.

Each further tableau (the *Generated Tableau*) is generated from some prior tableau (the *Generating Tableau*) by one of two methods:

> **R2** *Sequential generation*
>
> a)   Each line of the generated tableau is a new line of the same derivation as the generating tableau.
>
> b)   If a sentence of the form $\sim\sim$**X** occurs on the generating tableau, enter **X** on the generated tableau.
>
> c)   If a sentence of the form $\sim$(**X**v**Y**) occurs on the generating tableau, enter $\sim$**X** and $\sim$**Y** as separate lines on the generated tableau.
>
> d)   Reiterate all remaining sentences of the generating tableau as new lines of the generated tableau.

Tableaux 2 and 3 in the example illustrate sequentially generated tableaux. c) is illustrated in the example by lines 3, 4, 6, 7, 8, and 9. d) is illustrated by lines 5 and 10. Note that the rule I apply for c), which I have called '$\sim$v', is a new derived rule, constituted by simply applying DM followed by &E.

> **R3** *Branching generation:*
>
> a)   If a sentence of the form **X**v**Y** occurs on the generating tableau, start two new subderivations, one with assumption **X** and the other with assumption **Y**.
>
> b)   Reiterate **all** the remaining sentences of the generating tableau on each of the subderivations.
>
> c)   Each of the (initial parts of) the subderivations started by steps a) and b) constitutes a generated tableau.

Branching generation is illustrated in the example by tableaux 4, 5, 6, 7.

Tableaux 4, 6, and 7 illustrate what happens when both a sentence and the negation of a sentence appear on a tableau. No interpretation will make all the sentences on such a tableau true. So such a tableau will never provide an interpretation which will prove the original sentences consistent. We record this fact by extending the tableau by applying CD to derive 'A&$\sim$A'. We say that such a tableau is *Closed* and mark it with an '$\times$'.

We have applied CD to draw the explicit contradiction, 'A&$\sim$A', on closed tableaux because this contradiction will be helpful in deriving

'A&~A' in the outermost derivation. We will see that, if the original set of sentences is inconsistent, then all chains of tableaux will terminate with a closed tableau. Argument by cases will then allow us to export 'A&~A' from subderivations to outer derivations, step by step, until we finally get 'A&~A' as the final conclusion of the outermost derivation.

We make these ideas more precise with two further instructions:

> R4: If both a sentence and the negation of the same sentence appear on a tableau, apply CD to derive 'A&~A' as the last line of the tableau, and mark the end of the tableau with an '×' to indicate that it is *Closed*. Do not generate any new tableaux from a closed tableau.

> R5: If 'A&~A' appears on two subderivations, both generated by the same disjunction in the outer derivation, apply AC to write 'A&~A' as the final conclusion on the outer derivation.

Look again at tableaux 4, 6, and 7, as illustrations of R4. Lines 30 and 31 illustrate R5.

We now need to prove that semantic tableau derivations do what they are supposed to do. Here is the intuitive idea. We start with a set of sentences. The tableau procedure constitutes a way of determining whether or not this set is consistent. This works by systematically looking for all possible ways of making the original sentences true. If the systematic search turns up a way of making all the original sentences true (a model), then we know that the original set is consistent. Indeed, we will prove that if the original set is consistent, the procedure will turn up such an interpretation. Thus we know that if the procedure **fails** to turn up such an interpretation, the original set **must** be inconsistent. This is signaled by all chains of tableaux terminating with a closed tableau.

The procedure accomplishes these aims by resolving the original sentences into simpler and simpler sentences which enable us to see what must be true for the original set to be true. Each new tableau consists of a set of sentences, at least some of which are shorter than previous sentences. If all of the generated tableau's sentences are true, then all of the sentences on the generating tableau will be true. For a sequentially generated tableau, the new sentences give us what has to be true for the sentences on the generating tableau to be true. When we have branching generation, each of the two new tableaux gives one of the only two possible ways of making all sentences of the generating tableau true. In this way the procedure systematically investigates all ways in which one might try to make the original sentences true. Attempts that don't work end in closed tableaux.

We need to work these ideas out in more detail. We will say that

> A tableau is a *Terminal Tableau* if it has not generated any other tableau, and no rule for tableau generation applies to it.

It can happen that no rule applies to a tableau for one of two reasons:

The tableau can be closed. Or it might be open but have only minimal sentences (atomic or negated atomic sentences). We will discuss these two cases separately.

First we will prove

L18: An open terminal tableau describes an interpretation in which all sentences of the initial tableau are true.

An open terminal tableau has only minimal sentences, none of which is the negation of any other. The interpretation such a tableau specifies is the one which makes all its sentences true, that is, the assignment of t to all the tableau's unnegated atomic sentences and f to the atomic sentences which appear negated on the tableau. Let's call such an interpretation a *Terminal Interpretation,* for short.

Our strategy will be to do an induction. Suppose we are given an open terminal tableau, and so the terminal interpretation, **I**, which it specifies. The fact that all the sentences of the terminal tableau are true in **I** provides our basis step. For the inductive step you will show that instructions for constructing a tableau derivation guarantee that if all the sentences of a generated tableau are true in an interpretation, then all the sentences of the generating tableau are true in the same interpretation. Thus all the sentences of the tableau which generated the terminal tableau will be true in **I**. In turn, that tableau's generator will have all its sentences true in **I**. And so on up. In short, induction shows that all the *Ancestors* of the open terminal tableau are true.

To fill in the details of this sketch, you will first prove the inductive step:

L19: If tableau T_2 is generated from tableau T_1 and all sentences of T_2 are true in interpretation **I**, then all the sentences of T_1 are also true in **I**.

EXERCISE

13–11. Prove L19.

Since the proof of L18 will be inductive, we need to specify more clearly the sequence of cases on which to do the induction:

A terminal tableau's generator will be called the tableau's first *Ancestor*. In general, the i + 1st ancestor of a terminal tableau is the generator of the ith ancestor.

We will do the induction starting from a 0th case, namely, the terminal tableau. The ith case will be the terminal tableau's ith ancestor.

We are now ready to prove L18. Suppose we are given a semantic tableau derivation, with an open terminal tableau. This tableau specifies an interpretation, **I**, in which all the terminal tableau's sentences are true. The inductive property is: The nth ancestor of the terminal tableau has all its sentences true in **I**. The terminal tableau provides the basis case. By L19, if the nth ancestor of the terminal tableau has all its sentences true in **I**, then so does the n + 1st ancestor. Then, by induction, all the terminal tableau's ancestors have all their sentences true in **I**, which includes the derivation's initial tableau, as required to prove L18.

I have now said all I need about tableau derivations which terminate with one or more open tableaux. What happens if all the terminal tableaux are closed? In a word, rule R5 applies repeatedly until, finally, 'A&~A' appears as the final conclusion of the outermost derivation:

> L20: If in a semantic tableau derivation all the terminal tableaux are closed, then 'A&~A' appears as the derivation's final conclusion.

We will prove this with another induction.

We need a sequence of cases on which to do the induction. The natural choice is the level or depth of subderivations, as measured by the number of nested scope lines. But we want to start with the deepest level of subderivation and work our way back out. So we need to reverse the ordering: The first level of subderivations will be the deepest, the second will be the subderivations one level less deep, and so on. More exactly defined

> Given a tableau derivation, let k be the largest number of nested scope lines on the derivation (including the outermost scope line). The *Inverted Level* of each subderivation is k less the number of scope lines to the left of the subderivation.

(I will henceforth omit the word 'inverted' in 'inverted level'.)

The key to the proof will be the inductive step:

> L21: Let D be a semantic tableau derivation in which all terminal tableaus are closed. Then, if all of D's subderivations of level n have 'A&~A' as their final conclusion, so do all the subderivations of level n + 1.

(I construe 'subderivation' broadly to include the outermost derivation, a sort of null case of a subderivation.)

EXERCISE

13–12. Prove L21.

We are now ready to prove L20. Let D be a semantic tableau derivation in which all terminal tableaux are closed. Our inductive property will be: All the subderivations of level n have 'A&~A' as their final conclusion. At level 1 all subderivations have no sub-subderivations. So all of the subderivations must end in terminal tableaux. By assumption, all of these are closed. So the inductive property holds for level 1. L21 gives the inductive step. By induction, the derivations at all levels conclude with 'A&~A', which includes the outermost derivation.

We are at long last ready to prove T7. Suppose that **Z**, a finite set of sentences, is inconsistent. (Note that, if inconsistent, **Z** must have at least one sentence.) Make the sentences of this set the first tableau of a semantic tableau derivation. Suppose that the derivation has an open terminal tableau. Then, by L18, there is an interpretation which makes true all the sentences in **Z**. But this is impossible since **Z** is supposed to be inconsistent. Therefore all terminal tableaux are closed. Then L20 tells us that the derivation terminates with 'A&~A', so that **Z**⊢A&~A, as was to be shown.

We have one more detail to complete. My proof of T7 is subject to the restriction that 'v' and '~' are the only connectives which appear in any of the sentences. We easily eliminate this restriction by exchanging sentences with other connectives for logical equivalents which use 'v' and '~' instead. At each stage we deal only with the main connective or, for negated sentences, with the negation sign and the main connective of the negated sentence. We rewrite rule R2 for sequential generation to read:

R2 *Sequential generation:*

a) Each line of the generated tableau is a new line of the same derivation as the generating tableau.

b) If a sentence of the form ~~**X** occurs on the generating tableau, enter **X** on the generated tableau.

c) If a sentence of the form ~(**X**v**Y**) occurs on the generating tableau, enter both ~**X** and ~**Y** as separate lines on the generated tableau.

d) If a sentence of the form **X**&**Y** occurs on the generating tableau, enter both **X** and **Y** as separate lines on the generated tableau.

e) If a sentence of the form **X**⊃**Y** occurs on the generating tableau, enter ~**X**v**Y** on the generated tableau.

f) If a sentence of the form **X**≡**Y** occurs on the generating tableau, enter (**X**&**Y**)v(~**X**&~**Y**) on the generated tableau.

g) If a sentence of the form ~(**X**&**Y**) occurs on the generating tableau, enter ~**X**v~**Y** on the generated tableau.

h) If a sentence of the form ~(**X**⊃**Y**) occurs on the generating tableau, enter both **X** and ~**Y** as separate lines on the generated tableau.

i) If a sentence of the form ~(**X**≡**Y**) occurs on the generating tableau, enter (**X**&~**Y**)v(~**X**&**Y**) on the generated tableau.

j) Reiterate all remaining sentences of the generating tableau as new lines of the generated tableau.

We could provide a more complicated version of R2 which would produce more efficient tableau derivations, but it's not worth the effort since true efficiency is only obtained with the truth tree method. In the next exercises you will show that the proof for the special case, using only the connectives 'v' and '∼', extends to the general case covered by our reformulated R2.

---

k) Branching Generation
l) Derived Rule ~∨
m) Closed Tableau
n) Minimal Sentence
o) Terminal Tableau
p) Terminal Interpretation
q) Ancestors of a Tableau

Koenig's Lemma, Compactness, and Generalization to Infinite Sets of Premises

14

14–1. KOENIG'S LEMMA

My proofs of completeness, both for trees and for derivations, assumed finiteness of the set **Z** in the statement **Z⊨X**. Eliminating this restriction involves something called 'compactness', which in turn is a special case of a general mathematical fact known as 'Koenig's lemma'. Since we will need Koenig's lemma again in the next chapter, we will state and prove it in a form general enough for our purposes.

Suppose we have a branching system of points, or *Nodes,* such as the following:

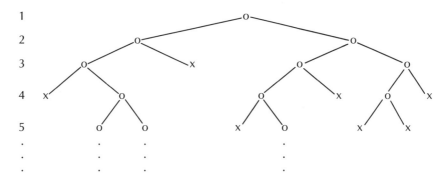

The nodes are connected by branching lines running downward; these are called *Paths*, or *Branches*. I have numbered the horizontal lines to help in referring to parts of the tree. We will consider only tree structures which have *Finite Branching*—that is, from any one node, only finitely many branches can emerge. To keep things simple, I will always illustrate with double branching, that is, with at most two branches emerging from a node. The restriction to two branches won't make an important difference.

Truth trees are one example of such a tree structure. Semantic tableau derivations are another, with each branch representing the formation of a new subderivation and each node representing all the tableaux on a subderivation before starting new subderivations. Some of the paths end with a '×', as when we close a path in a truth tree or close a tableau in a tableau derivation. We say that such a path is *Closed*. A tree might have only finitely many horizontal lines, That is, there might be a line number, n, by which all paths have ended, or closed. Or such a tree might have infinitely many lines. What we want to prove is that if such a tree is infinite (has infinitely many horizontal lines with at least one open path extending to each line), then there is an infinite path through the tree.

Perhaps this claim will seem obvious to you (and perhaps when all is said and done it **is** obvious). But you should appreciate that the claim is not just a trivial logical truth, so it really does call for demonstration. The claim is a conditional: *If* for **every** line **there is** an open path extending to that line, *then* **there is** an open path which extends to **every** line. The antecedent of the conditional is a doubly quantified sentence of the form $(\forall u)(\exists v)R(u,v)$. The consequent is the same, except that the order of the quantifiers has been reversed: $(\exists v)(\forall u)R(u,v)$. Conditionals of this form are not always true. From the assumption that everyone is loved by someone, it does not follow that there is someone who loves everyone. The correctness of such conditionals or their corresponding arguments requires special facts about the relation **R**.

The tree structure provides the special facts we need in this case. Let's assume that we have an infinite tree, that is, a tree with infinitely many horizontal lines and at least one open path extending to each line. The key is to look at infinite subtrees. For example, look at line 3. The first, third, and fourth nodes can each be viewed as the first node in its own subtree, that is, the system of paths which starts with the node in question. The first node of line 3 heads a subtree which does not end, at least not as far as we can tell by as much of the tree as I have drawn. The same is true for the third node of line 3. But the fourth node heads a subtree that we can see is finite: All paths starting from that node close.

Now consider all of the nodes of line 3 again. Suppose that **all** of the subtrees headed by these nodes are finite. Then the whole tree would be finite. Line 3 has only four nodes, and if each has below it only finitely many nodes, then there are only finitely many nodes in the whole tree.

In such cases there are no more than four times the maximum number of nodes in the subtrees headed by line 3 nodes, plus the three nodes in lines 1 and 2. Conversely, if the whole tree is infinite, at least one node of line 3 must head an infinite subtree.

We can use induction to prove that the same will be true of any line of an infinite tree:

> L22: In any infinite tree, every line has at least one node which heads an infinite subtree.

Suppose we have an infinite tree. Our inductive property will be: The nth line has at least one node which heads an infinite tree. Line 1 has this property, by assumption of the argument. This gives the basis step of the induction. For the inductive step, assume the inductive hypothesis that line n has the inductive property. That is, line n has at least one node which heads an infinite tree. Let **N** be the leftmost such node. Consider the nodes on line n + 1 below node **N**. If both of these nodes were to head only finite subtrees, then **N** would also head only a finite subtree, contrary to the inductive hypothesis. So at least one of these nodes of line n + 1 must also head an infinite subtree. In sum, if line n has the inductive property, so does line n + 1, completing the inductive proof of L22.

It is now easy to establish

> L23 (Koenig's lemma): In any infinite tree there is an infinite path.

Proof: Given an infinite tree, start with the top node and extend a path from each line to the next by choosing the leftmost node in the next line which heads an infinite tree. L22 guarantees that there will always be such a node. Since at each stage we again pick a node which heads an infinite tree, the process can never end. (See Exercise 14–1.)

14–2. COMPACTNESS AND INFINITE SETS OF PREMISES

In my proofs of completeness, the statement that if $Z \vDash X$, then $Z \vdash X$, I assumed that **Z** is finite. But in my original definition of $Z \vDash X$ and $Z \vdash X$, I allowed **Z** to be infinite. Can we lift the restriction to finite **Z** in the proofs of completeness?

There is no problem with $\vdash$. By $Z \vdash X$, for infinite **Z**, we just mean that there is a proof which uses some finite subset of **Z** as premises. Counting **Z** as a subset of itself, this means that (whether **Z** is finite or infinite) **X** can be derived from **Z** iff **X** can be derived from some finite subset of **Z**. That is (using '$Z' \subset Z$' to mean that **Z'** is a subset of **Z**)

(1) $Z \vdash X$ iff $(\exists Z')(Z' \subset Z$ and Z' is finite and $Z' \vdash X)$.

EXERCISE

14–1. Consider a tree that looks like this:

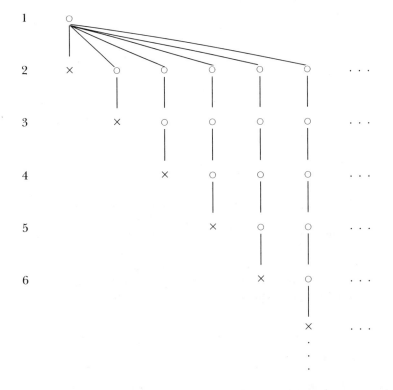

This tree differs from the ones we have been considering because it allows *Infinite Branching*—that is, from one node (here, the first node) infinitely many new branches emerge. These branches also extend farther and farther down as you move from left to right, so that the tree extends infinitely downward as well as to the right. For each integer, n, there is an open path that extends to the nth line. But there is no infinite path through the tree!

This example helps to show that Koenig's lemma is not just a trivial truth. Thinking about this example will also help to make sure you understand the proof of Koenig's lemma.

Explain why the proof of Koenig's lemma breaks down for trees with infinite branching. My proof actually assumed at most double branching. Rewrite the proof to show that Koenig's lemma works when the tree structure allows any amount of finite branching.

What we need is a similar statement for ⊨:

(2)   **Z**⊨**X** iff (∃**Z**′)(**Z**′⊂ **Z** and **Z**′ is finite and **Z**′⊨**X**).

(1) and (2) will enable us quickly to connect completeness for finite **Z**′ with completeness for infinite **Z**.

Using L1 we see that (2) is equivalent to

(3)   **Z**∪{~**X**} is inconsistent iff (∃**Z**′)(**Z**′⊂**Z** and **Z**′ is finite and **Z**′∪{~**X**} is inconsistent).

Compactness is just (3), but stated slightly more generally, without the supposition that the inconsistent set has to include the negation of some sentence:

T8 *(Compactness):* **Z** is inconsistent iff **Z** has an inconsistent finite subset. Equivalently, **Z** is consistent iff all its finite subsets are consistent.

Compactness with the help of L1 will immediately give us

T9 (Completeness): If **Z**⊨**X**, then **Z**⊢**X**, where **Z** now may be infinite.

⊢ may be derivability by trees or derivations (or, indeed many other systems of proof). All that we require here is (1), compactness, and completeness for finite sets **Z** in the system of proof at hand.

EXERCISES

14–2. Prove the equivalence of the two statements of compactness in T8.

14–3. Prove completeness for arbitrary sets of sentences. That is, prove that if **Z**⊨**X**, then **Z**⊢**X**, where **Z** may be infinite. Do this by using compactness and L1 to prove (2). Then use (2) and (1), together with the restricted form of completeness we have already proved (with **Z** restricted to being a finite set) to lift the restriction to finite **Z**.

The key here is compactness, and the key to compactness is Koenig's lemma. In outline, we will create a tree the paths of which will represent lines of a truth table. Finite subsets of an infinite set of sentences, **Z**, will be made true by paths (truth table lines) reaching down some finite number of lines in our tree. Koenig's lemma will then tell us that there is an infinite path, which will provide the interpretation making everything in **Z** true, showing **Z** to be consistent.

Here goes. Since our language has infinitely many sentence letters, let's call the sentence letters 'A_1', 'A_2', . . . , 'A_n'. . . . Consider the tree which starts like this:

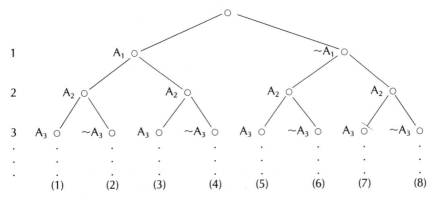

Each branch through the third line represents one of the eight possible truth value assignments to 'A_1', 'A_2', and 'A_3'. Branch (1) represents 'A_1', 'A_2', and 'A_3' all true. Branch (2) represents 'A_1' and 'A_2' true and 'A_3' false. Branch (3) represents 'A_1' true, 'A_2' false, and 'A_3' true. And so on. Line 4 will extend all branches with the two possible truth value assignments to 'A_4', with 'A_4' true on one extension and 'A_4' false on the other. Continuing in this way, each initial segment of a branch reaching to line n represents one of the truth value assignments to 'A_1' through 'A_n', and every possible truth value assignment is represented by one of the branches.

Now let us suppose that the set, **Z**, is composed of the sentence logic sentences $X_1, X_2, . . . , X_n$ . . . , all written with the sentence letters 'A_1', 'A_2', . . . , 'A_n'. . . . Let $Z_n = \{X_1, X_2, . . . X_n\}$. That is, for each n, Z_n is the finite set composed of the first n sentences in the list X_1, X_1. . . . Finally, let us suppose that each Z_n is consistent, that is, that Z_n has a model, an interpretation, **I**, which assigns truth values to all sentence letters appearing in the sentences in Z_n and which makes all the sentences in Z_n true.

Our tree of truth value assignments will have initial path segments which represent the models which make the Z_n's consistent. Koenig's lemma will then tell us that there will be an infinite path which makes all the $X_1, X_2, ...$ true. To show this carefully, let us prune the truth value tree. For each Z_n, starting with Z_1, let i_n be the first integer such that all the sentence letters in the sentence in Z_n occur in the list 'A_1', 'A_2', . . . , 'A_{i_n}'. Then the initial paths through line i_n will give all the possible interpretations to the sentences in Z_n. Mark as closed any path which does not represent a model of Z_n, that is, which makes any sentence in Z_n false. Since each Z_n is consistent, there will be at least one open path reaching to line i_n.

I have provided an outline of a proof of lemma 24:

> L24: Let X_1, X_2 . . . X_n be an infinite sequence of sentences, each initial subsequence of which is consistent. Let T be a tree the paths which represent all the truth value assignments to the sentence letters occurring in X_1, X_2. . . . Let each path be closed at line i_n if the path's initial segment to line i_n makes any sentence X_1 through X_n false, where line i_n is the first line paths to which assign truth values to all sentence letters in X_1 through X_n. Then, for every line in T, there is an open path that reaches to that line.

EXERCISE

14–4. Prove lemma L24. Wait a minute! What remains to be done to prove L24? That depends on how thorough you want to be. There are details I didn't discuss. What if the vocabulary used is finite? What if the vocabulary of some Z_n already includes the vocabulary of Z_{n+1}? More interestingly, perhaps you can find a simpler proof of L24 than the one I suggested. Or better still, you may be able to reformulate L24 so that your L24 is less complicated to prove but still functions to make the proof of compactness easy, in something like the way I will describe in the following paragraphs.

Proving compactness is now easy. Suppose that all of Z's finite subsets are consistent. If Z itself is finite, then, because any set counts as one of its own subsets, Z is consistent. If Z is infinite, we can order its sentences in some definite order. For example, write out each connective and parenthesis with its English name ('disjunction', 'negation', 'right parenthesis', etc.) and think of each sentence logic sentence thus written out as a very long word. Then order the sentences (as words) as one does in a dictionary. (This is called a *Lexicographical Ordering*.) Since all finite subsets of Z are consistent, each initial segment of the ordered list of sentences is a consistent set. L24 applies to tell us that there is a tree, the initial finite open paths of which represent models of the initial segments of the list of sentences. L24 further tells us that for each line of the tree, there will be at least one open path that reaches that line. Koenig's lemma then tells us that there will be at least one path through the whole tree (an infinite path if the tree is infinite). This path will represent a model for all the sentences in the set, establishing the consistency of Z.

EXERCISES

14–5. Complete the proof of compactness by showing that if **Z** is consistent, then so are all of its finite subsets.

14–6. In my proof of soundness for trees I also limited **Z** in the statement **Z⊢X** to be a finite set. There was no reason for doing so other than the fact that for trees it was convenient to treat soundness and completeness together, and I needed the restriction to finite **Z** in the proof of completeness.

Assume soundness for finite **Z**, that is, assume that for all finite **Z**, if **Z⊢X**, then **Z⊨X**. Prove the same statement for infinite **Z**. Your proof will be perfectly general; it will not depend on which system of proof is in question. You will not need to use compactness, but you will need to use the result of exercise 10–9.

CHAPTER CONCEPTS

Here are this chapter's principal concepts. In reviewing the chapter, be sure you understand them.

   a) Tree Structure
   b) Node of a Tree
   c) Path (or Branch) in a Tree
   d) Koenig's Lemma
   e) Compactness
   f) Finite Branching
   g) Infinite Branching
   h) Tree of Truth Value Assignments
   i) Lexicographical Ordering

Interpretations, Soundness, and Completeness for Predicate Logic

15

15–1. INTERPRETATIONS

In chapter 2 I introduced the idea of an interpretation for a predicate logic sentence, that is, of a case which determines the truth value for closed sentences of predicate logic. In the definition of chapter 2 I required that every object in the domain of an interpretation have at least one name. I included this requirement because with it I could give a simple and intuitive truth definition for existentially and universally quantified sentences: I said that an existentially quantified sentence is true in any interpretation just in case at least one of its substitution instances is true in the interpretation. And I said that a universally quantified sentence is true in an interpretation just in case all of its substitution instances are true in the interpretation.

Requiring every object to have a name may have been expedient for teaching fundamentals, but ultimately the requirement is unsatisfactory. Our system of logic should be able to deal with situations in which some objects go unnamed. So henceforth, by an interpretation for predicate logic, I will mean exactly what I meant in chapter 2, except that I will no longer require every object to have a name. I also will streamline the definition somewhat by counting atomic sentence letters as *Zero Place Predicates:*

> D20: An *Interpretation* consists of a nonempty domain of objects, a list of names, and a list of (zero place, one place, two place, and in general many

place) predicates. The list of names may be empty, but there must be at least one predicate. For each name, the interpretation specifies the object in the domain which is named by that name; and for each predicate the interpretation specifies its truth value if it is a zero place predicate (an atomic sentence letter), or the objects in the domain of which the predicate is true if it is a one place predicate, or the ordered lists of objects of which the predicate is true if it is a two, three, or many place predicate. If a predicate is not true of an object or ordered list of objects, it is false of that object or list of objects.

This definition allows us to consider situations in which there are objects without names in the object language. But it makes hash of my definition of truth in an interpretation for quantified sentences.

Before we begin, precision requires a comment on notation. Remember that '$(\exists \mathbf{u})P(\mathbf{u})$' is an expression of the metalanguage ranging over closed existentially quantified sentences, with **u** the existentially quantified variable. Ordinarily, $P(\mathbf{u})$ will be an open sentence with **u** the only free variable, which is the way you should think of '$P(\mathbf{u})$' while getting an intuitive grasp of the material. But strictly speaking, '$(\exists \mathbf{u})P(\mathbf{u})$' ranges over closed existentially quantified sentences, the **s**-substitution instances of which are $P(\mathbf{s})$, the expressions formed by substituting **s** for all free occurrences of **u** in $P(\mathbf{u})$—**if there are any free occurrences of u**. This detail accommodates vacuously quantified sentences, such as '$(\exists x)A$', as discussed in exercise 3–3.

To work toward new truth definitions for the quantifiers, let's think through what we want these definitions to do. Intuitively, $(\exists \mathbf{u})P(\mathbf{u})$ should be true in an interpretation iff there is some object in the domain of the interpretation of which the open sentence, $P(\mathbf{u})$, is true. When all objects in the domain had names, we could express this condition simply by saying that there is at least one name, **s**, in the interpretation for which the substitution instance, $P(\mathbf{s})$, is true in the interpretation. But now the object or objects in virtue of which $(\exists \mathbf{u})P(\mathbf{u})$ is true might have no names, so this strategy won't work.

We can get around this problem by appealing to the fact that, even if the interpretation we are considering does not include a name for the object we need, there will always be another interpretation which **does** have a name for this object and which is otherwise exactly the same.

In more detail, here is how the idea works. Suppose we have an interpretation, **I**, and a sentence $(\exists \mathbf{u})P(\mathbf{u})$. Intuitively speaking, $(\exists \mathbf{u})P(\mathbf{u})$ is true in **I** when **I** has an object, **o**, of which, intuitively speaking, the open sentence $P(\mathbf{u})$ is true. We cannot say that $(\exists \mathbf{u})P(\mathbf{u})$ is true of **o** by saying that **o** has a name, **s**, in **I** such that $P(\mathbf{s})$ is true in **I**. We are considering an example in which **o** has no name in **I**. But we get the same effect in this way: We consider a second interpretation, **I**$'$, which is **exactly like I**, except that in **I**$'$ we assign **o** a name. We can always do this, because if **I** is one interpretation, we get a second interpretation, **I'**, which has exactly the same domain of objects, the same list of predicates, the same specification of what is true of what, but which differs from **I** only by assigning the name **s** to object **o.**

We do also have to require that **s** not be a name which occurs in (∃**u**)**P**(**u**). If, in going from **I** to **I'**, we move a name from one object to another, and this name occurs in (∃**u**)**P**(**u**), we may disturb some other aspect of the truth conditions for (∃**u**)**P**(**u**).

Some new terminology will help in transforming this intuitive idea into a precise definition:

> D21: $\mathbf{I_s}$ is an *s-Variant* of **I** iff $\mathbf{I_s}$ assigns the name **s** to some object in its domain and $\mathbf{I_s}$ differs from **I** at most by having name **s** or by assigning **s** to a different object.

With the help of the idea of an **s**-variant, we can say

> D22: (∃**u**)**P**(**U**) is true in interpretation **I** iff, for some name, **s**, which does not appear in (∃**u**)**P**(**u**), there is an **s**-variant, $\mathbf{I_s}$, of **I** in which **P**(**s**) is true.

EXERCISE

15–1. Give an example of a sentence and an interpretation which shows that D22 would not work as intended if it did not include the requirement that **s** not appear in (∃**u**)**P**(**u**).

The truth definition for the universal quantifier works in exactly the same way, except that we use 'all **s**-variants' instead of 'some **s**-variant'. We want to specify the conditions under which (∀**u**)**P**(**u**) is true in **I**. Intuitively, the condition is that **P**(**u**) be true of **all** objects in **I**. We capture this idea with the requirement that **P**(**s**) be true in **all s**-variants of **I**:

> D23: (∀**u**)**P**(**u**) is true in interpretation **I** iff, for some name, **s**, which does not appear in (∀**u**)**P**(**u**), **P**(**s**) is true in all **s**-variants of **I**.

EXERCISE

15–2. Give an example of a sentence and an interpretation which shows that D23 would not work as intended if it did not include the requirement that **s** not appear in (∀**u**)**P**(**u**).

I hope you will find these new truth definitions for quantifiers to have some plausibility. But they are a bit abstract and take some getting used to. The only way to become comfortable with them is to work with them. We can get the needed practice, and at the same time lay the groundwork for the next sections, by proving some basic lemmas.

Consider a predicate logic sentence, **X**, and an interpretation, **I**. Now consider some name which does not occur in **X**. If we reassign the name to some new object in the interpretation, this should make no difference to the truth value of **X** in **I**. **X** does not constrain the referent of the name in any way. The same thing goes for a predicate symbol not occurring in **X**. Intuitively, **X** and the unused predicate have no bearing on each other. So what the predicate is true of (or the truth value of a zero place predicate) should make no difference to the truth or falsity of **X**:

> L25: Let **X** be a sentence and **I** and **I'** two interpretations which have the same domain and which agree on all names and predicates which occur in **X.** Then **X** is true in **I** iff **X** is true in **I'**.

By 'agreeing on all names and predicates which occur in **X**', I mean that, for each name which appears in **X**, **I** and **I'** assign the same object to that name, and for each predicate appearing in **X**, **I** and **I'** specify the same truth value or the same collection of objects of which the predicate is true. For names and predicates not appearing in **X**, **I** and **I'** may make different assignments.

We prove L25 by induction on the number of connectives in **X**. For the basis case, consider an atomic **X** and an **I** and **I'** with the same domain which agree on all names and predicates in **X**. An interpretation explicitly provides the truth values in terms of the extensions of the used predicates and names (e.g., 'Pa' is true in **I** just in case the thing named 'a' is in the extension which **I** assigns to 'P'). Since **I** and **I'** agree on the predicates and names in **X**, they assign **X** the same truth value.

For the inductive case, assume, as inductive hypothesis, that L25 holds for all **X** with n or fewer connectives and all **I** and **I'** agreeing on **X**, as before. We must separately consider each of the connectives. For example, suppose that **X** has the form **Y&W**. Then **X** is true in **I** iff both **Y** and **W** are true in **I**. But since **Y** and **W** both have fewer connectives than **X**, we can apply the inductive hypothesis to conclude that **Y** is true in **I** iff **Y** is true in **I'**; and **W** is true in **I** iff **W** is true in **I'**. Finally, **Y** and **W** are both true in **I'** iff **X** (=**Y&W**) is true in **I'**, which is what we need to show in this part of the argument.

EXERCISE

15–3. Carry out the inductive step of the proof of L25 for the other sentence logic connectives, modeling your proof on the example just given for '&'.

Now assume that **X** has the form $(\exists u)P(u)$. The ideas are not hard, but keeping everything straight can be confusing. So let's introduce some further terminology: For **I′** I will write **I(X)** to remind us that **I(X)** is an interpretation with the same domain as **I** and just like **I** so far as names and predicates in **X** are concerned, but differing arbitrarily from **I** on other predicates and names. In considering the case of **X** = $(\exists u)P(u)$, instead of writing out **I**$((\exists u)P(u))$, I will write just **I(P)**. Finally, I will write **I(P,s)** for an otherwise arbitrary interpretation agreeing with **I** on domain, on **P**, and on **s**.

So suppose that $(\exists u)P(u)$, **I**, and **I(P)** have been given. Suppose that **I** makes $(\exists u)P(u)$ true. Definition D22 then tells us that there is a name, **s**, not appearing in $(\exists u)P(u)$, and an s-variant of **I**, **I$_s$**, where **P(s)** is true in **I$_s$**. Now we change **I$_s$**. We keep **I$_s$**'s assignment of **s** and of all the names and predicates in $(\exists u)P(u)$, and we change everything else to look just like **I(P)**. The resulting interpretation, **I(P,s)**, is an s-variant of **I(P)**. Furthermore, the inductive hypothesis applies to tell us that, since **P(s)** is true in **I$_s$**, **P(s)** is true in **I(P,s)**. D22 applies to these facts to yield the conclusion that $(\exists u)P(u)$ is true in **I(P)**.

I have shown that if $(\exists u)P(u)$ is true in **I**, it is true in **I(P)**. But exactly the same argument works in the reverse—direction—if **I(P)** agrees with **I** on all vocabulary in $(\exists u)P(u)$, then **I** agrees with **I(P)** on this vocabulary. So we may conclude that $(\exists u)P(u)$ is true in **I** iff it is true in **I(P)**, as was to be shown. (I did not use an iff in the chain of inferences in the previous paragraph because doing so makes it harder to keep clear about the existential quantifiers, 'there is an **s**' and 'there is an **I$_s$**'. I will avoid certain 'iffs' in the proof of the next lemma for the same reason.)

EXERCISE

15–4. Carry out the inductive step of the proof of L25 for the universal quantifier.

Let's move on to another very intuitive fact, but one which is a bit tricky to prove. Consider a sentence of the form **R(s,t)**, a perhaps very complex sentence in which the names **s** and **t** may (but do not have to) occur. Let **I** be an interpretation in which **s** and **t** refer to the same object. Then it should not make any difference to the truth of **R(s,t)** in **I** if we replace any number of occurrences of **s** with occurrences of **t** or occurrences of **t** with occurrences of **s**. In **I**, **s** and **t** are just two different ways of referring to the same thing. **R(s,t)** says something about this thing, and how one refers to this thing should not make any difference to the truth of **R(s,t)** in **I**. (At this point it would be a good idea to review the discussion of extensional semantics in section 9–2.)

L26: Let **R(s,t)** be a closed sentence in which the names **s** and **t** may occur. Let **I** be an interpretation in which the names **s** and **t** refer to the same object. Let **R′(s,t)** arise by replacing any number of instances of **s** by **t** or instances of **t** by **s**. then **R(s,t)** is true in **I** iff **R′(s,t)** is true in **I**.

I have stipulated that **s** and **t** do not have to occur in **R(s,t)** to cover the important case in which **all** occurrences of **s** in a sentence **P(s)** get replaced by occurrences of **t**.

EXERCISE

15–5. Begin the proof of L26 by carrying out the basis step and the inductive step for the sentence logic connectives.

The complications in the inductive step for L26 call for writing it out in some detail. In what follows, take care to understand what I mean by '**r** = **s**'. '**r**' and '**s**' are metavariables over **names**. So '**r** = **s**' means that the name picked out by '**r**' is identical to the name picked out by '**s**', that is, that **r** and **s** are the same name. '**r** = **s**' does **not** mean the object referred to by the name picked out by '**r**' is the same as the object referred to by a different name picked out by '**s**'.

Now let's assume (inductive hypothesis) that L26 holds for all **R(s,t)** with n or fewer connectives. And let's consider the case of **R(s,t)** with the form **(∃u)Q(u,s,t)**. **R′(s,t)** is then the sentence **(∃u)Q′(u,s,t)**. Let interpretation **I** be given with names **s** and **t** having the same referent. In outline, the argument runs as follows:

(1) Suppose that **I** makes **(∃u)Q(u,s,t)** true. (Assumption)

(2) Then there is a name, **r**, and an **r**-variant, **I**$_r$ of **I**, such that **I**$_r$ makes **Q(r,s,t)** true. (By (1) and D22)

(3) Suppose that **r** ≠ **s** and **r** ≠ **t**. (Assumption, to be discharged)

(4) Then **I**$_r$ makes **Q′(r,s,t)** true. (By the inductive hypothesis applied to (2) and (3))

(5) Then **I** makes **(∃u)Q′(u,s,t)**. (By D22 applied to (4))

I want to be sure you understand step (4) and the role of step (3). First, you might have thought that D22 guarantees (3). But that happens only if both **s** and **t** actually occur in **(∃u)Q(u,s,t)**. Since we want out proof to cover, for example, a sentence in which just **t** occurs and in which we replace all occurrences of **t** with occurrences of **s**, we have allowed that **s** and **t** don't have to occur. Next, remember that to apply the inductive hypothesis to switch around the names **s** and **t**, we need to be considering an interpretation in which **s** and **t** both refer to the same object. By assumption, **I** is such an interpretation. But in step (4) we need this to be true of $\mathbf{I_r}$. If $\mathbf{r} \neq \mathbf{s}$ and $\mathbf{r} \neq \mathbf{t}$, we're OK. According to D22, $\mathbf{I_r}$ arises from $\mathbf{I}$ by at most reassigning $\mathbf{r}$ to a new referent. When $\mathbf{r} \neq \mathbf{s}$ and $\mathbf{r} \neq \mathbf{t}$, $\mathbf{s}$ and $\mathbf{t}$ still have their mutual referent, so the inductive hypothesis can be applied.

To get ready to discharge the assumption (3), let's see what can go wrong if (3) fails. Let's suppose that $\mathbf{r} = \mathbf{s}$. In this case, when we apply D22 to make $\mathbf{I_r}$ out of $\mathbf{I}$, we might have the situation pictured for $\mathbf{I_r}$ in figure 15–1.

In $\mathbf{I}$, $\mathbf{s}$ and $\mathbf{t}$ both refer to the object $\mathbf{o_t}$. We apply D22, which says that there is an $\mathbf{r}$-variant, $\mathbf{I_r}$, of $\mathbf{I}$, differing at most from $\mathbf{I}$ by assigning a new referent, which I'm calling '$\mathbf{o_r}$', to $\mathbf{r}$ ($\mathbf{o_r}$ is an object which makes the existential quantification true). But if $\mathbf{r} = \mathbf{s}$, this means assigning $\mathbf{r}$, that is, $\mathbf{s}$, to the object $\mathbf{o_r}$, which in general will be distinct from $\mathbf{o_t}$. So in $\mathbf{I_r}$ we may not have available the condition that $\mathbf{s}$ and $\mathbf{t}$ have the same referent, the condition needed to apply the inductive hypothesis.

To get around this difficulty I will argue by cases. Case 1: Neither $\mathbf{s}$ nor $\mathbf{t}$ actually occurs in $(\exists\mathbf{u})\mathbf{Q}(\mathbf{u},\mathbf{s},\mathbf{t})$. Then there is nothing to prove, since there are no occurrences of $\mathbf{s}$ and $\mathbf{t}$ to switch around. Case 2: $\mathbf{s}$ and $\mathbf{t}$ both occur in $(\exists\mathbf{u})\mathbf{Q}(\mathbf{u},\mathbf{s},\mathbf{t})$. D22 requires that $\mathbf{r}$ not occur in $(\exists\mathbf{u})\mathbf{Q}(\mathbf{u},\mathbf{s},\mathbf{t})$. So in this case $\mathbf{r} \neq \mathbf{s}$ and $\mathbf{r} \neq \mathbf{t}$, we have assumption (3) available, and the proof (1)–(5) can proceed.

Case 3: $\mathbf{t}$ but not $\mathbf{s}$ actually occurs in $(\exists\mathbf{u})\mathbf{Q}(\mathbf{u},\mathbf{s},\mathbf{t})$. (The case in which $\mathbf{s}$ but not $\mathbf{t}$ occurs is the same.) To remind us that $\mathbf{s}$ occurs vacuously, I will put parentheses around $\mathbf{s}$, like this: $(\exists\mathbf{u})\mathbf{Q}(\mathbf{u},(\mathbf{s}),\mathbf{t})$. If, in this case, $\mathbf{r}$ happens by luck to be distinct from $\mathbf{s}$, the proof (1)–(5) applies. So I will also assume that $\mathbf{r} = \mathbf{s}$. In this case we have the situation for $\mathbf{I_r}$ pictured in figure 15–1, and the inductive hypothesis will not apply because $\mathbf{s}$ and $\mathbf{t}$ no longer have the same referent. In addition, we won't be able to apply

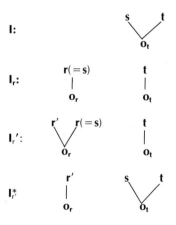

Figure 15–1

D22 in step (5). When **r** = **s**, **r**, that is, **s**, will get put in for occurrences of **t** when we exchange **Q(r,(s),t)** for **Q′(r,(s),t)**. Then when we try to apply D22 to reform the existential quantification, the **u** will get put into the wrong places.

To resolve these difficulties, I must accomplish two things. I must show that I can pick another name, **r′**, with **r′** ≠ **s** and ≠ **t**, and assign **r′** to **o_r**. Then I must **reassign s** as a name of **o_t**. If I do these two things, then **s** and **t** will again have the same referent, so that I can apply the inductive hypothesis in step (4); and I will again be using a name, **r′** ≠ **s** and ≠ **t**, so that D22 will unproblematically apply in step (5).

Once this problem is clearly explained it is easy to solve, with the help of lemma L25. I pick a new name, **r′**, not occurring in **Q(r,(s),t)**, ≠ **s** and ≠ **t**. L25 tells us that **Q(r,(s),t)** has the same truth value in a new interpretation, $I_{r'}$, that it had in I_r, where $I_{r'}$ is just like I_r except that **r′** has been assigned as an additional name of **o_r**. Next I apply the inductive hypothesis to **Q(r,(s),t)** and the interpretation $I_{r'}$. In $I_{r'}$, **r′** and **r** (that is, **s**) both name **o_r**. So the inductive hypothesis allows me to replace all occurrences of **r** with **r′**. I now have Q(**r′**,(s),t) true in $I_{r'}$, with **s** not actually occurring in Q(**r′**,(s),t). Consequently, I can again apply L25 to tell me that **Q(r′,(s),t)** is also true in I_r^*, an interpretation just like $I_{r'}$ except that **s** has been reassigned to **o_t**. At this point I_r^* is an **r′**-variant of **I**, **r′** ≠ **s** and ≠ **t**, and **s** and **t** are both referents of **o_t** so that I can carry out steps (4) and (5) of the foregoing proof using I_r^*, instead of $I_{r'}$.

We are almost done. I have shown that if **I** makes (∃**u**)**Q(u,s,t)** true, then **I** makes (∃**u**)**Q′(u,s,t)** true. But the argument works in exactly the same way in the opposite direction. So we have shown that **I** makes (∃**u**)**Q(u,s,t)** true iff it makes (∃**u**)**Q′(u,s,t)** true, completing this part of the proof of L26.

EXERCISES

15–6. In a more advanced logic text, this sort of informal proof would be written up much more briefly. I have spelled it out in some detail to help you learn how to read and study such a proof. To further practice study of an informal proof and to appreciate better how complicated it really is, formalize the proof as a natural deduction. Use '**Mod(I,X)**' for '**X** is true in **I**', '(∃**r**)' for 'There is a name, **r**', '(∃I_r)' for 'There is an **r**-variant, I_r, of **I**', and so on. I suggest that you formalize the initial proof (1)–(5), with the undischarged assumption of step (3), being sure to make explicit the tacit appeal to ∃E. Then fill in the full argument explained in the discussion which follows (1)–(5). The most efficient natural deduction may have a significantly different organization than the informal presentation, which was designed to help you see what is going on as opposed to presenting the argument in as few steps as possible.

Students of truth trees may also have fun doing this argument as a truth tree proof, although this is less helpful in exposing the structure of the informal argument in English.

15–7. Carry out the inductive step of the proof of L26 for universally quantified sentences. You may do this most efficiently by commenting on how to modify the proof for the case of existentially quantified sentences.

Now that I have shown you how to proceed with this kind of argument, I am going to ask you to prove the rest of the lemmas we will need. When not otherwise specified, **P(u)** can be any open sentence with **u** the only free variable, **I** any interpretation, and so on.

Lemmas L27 and L28 show that the truth definitions for the quantifiers are equivalent to conditions which, superficially, look stronger than the definitions:

> L27: Let **s** be **any** name not appearing in $(\exists u)P(u)$. Then $\textbf{Mod}[I,(\exists u)P(u)]$ iff there is an **s**-variant, I_s, of **I** such that $\textbf{Mod}[I_s, P(s)]$.

> L28: Let **s** be **any** name not appearing in $(\forall u)P(u)$. Then $\textbf{Mod}[I,(\forall u)P(u)]$ iff $\textbf{Mod}[I_s,P(s)]$ for all **s**-variants, I_s, of **I**.

EXERCISE

15–8. Prove L27 and L28. Apply L25 and L26 to D22 and D23. You will not need to do an induction.

> L29: $\sim(\forall u)P(u)$ is logically equivalent to $(\exists u)\sim P(u)$ and $\sim(\exists u)P(u)$ is logically equivalent to $(\forall u)\sim P(u)$.

EXERCISE

15–9. Prove L29. Remember that logical equivalence is the semantic notion of having the same truth value in all interpretations. You will not need to use induction. Instead, simply apply L27 and L28.

When you have finished your proof of L29, look it over and find the places at which you used, as informal logical principles applied in the metalanguage, just the negated quantifier rules which you were proving as generalizations about the object language! It is a noteworthy, and perhaps disturbing, fact that we cannot prove anything about the object language formulation of logic without assuming logical principles at least as strong in the metalanguage. What, then, do we gain in the process? Precision and clarity.

L30: Suppose that **Mod[I,P(s)]**. Then **Mod[I,(∃u)P(u,s)]**, where **P(u,s)** arises from **P(s)** by substituting **u** for any number of occurrences of **s** in **P(s)**.

L31: Suppose that **Mod[I,(∀u)P(u)]**. Let **I′** differ from **I** only in assignment of names not occurring in **(∀u)Pu,** and let **s** be any name in **I′**. Then **Mod[I′,P(s)]**.

Note that in L31, **s** may be a name appearing in **(∀u)P(u)**. L31 is a generalization of the principle that all substitution instances of a universally quantified sentence are true, a generalization we will need in the following sections.

EXERCISES

15–10. Prove L30. You will use L26 and D22 and no induction.

15–11. Prove L31, using L25, L26, and L28. The fact that **s** may appear in **(∀u)P(u)** may give you trouble in this problem. The trick is not to use the name **s** for the **s**-variant in D23. Use some other name, **t**, which does not appear in **(∀u)P(u)** and then apply L25 and L26 to **s** and **t**.

L32: Let **I** be an interpretation in which every object in its domain has a name. Then

    a) **Mod[I,(∃u)P(u)]** iff **Mod[I,P(s)]** for some name, **s**, that appears in **I**.
    b) **Mod[I,(∀u)P(u)]** iff **Mod[I,P(s)]** for all names, **s**, that appear in **I**.

L32 simply says that the truth definitions for quantifiers given in chapter 2 work in the special case in which all objects in an interpretation's domain have names.

EXERCISE

15–12. Using any prior definitions and lemmas from this section that you need, prove L32.

We are now ready to extend our previous proofs of soundness and completeness for sentence logic to predicate logic. Most of the real work has been done in the lemmas of this section and in Koenig's lemma from chapter 14. I am only going to outline the proofs and ask you to fill in the details. In the next three sections I will only treat predicate logic without identity or function symbols, and I will treat only finite sets of sentences in the completeness proofs.

15–2. SOUNDNESS AND COMPLETENESS FOR TREES

When we extend trees for sentence logic to predicate logic, we add four new rules: ∃, ~∃, ∀, and ~∀. Roughly speaking, what we need to do is to check that these rules are downwardly and upwardly correct. There is, however, a complication: infinite trees.

Before going further, please review section 8–4. In sentence logic every tree ends, including all open trees. That is because we need to work on each sentence only once, and when working on a sentence the sentences on the output list are all shorter than the input sentence. But in predicate logic we may have to work on sentences of the form $(\forall u)(\exists v)R(u,v)$ more than once. When we instantiate $(\forall u)(\exists v)R(u,v)$ with a name, **s**, we get an existentially quantified sentence, $(\exists v)R(s,v)$. When we apply ∃ to this sentence, we **must** use a new name, **t**, which we must then substitute back into $(\forall u)(\exists v)R(u,v)$, producing another existentially quantified sentence, which will produce another new name, and so on.

The overall tree strategy still works as before: We make longer sentences true by making shorter sentences true, until we get to minimal sentences which describe an interpretation. The process may now go on forever, but we can still think of infinite open paths as describing interpretations in which all sentences on the paths are true.

Because trees can be infinite, we need to reconsider what is involved in a finished tree. We do not need to revise our definition, D9, but we do need to make sure that if a tree does not close in a finite number of steps that it can be finished in the sense given by D9. That is, we must make sure that there is some systematic way of applying the rules which guarantees that, for each sentence to which a rule can be applied, eventually the rule is applied.

Here's a system which supplies the guarantee. We segment our work on a tree into stages. At stage n we work only on sentences that appear on lines 1 through n. Stage n continues until all sentences on lines 1 through n which can be checked have been checked and until all names occurring in lines 1 through n have been substituted into all universally quantified sentences occurring in lines 1 through n. Of course, at the end of stage n, the tree may have grown to many more than n lines. But that does not matter. Every checkable sentence occurs by some line, n, and so will eventually get checked by this process, and every name and every universally quantified sentence occurs by some line n, so every universally quantified sentence will eventually be instantiated by every name. Of course, this system is not efficient. But efficiency is not now the point. We want to show that there is a system which is guaranteed not to leave anything out.

The next point to establish is that if a tree is infinite it has an infinite open branch. Koenig's lemma tells us that if a tree is infinite, it has an infinite branch, and since closed branches are finite, this infinite branch must be open.

Open branches, infinite or finite, describe interpretations in pretty much the way they do for sentence logic. Given an open branch, collect all the names that occur on the branch and set up a domain of objects, each one named by one of the names on the branch, with no two names assigned to the same object. Then let the minimal sentences on the branch specify what is true of what. Atomic sentence letters are treated as in sentence logic. If an atomic sentence of the form **P(s)** appears on the branch, in the branch's interpretation **P** is true of **s**. If an atomic sentence of the form ~**R(s,t)** appears, then in the branch's interpretation **R** is false of the pair of objects named by **s** and **t** (in that order). And so on. The minimal sentences will generally fail to specify all atomic facts. The unspecified facts may be filled in arbitrarily.

For sentence logic we formulated rule correctness in terms of **any** interpretation: Any interpretation which makes an input sentence true makes at least one output list true. And any interpretation which makes an output list true makes the input sentence true. This won't work for quantified sentences.

For upward correctness of the ∀ rule, consider some sentence, (∀u)P(u), and some interpretation, **I**, in which there are more objects than are named on an open branch. Even if all of the output sentences of the ∀ rule—that is, even if all of the substitution instances of (∀u)P(u) which appear on this branch—are true in **I**, (∀u)P(u) might not be true in **I**. To be true in **I**, (∀u)P(u) must be true for **all** objects in **I**, whether the object concerned has a name or not.

For downward correctness we need the following: Given an interpretation in which the first n lines of a branch are true, there is an interpretation which makes true all of these sentences as well as the sentences in an output list resulting from applying a rule. But for the ∃ rule, not just any interpretation in which the first n lines, including (∃u)P(u), are true will serve. Such an interpretation might not have a name for an object which makes (∃u)P(u) true. Worse, the interpretation might have such a name but the resulting substitution instance might conflict with another sentence already on the branch.

This last problem is what necessitated the new name rule, and it is essential that you understand how that requirement fits in here. Suppose that our branch already has '(∃x)Bx' and '~Ba' and that the interpretation, **I**, which makes these two sentences true has just one name, 'a', and two objects, the first, named by 'a', which is not B and the second, which has no name in **I** and is B. This **I** is a consistent interpretation for '(∃x)Bx' and '~Ba', but we cannot use it in forming a substitution instance which shows '(∃x)Bx' to be true. We must extend or change our interpretation by assigning a new name, 'b', to the unnamed object. Then the truth of '(∃x)Bx' is made explicit by including 'Bb' on the branch.

The new name feature of the ∃ rule ensures that we always proceed in the way just described. When it comes time to describe downward correctness of the ∃ rule, the downward correctness must be given a corresponding description. As in the last example, the **I** which makes the initial sentences on the branch true may not have the required new name. Or **I** may have the name but, since the name does not occur in any of the sentences so far considered on the branch, the name could refer to the wrong object. (Think of lemma 25 in making sure you understand this last point.) For lack of the right name referring to the right object, the **I** which makes true the first n sentences on a branch may not also make true the substitution instance which comes by applying the ∃ rule with its new name requirement. But there will always be an **s**-variant of **I**, **I$_s$**, resulting by assigning the new name **s** to the right object, which will make true (∃u)P(u)'s substitution instance, **P(s)**. Since **s** is new to the branch, lemma 25 guarantees that all the prior sentences in the branch will still be true in **I$_s$**.

The foregoing remarks should motivate the following revisions of D15 and D16:

> D15′: A tree method rule is *Downwardly Correct* iff it meets the following condition for all interpretations, **I**, and all line numbers, n: Suppose that **I** is an interpretation which makes true all sentences along a branch from lines 1 through n. Suppose that the input sentence for the rule lies on this branch, on one of the lines 1 through n, and the sentences on the output lists lie on the lines immediately succeeding n. Then there is an **s**-variant of **I** which makes true all of the sentences on the original branch, lines 1 through n, and also all of the sentences on at least one of the output lists.

> D16′: A tree method rule is *Upwardly Correct* iff in any interpretation, **I**, which is described by an open branch, if all the sentences on an output list on that branch are true in **I**, then the input sentence is true in **I**.

Note that upward correctness concerns **only** interpretations which are described by the open branch in question.

Before checking rule correctness, we need to clarify what is to count as the output list for an application of the ∀ rule. For upward correctness, the output list resulting when ∀ is applied to (∀u)P(u) includes all the substitution instances of (∀u)P(u) on the finished branch. For downward correctness the output list includes only those substitution instances on the branch as it exists just after the ∀ rule is applied to (∀u)P(u) but before any further rules are applied.

You can now proceed to check downward and upward correctness of the quantifier rules.

EXERCISES

15–13. Using lemma L29, show that the rules ~∃ and ~∀ are downwardly and upwardly correct according to D15′ and D16′ (though, for these two rules, the difference with D15 and D16 is inessential).

15–14. Prove that the ∃ rule is upwardly correct. You only need apply definition D22.

15–15. Prove that the ∀ rule is upwardly correct. You need to apply lemma L32.

15–16. Prove that the ∃ rule is downwardly correct. You need lemmas L25 and L27. Note carefully the role of the new name requirement in your proof.

15–17. Prove that the ∀ rule is downwardly correct. You need lemma L31. Don't forget to treat the case in which ∀ applies to a sentence on a branch with no names. This case will require L25.

We have now done all the real work in proving downward and upward adequacy:

T10: The truth tree method for predicate logic is downwardly adequate.

T11: The truth tree method for predicate logic is upwardly adequate.

Given the revised definitions of upward rule correctness, the proof of upward adequacy works pretty much as it does for sentence logic. Downward adequacy requires some change, in ways which I have already indicated. Suppose that an initial set of sentences has a model. For sentence logic we showed that each time we applied a rule there is at least one extension of the initial segment of a branch all the sentences of which are true in the original model. Now we show instead that each time we apply a rule there is at least one extension of the initial segment of a branch all the sentences of which are true in an s-variant of the model for the prior branch segment. D15′ has been designed to make the inductive proof of this statement straightforward.

EXERCISES

15–18. Prove downward adequacy for predicate logic trees.

15–19. Prove upward adequacy for predicate logic trees. To extend the proof of section 12–2, you will need to revise the definition of 'length of a sentence'. The natural alternative is to let the length of a predicate logic sentence be the number of predicates and connectives. But on this definition the input and output sentences of the $\sim\exists$ and $\sim\forall$ rules have the same length. With a little care you can still do the induction with this definition. Or you can define length by letting an initial negation followed by a quantifier count as three units of length and letting each occurrence of '$\equiv$' count as two units.

T10 and T11, downward and upward adequacy, immediately give

> T12: The truth tree method for predicate logic is sound.

and

> T13: The truth tree method for predicate logic is complete.

in exactly the way they do for sentence logic.

15–3. SOUNDNESS FOR PREDICATE LOGIC DERIVATIONS

To extend the proof for sentence logic, we need to prove rule soundness for the four new predicate logic rules. Two are easy applications of definitions and lemmas given in section 15–1:

> L33 (Soundness for $\exists$I): If $Z \vDash P(s)$, then $Z \vDash (\exists u)P(u,s)$, where $(\exists u)P(u,s)$ is an existential generalization of $P(s)$, that is, $P(u,s)$ results from $P(s)$ by replacing any number of occurrences of s with u.

> L34 (Soundness for $\forall$E): If $Z \vDash (\forall u)P(u)$, then $Z \vDash P(s)$, where $P(s)$ is a substitution instance of $(\forall u)P(u)$, that is, s is substituted for all free occurrences of u in $P(u)$.

> *EXERCISES*
>
> 15–20. Apply lemma L30 to prove lemma L33.
> 15–21. Apply lemma L31 to prove lemma L34.

Let's look at $\forall$I in a bit more detail. We want to prove

> L35 (Soundness for $\forall$I): Assume that the name s does not occur in Z or in $(\forall u)P(u)$. On this assumption, if $Z \vDash P(s)$, then $Z \vDash (\forall u)P(u)$, where $(\forall u)P(u)$ is the universal generalization of $P(s)$, that is, $P(u)$ results by replacing **all** occurrences of s in $P(s)$ with u.

Let's consider an arbitrary interpretation, **I**, in which all the sentences in **Z** are true. What will it take for (∀**u**)**P**(**u**) to be true also in **I**? Lemma L28 tells us that given any name, **s**, not appearing in (∀**u**)**P**(**u**), we need only show that **P**(**s**) is true in all **s**-variants of **I**. What we need to do is squeeze the conclusion that **P**(**s**) is true in all the **s**-variants of **I** out of the assumption that **Z**⊨**P**(**s**) and the hypothesis that **Mod**(**I**,**Z**).

But this is easy. The assumption that **s** does not occur in **Z** allows us to apply lemma L25 as follows: **I** is a model for **Z**. Since **s** does not occur in **Z**, L25 tells us that any **s**-variant of **I** is also a model of **Z**. Then the assumption that **Z**⊨**P**(**s**) tells us that any **s**-variant of **I** makes **P**(**s**) true.

You should carefully note the two restrictions which play crucial roles in this demonstration. In order to apply lemma L25, **s** must not appear in **Z**. Also, in order to apply lemma L28, **s** must not appear in (∀**u**)**P**(**u**). The latter restriction is encoded in the ∀I rule by requiring that (∀**u**)**P**(**u**) be the universal generalization of **P**(**s**).

In a similar way, the restrictions built in the ∃E rule play a pivotal role in proving

> L36 (Soundness for ∃E): Assume that **s** does not appear in **Z**, in (∃**u**)**P**(**u**), or in **X**. Then if **Z**∪{(∃**u**)**P**(**u**),**P**(**s**)}⊨**X**, then **Z**∪{(∃**u**)**P**(**u**)}⊨**X**.

You will immediately want to know why the restrictions stated in L36 are not the same as the restriction I required of the ∃E rule, that **s** be an isolated name. If you look back at section 5–6, you will remember my commenting that requiring **s** to be an isolated name involves three more specific requirements, and that other texts state the ∃E rule with these three alternative requirements. These three requirements are the ones which appear in the assumption of L36. Requiring that **s** be an isolated name is a (superficially) stronger requirement from which the other three follow. Since we are proving soundness, if we carry out the proof for a weaker requirement on a rule, we will have proved it for any stronger requirement. You can see this immediately by noting that if we succeed in proving L36, we will have proved any reformulation of L36 in which the assumption (which states the requirement) is stronger.

Of course, by making the requirement for applying a rule stronger (by making the rule harder to apply), we might spoil completeness—we might make it too hard to carry out proofs so that some valid arguments would have no corresponding proofs. But when we get to completeness, we will check that we do not get into that problem.

Let's turn to proving L36. The strategy is like the one we used in proving L35, but a bit more involved. Assume that **I** is a model for **Z** and (∃**u**)**P**(**u**). Since **s** does not appear in (∃**u**)**P**(**u**), there is an **s**-variant, **I**$_s$ of **I**, such that **P**(**s**) is true in **I**$_s$. Since **s** does not appear in (∃**u**)**P**(**u**) or in **Z**, and since **I** and **I**$_s$ differ only as to **s**, lemma L25 tells us that (∃**u**)**P**(**u**) and

Z are also true in $\mathbf{I}_s$. The hypothesis, that $\mathbf{Z} \cup \{(\exists \mathbf{u})\mathbf{P(u)}, \mathbf{P(s)}\} \vdash \mathbf{X}$, then tells us that **X** is true in $\mathbf{I}_s$. Finally, since **s** is assumed not to appear in **X** and **I** and $\mathbf{I}_s$ differ only as to **s**, lemma L25 again applies to tell us that **X** is true in **I**.

The soundness of the quantifier rules immediately gives us

> T14 (Soundness for predicate logic derivations): For any set of sentences, **Z**, and sentence, **X**, if **Z**⊢**X**, then **Z**⊨**X**.

The proof is a trivial extension of the proof for sentence logic, but to fix the ideas you should carry out this extension.

EXERCISE

15–22. Prove T14. You only need to extend the inductive step in the proof of T5 to cover the cases of the four quantifier rules.

15–4. COMPLETENESS FOR PREDICATE LOGIC DERIVATIONS

For completeness, we also follow the same overall strategy as we did for sentence logic. Starting with an initial tableau of sentences, we generate a new tableau the sentences of which make the sentences on the original tableau true. The sentences on the generated tableau are, on the whole, shorter than on the generating tableau. Roughly speaking, we eventually get down to minimal sentences which characterize an interpretation on which all the sentences of ancestor tableaux are true. But there will be some new wrinkles.

We have to say how quantified and negated quantified sentences will be treated on a tableau. For negated quantified sentences, we apply the rules of logical equivalence for negated quantifiers, pushing the negation sign through the quantifier and switching the quantifier. That will leave us with only quantified sentences, with no negation signs in front, with which we have to deal.

We will make a universally quantified sentence true by making all its substitution instances true. We will make an existentially quantified sentence true by making one substitution instance true. But we will have to make this substitution instance the assumption of a new subderivation so that we will be able to apply the ∃E rule to contradictions to get 'A&~A' as the final conclusion of the outermost derivation.

These ideas get incorporated by extending the rules for sequential and branching generation:

R2' *Sequential generation:* Extend the statement of the rule with the following steps (to be applied before the instruction to reiterate remaining sentences).

a) If a sentence of the form ~(∃u)P(u) appears on the generating tableau, enter (∀u)~P(u) on the generated tableau.

b) If a sentence of the form ~(∀u)P(u) appears on the generating tableau, enter (∃u)~P(u) on the generated tableau.

c) If a sentence of the form (∀u)P(u) occurs on the generating tableau, enter on the generated tableau all the substitution instances formed with names which appear on the generating tableau. If no names appear on the generating tableau, pick one name arbitrarily and use it to form a substitution instance entered on the generated tableau. **Also** reiterate (∀u)P(u) on the generated tableau.

We must reiterate (∀u)P(u) on the generated tableau because, as you will soon see, new names can arise on later tableaux. These new names must be substituted into (∀u)P(u) to make (∀u)P(u) true for all its substitution instances. So we must carry (∀u)P(u) along on each tableau to have it for forming substitution instances any time that a new name arises.

R3' *Branching generation:* If any sentence of the form XvY occurs on the generating tableau, apply R3 exactly as stated. If no XvY occurs but there is a sentence of the form (∃u)P(u) on the generating tableau, pick a **New Name,** that is, a name which does not appear anywhere on the generating tableau. Use the new name to form a substitution instance of (∃u)P(u), and use this substitution instance as the assumption starting a new subderivation. Reiterate all other sentences on the generating tableau in the subderivation to complete the generated tableau, just as in R3.

As students of the tree method already know, these rules create a problem. Suppose that a sentence of the form (∀u)(∃v)R(u,v) appears on a tableau. R2' tells us to enter at least one substitution instance, (∃v)R(s,v), on the next tableau and to reiterate (∀u)(∃v)R(u,v) itself. R3' will then tell us to start a new subderivation with R(s,t), t a new name. Of course, (∀u)(∃v)R(u,v) also gets reiterated onto the subderivation. But now we will have to do the same thing all over again. The new name, t, will have to go into (∀u)(∃v)R(u,v), giving a new existentially quantified sentence, (∃v)R(t,v), which will call for a new subderivation with yet another new name, which will have to go back into the reiterated (∀u)(∃v)R(u,v). We are off and running in a chain of subderivations that will never end.

A first impulse is to wonder if the generation rules couldn't be written better, so as to avoid this problem. They can be written so as to avoid exactly this form of the problem, but it turns out that no matter how the rules are written, some problem with essentially the same import will arise. Indeed, proving this is a further important fact about logic.

Here is an overview of what the problem involves. The semantic tableau procedure provides a mechanical method for searching for a derivation which establishes the validity of a given argument, or equivalently, a mechanical method for searching for an interpretation of a given finite set of sentences. In sentence logic, the method is guaranteed to terminate. A method which thus terminates is guaranteed to give a definite yes or no answer to the original question ('Is the argument valid?' or 'Is the initial set of sentences consistent?'). Such a method, guaranteed eventually to turn up a yes or no answer, is called a *Decision Procedure.*

Now, here is the general form of our current problem. Given an exceedingly plausible assumption about what will count as a mechanical decision procedure, one can prove that there is no decision procedure for predicate logic. In our formulation we fail to get a decision procedure because we may get an infinite sequence of sub-sub . . . -sub-derivations. If our tableau procedure has failed to close at some stage, we may not be able to tell for sure whether that is because we just haven't pursued it far enough, or because it will go on forever. This is not just a weakness of our rules. One can prove that any sound and complete system of predicate logic will suffer in the same way. Roughly speaking, the problem arises from the requirement on the ∃E rule, which we must have in order to ensure soundness.

Since there is no point in searching for better rules, we will have to see what we can make of our R2' and R3' in fashioning a completeness proof.

Consider a set of sentences, for example, just the sentence $(\forall u)(\exists v)R(u,v)$ for which our tableau procedure generates an infinite sequence of tableaux. We will need the fact that we can then, so to speak, draw an unending path through the nested sequence of subderivations. Koenig's lemma assures us that we can always do so. Refer back to the tree structure at the beginning of chapter 14 and imagine that each node represents a subderivation, beginning with the outermost derivation at the top node. Moving from one node to two nodes beneath represents the process of starting two new subderivations by working on a sentence of the form XvY. When we start one new subderivation by working on a sentence of the form $(\exists u)P(u)$, we start one new node, that is, a "branch" with one rather than two new forks. When a subderivation closes, the corresponding path on the tree structure closes. Koenig's lemma tells us that if such a tree structure is infinite, then there is an infinite open path through the tree.

We now know that if a tableau derivation does not close (is infinite or does not have all its terminal tableaux closed) then there is an open path of subderivations through the derivation. The path might be finite or it might be infinite. Each such path provides an interpretation, which we will again call a *Terminal Interpretation.* But we want to characterize the idea of a terminal interpretation so that it will work for infinite as well as finite cases. Since an infinite path through a derivation has no terminal tableau, we cannot let the terminal interpretation simply be one provided by the terminal tableau.

Here's the recipe for the terminal interpretation represented by an infinite path. Collect all the names that occur on the path, and set up a domain of objects, each one named by one of the names on the path, with no two names assigned to the same object. Then look at all the minimal sentences which appear on the path. If an atomic sentence letter appears, the interpretation will make it true. If an atomic sentence letter appears negated, the interpretation will make the atomic sentence letter false. If an atomic sentence of the form **P**(s) appears, the interpretation will make the predicate **P** true of the object named by **s**. Similarly, if ∼**P**(s) appears, the interpretation will make **P** false of the object named by **s**. Two and more place predicates are treated similarly. If this recipe fails to specify all the atomic facts of the interpretation, fill in the missing facts arbitrarily. In sum

> D24: A *Terminal Interpretation* represented by an open path has as its names all the names which occur on the path and as its domain a set of objects, each named by exactly one of the names. The interpretation assigns truth values to atomic sentence letters and determines which predicates are true of which objects (pairs of objects, and so on) as described by the minimal sentences on the path. Any facts not so specified by the minimal sentences may be filled in arbitrarily.

Note, incidentally, that this recipe gives a consistent interpretation. Since the path is open, it cannot contain both an atomic sentence and its negation. So this recipe will not make an atomic sentence both true and false. That is, it will not both say and deny that a predicate is true of an object.

The main work we need to do is to prove the analogy of lemma 18, namely

> L37: The sentences of the initial tableau are all true in a terminal interpretation represented by an open path.

We prove this by proving that a terminal interpretation makes true all the sentences in all the tableaux along its path, arguing by induction on the length of the sentences.

We need to take a little care in saying what the length of a sentence is. To keep things initially simple, let us first consider a special case—analogous to our procedure in section 13–4: Suppose that 'v', '∼', and the quantifiers are the only connectives occurring in any of the initial sentences. Then we can take the length of a sentence simply to be the number of connectives occurring in the sentence.

To carry out the inductive argument, suppose that we have an open path and a terminal interpretation, **I**, represented by that path. By the definition of a terminal interpretation, all atomic and negated atomic sentences, and so all sentences of length 0 or 1, along this path are true in **I**.

For the inductive hypothesis, suppose that all sentences of length no greater than n along the path are true in **I**. Let **X** be a sentence of length n + 1. Suppose that **X** has the form ~(Y∨Z). Then rule R2 for sequential generation tells us that ~**Y** and ~**Z** will both be on the path, since they will be on the tableau generated by the tableau on which ~(Y∨Z) occurs. ~**Y** and ~**Z** are both shorter than ~(Y∨Z), and the inductive hypothesis tells us that ~**Y** and ~**Z** are both true in **I**. Hence ~(Y∨Z), that is, **X**, is true in **I**. When **X** has the form ~~**Y** the argument goes quite like the case of ~(Y∨Z).

Next, we must consider **X** of the form Y∨W. Such **X** gives rise to two generated tableaux, one including **Y** and one including **W**. One of these generated tableaux must be on the open path. Suppose it is the one with **Y**. Since (by the inductive hypothesis) all sentences along this path with n or fewer connectives are true, **Y**, and so Y∨W, are true. If **W** rather than **Y** is on the path, the same argument applies.

Suppose that **X** has the form (∃u)P(u). Then rule R3′ specifies that there is a subderivation along the path that includes a substitution instance, **P(s)**, which the inductive hypothesis tells us is true in **I**. Definition D22 applies to tell us that then (∃u)P(u), that is, **X**, is true in **I**.

Now suppose that **X** has the form (∀u)P(u). Rule R2′ specifies that, for each tableau in which (∀u)P(u) appears, all its substitution instances formed with names in that tableau appear in the next sequentially generated tableau. (∀u)P(u) is also reiterated, so that any name which comes up will eventually get instantiated along the path. By the inductive hypothesis, all these substitution instances are true in **I**. Remember that in a terminal interpretation there is exactly one object named by each name, and we have just seen that all of these names eventually get used to form true substitution instances of (∀u)P(u). So lemma L32 applies to tell us that (∀u)P(u), that is, **X**, is also true in **I**.

Make sure that you understand how this last step in the inductive proof makes essential use of the fact that (∀u)P(u) is always reiterated, to ensure that when new names come up in later tableaux, they will always be used to instantiate (∀u)P(u).

We still need to consider sentences of the form ~(∃u)P(u) and ~(∀u)P(u). Rule R2′ applies to such sentences to produce sentences, respectively, of the form (∀u)~P(u) and (∃u)~P(u). There might seem to be a problem here because ~(∃u)P(u) and (∀u)~P(u) have the same number of connectives, as do ~(∀u)P(u) and (∃u)~P(u). But we can still complete the inductive step. Suppose that ~(∃u)P(u) has n + 1 connectives and appears on the path. R2′ tells us that (∀u)~P(u), also having n + 1 connectives, also appears on the path. But we have already seen that the inductive hypothesis ensures us of the truth of (∀u)~P(u) in the terminal interpretation, **I**. Lemma L29 then tells us that ~(∃u)P(u) is also true in **I**. Of course, the case for ~(∀u)P(u) works the same way.

To complete the proof of L37 we must lift the restriction and allow sentences to include all the sentence logic connectives. This creates a new difficulty. For example, R2 instructs us to generate $(\mathbf{X}\&\mathbf{Y})\vee(\sim\mathbf{X}\&\sim\mathbf{Y})$ from $\mathbf{X}\equiv\mathbf{Y}$. But $(\mathbf{X}\&\mathbf{Y})\vee(\sim\mathbf{X}\&\sim\mathbf{Y})$ has four **more** connectives than $\mathbf{X}\equiv\mathbf{Y}$ rather than fewer.

We can resolve this impasse by assigning weights to the connectives. '$\sim$', '$\vee$', and the quantifiers are each worth one "point," '$\supset$' and '$\&$' each get three "points," and '$\equiv$' gets six "points." The length of a sentence is now just the number of these "points" added up for all the connectives in the sentence. (This technique can also be applied to arrange for $\sim(\exists\mathbf{u})\mathbf{P}(\mathbf{u})$ and $\sim(\forall\mathbf{u})\mathbf{P}(\mathbf{u})$ to be longer than $(\forall\mathbf{u})\sim\mathbf{P}(\mathbf{u})$ and $(\exists\mathbf{u})\sim\mathbf{P}(\mathbf{u})$.)

EXERCISE

15–23. Complete the inductive step of the argument for lemma L37 with all of the sentence logic connectives.

We have proved L37, the analogue of L18 needed for proving completeness for sentence logic derivations. The proof for sentence logic derivations also used L20, which says that if all terminal tableaux close, then 'A&~A' appears as the derivation's final conclusion. We must reformulate the statement ever so slightly because, with the possibility of infinite derivations, some paths might not have terminal tableaux. So we will say

> D25: a semantic tableau derivation is *Closed* if all sequences of subderivations terminate in a closed tableau.

You will then prove the analogy of L20:

> L38: If a semantic tableau derivation is closed, then 'A&~A' appears as the derivation's final conclusion.

The key to L20 is the inductive step, L21. Again, we only need to reformulate to accommodate our more specific definition of a closed tableau derivation:

> L39: Let **D** be a closed semantic tableau derivation. Then, if all of **D**'s subderivations of level i have 'A&~A' as their final conclusion, so do all the subderivations of level i + 1.

EXERCISE

15–24. Prove L39. You only need to check the inductive step for rule R3′, involving subderivations started with a substitution instance of a sentence of the form $(\exists\mathbf{u})\mathbf{P}(\mathbf{u})$. Be sure you see how the new

> name requirement in the statement of R3′ functions crucially in your proof.

If you now go back and read the short paragraph proving T7 and change just the words 'L18' and 'L20' to 'L37' and 'L38', you will see that we have a proof of T7, where the set of sentences **Z** may now include predicate logic sentences. T7 applies exactly as it did in section 12-3 to establish

> T15 (Completeness for predicate logic derivations): For any finite set of sentences, **Z**, and any sentence **X**, if **Z**⊨**X**, then **Z**⊢**X**.

15–5. COMPACTNESS, IDENTITY, AND FUNCTIONS

In this section I am going to get started in cleaning up some details. But I am going to let you do most of the work. Students of truth trees and of derivations will be able to apply the material of this section appropriately to what they have learned.

My completeness proofs for predicate logic assumed a finite set of sentences, **Z**. To get a full statement of completeness, where **Z** can be infinite, we need to show that the compactness result, T8, which we proved in chapter 14, also holds for predicate logic. To accomplish this we need to modify the idea of a tree of truth value assignments.

Here's what we do. We can consider all possible closed atomic sentences written out in some definite order: the first atomic sentence letter, the second, the first one place predicate with the first name, the second . . . : 'A', 'B', 'Pa', 'Pb', 'Raa'. . . . To make sure that this is possible, again consider that we could write each such description of the atomic sentences in English and order them as in a dictionary.

Say the closed atomic sentences are $X_1, X_2, X_3, \ldots$ Then we can diagram all possible truth value assignments to these atomic sentences in the form of a tree:

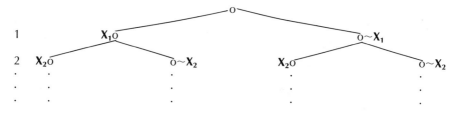

The third line will catalogue the alternative truth values for X_3 underneath all the possibilities covered in lines 1 and 2, and so on.

Note that each path through this tree represents an interpretation, indeed, just the sort of interpretations represented by open paths on a truth tree or semantic tableau derivation. We have seen, in the completeness proofs, how there must be at least one such interpretation for each consistent finite set of sentences. We now proceed very much as we did in predicate logic. Let Z be an infinite set of sentences all of the finite subsets of which are consistent. We list the sentences in some definite order, and consider the initial finite segments of this ordering: $Z_1, Z_2, Z_3, \ldots$ As we work down the lines of the tree, we close branches which conflict with some sentences in one of the Z_i. Since all of the Z_i are consistent, for each line of the tree, there will be an open branch reaching down to that line. Koenig's lemma tells us that there is then an infinite path through the tree. But (if you make the right sort of arrangement of when paths get closed) you will see that this infinite path represents an interpretation which makes true all the sentences in all the Z_i. That is, this interpretation is a model of Z.

EXERCISE

15–25. Following the suggestions of the argument sketch given in the last paragraph, give a detailed proof of compactness for predicate logic.

Actually, we have done the work to prove the *Löwenheim Skolem Theorem,* a much stronger result, of fundamental importance in logic and set theory. In all my discussion of infinite interpretations, I have not mentioned the fact that there are different kinds of infinities. The infinity of the integers is the smallest, called, for obvious reasons, a *Countable Infinity.* However, other infinities are, in a certain sense, "larger." Consider, for example, the infinity of the real numbers (numbers representable by a finite or an infinite decimal fraction, such as 27.75283 . . .). The infinity of the real numbers is larger, or *Uncountable,* in the sense that there is no one-to-one correspondence between the integers and the real numbers. We cannot list the real numbers with the integers the way we can an infinite set of sentences.

The Löwenheim Skolem theorem says that if a set of sentences has a model with a finite, countable, or uncountable domain, then it has a finite or a countable model. For finite sets of sentences, these models are generated by open paths on a truth tree or semantic tableau derivation. If a finite set has a model (finite, countable, or uncountable) then there is an open path. But then the open path represents a finite or countably infinite model. The compactness theorem then shows how the same is true of infinite consistent sets of sentences. (If our object language does not include identity, then there is always a countable model. But '=' allows us to write a sentence which, for example, is only true in an interpretation with exactly one object. Can you produce such a sentence?)

My soundness and consistency proofs assumed that our object language contained neither identity nor function symbols. For the moment, let's consider just identity. To begin with, we must refine the characterization of an interpretation with requirements which should seem natural if '=' really means 'identity':

> D20' (Interpretations for languages with identity): An interpretation is as described in D20 with the following two additional requirements:
>
> a)   A sentence of the form **s**=**t** is true in an interpretation iff **s** and **t** name the same object.
> b)   For all **atomic** sentences of the form **R(s,t)**, if **s**=**t** is true in an interpretation, then **R(s,t)** and **R'(s,t)** have the same truth value in the interpretation, where **R'(s,t)** arises from **R(s,t)** by replacing any number of occurrences of **s** with **t** or of **t** with **s**.

Clause b) covers sentences such as 'Qab': If 'a=c' is true in an interpretation, then 'Qab' and 'Qcb' have the same truth value in the interpretation.

A good many of the semantical facts surrounding identity turn on the following lemma, which simply generalizes clause b) to the case of any closed sentence:

> L40: Let **I** be an interpretation for predicate logic with identity. Then, for all sentences of the form **R(s,t)**, if **s**=**t** is true in **I**, **R(s,t)** and **R'(s,t)** have the same truth value in **I**, where **R'(s,t)** arises from **R(s,t)** by replacing any number of occurrences of **s** with **t** or of **t** with **s**.

EXERCISE

15–26. Prove L40.

You are now in a position to examine how our soundness proofs need to be modified if our language includes identity. Identity involves new rules, the roles of which need to be checked in the proofs.

EXERCISES

15–27. (Trees) Show that the truth tree = rule is downwardly correct. To treat the ≠ rule, note that we can reconstrue it in the following way: Whenever a sentence of the form **s**≠**s** appears on a branch, also write the sentence **s** = **s** on that branch. Explain why this rule comes to the same as the ≠ rule as stated in chapter 9. Prove that the rule in this form is downwardly correct.

15–28. (Derivations) State and prove rule soundness for the two derivation rules for identity. Comment on whether and, if so, how these rules require any changes in the inductive proof of soundness for derivations.

We can turn now to completeness. For semantic tableau derivations we must add two new parts to the rules for sequential generation, corresponding exactly to the = I and = E rules: Whenever a name **s** occurs on a tableau, include the sentence **s** = **s** on the sequentially generated tableau. And if two sentences of the form **s** = **t** and **R(s,t)** appear on a tableau, include the sentences **R′(s,t)** on the sequentially generated tableau. Then, for both trees and semantic tableau derivations, we change how we read an interpretation off an open branch. Before, every name was assigned a distinct object. Now each name will be assigned a distinct object unless a sentence of the form **s** = **t** appears on the branch. Then **s** and **t** are assigned the same object. This corresponds to clause a) in D20′. Clause b) in D20′ is already ensured by the identity rules for trees and for tableau generation.

EXERCISES

15–29. (Trees) Show that clause b) of D20′ will be satisfied in the interpretation represented by an open branch. Comment on the status of lemma L40 in describing an open branch. That is, note the way in which, in effect, proof of upward adequacy automatically covers the work done by lemma L40. Then check that the tree method with identity is upwardly adequate. Though intuitively quite clear, a formal proof requires care, since the input and output sentences for the = rule all have the same predicates and connectives, so that none of our prior methods of attributing lengths to sentences will apply here.

15–30. (Derivations) Show that clause b) of D20′ will be satisfied in the interpretation represented by an open branch. Comment on the status of lemma L40 in describing an open branch. That is, note the way in which, in effect, proof of lemma L37 automatically covers the work done by lemma L40. Then check that lemma L37 is still correct. Just as with the case for trees, proof requires care, since none of our prior means of assigning lengths to sentences will work here.

Finally, let's take a brief look at function symbols. Again, we must extend the definition of an interpretation:

> D20″ (Interpretations for languages with function symbols): An interpretation is as described in D20 or D20′, with the following addition: For each function symbol, **f**, and each object, **o**, in the domain of the interpretation, the interpretation assigns a unique object **o**′ = **f(o)**, as the value of **f** applied to **o**. If **s** is a closed term referring to object **o***, then **f(s)** is a term referring to **f(o*)**.

The last sentence in D20″ constitutes a recursive definition. If **s** is a name, referring to **o**, then **f(s)** refers to **f(o)**, **ff(s)** refers to **ff(o)**, and so on.

As with identity, once we have made this extension of the notion of an interpretation, most of the work is done.

EXERCISES

15–31. (Trees) Check the downward correctness of the quantifier rules when the language includes function symbols.

15–32. (Derivations) Check the proof of rule soundness for the quantifier rules when the language includes function symbols.

15–33. (Trees) Check that the proof of upward adequacy works when interpretations are read off open branches in accord with definition D20″.

15–34. (Derivations) Check lemma L37 when interpretations are read off open branches in accord with definition D20″.

15–6. CONCLUSION

You have worked hard trying to understand these proofs of soundness and completeness. I too have worked hard, first in understanding them and then in my efforts to write them up in a clear and accessible form. Working on the strength of the presentations of others, I will be very happy if I have made some small contribution to improving the accessibility of soundness and completeness and if I have avoided both horns of the dilemma of too much complication versus inaccuracies in the proofs. Whatever I have accomplished, I am sure that my presentation can be improved. I welcome your comments and suggestions. In the meantime, you should not be discouraged if you have found part II of this text to be very difficult. Soundness and completeness are substantial mathematical results. If you understand them only in a fragmentary way, you can greatly improve your grasp by patiently going over these chapters again.

CHAPTER CONCEPTS

In reviewing this chapter, be sure you have a firm grasp on the following:

a) Interpretation
b) Unnamed Object
c) s-Variant
d) Truth of an Existentially Quantified Sentence
e) Truth of a Universally Quantified Sentence
f) Infinite Tree
g) Infinite Semantic Tableau Derivation
h) Downward correctness of a Truth Tree Rule
i) Upward correctness of a Truth Tree Rule
j) Interpretation Represented by an Infinite Truth Tree Branch
k) Restrictions on the Derivation Rule for ∀I
l) Restrictions on the Derivation Rule for ∃E
m) Terminal Interpretation in a Semantic Tableau Derivation
n) Closed Semantic Tableau Derivation
o) Compactness for Predicate Logic
p) Interpretation for a Language with Identity
q) Interpretation for a Language with Function Symbols

Index

DERIVED SENTENCE LOGIC RULES FOR NATURAL DEDUCTION

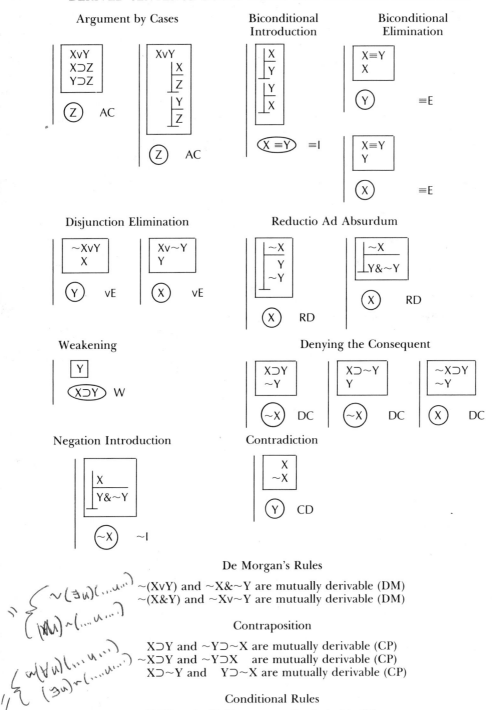

Argument by Cases

XvY
X⊃Z
Y⊃Z

(Z) AC

XvY
| X
| Z
| Y
| Z

(Z) AC

Biconditional Introduction

| X
| Y
| Y
| X

(X≡Y) ≡I

Biconditional Elimination

X≡Y
X

(Y) ≡E

X≡Y
Y

(X) ≡E

Disjunction Elimination

~XvY
X

(Y) vE

Xv~Y
Y

(X) vE

Reductio Ad Absurdum

| ~X
| Y
| ~Y

(X) RD

| ~X
| Y&~Y

(X) RD

Weakening

Y

(X⊃Y) W

Denying the Consequent

X⊃Y
~Y

(~X) DC

X⊃~Y
Y

(~X) DC

~X⊃Y
~Y

(X) DC

Negation Introduction

| X
| Y&~Y

(~X) ~I

Contradiction

X
~X

(Y) CD

De Morgan's Rules

~(XvY) and ~X&~Y are mutually derivable (DM)
~(X&Y) and ~Xv~Y are mutually derivable (DM)

Contraposition

X⊃Y and ~Y⊃~X are mutually derivable (CP)
~X⊃Y and ~Y⊃X   are mutually derivable (CP)
X⊃~Y and   Y⊃~X are mutually derivable (CP)

Conditional Rules

X⊃Y and ~XvY are mutually derivable (C)
~(X⊃Y) and   X&~Y are mutually derivable (C)